E-Business:
The Practical Guide to the Laws

SPIRO BUSINESS GUIDES
E-COMMERCE

Spiro Business Guides are designed to provide managers with practical, down-to-earth information, and they are written by leading authors in their respective fields. If you would like to receive a full listing of current and forthcoming titles, please visit www.spiropress.com or email spiropress@capita-ld.co.uk or call us on +44 (0)870 400 1000.

E-BUSINESS:
THE PRACTICAL GUIDE TO THE LAWS

AMANDA C. BROCK

LLB(HONS), MCJ, LLM

SOLICITOR

Consultant Editor:

Rafi Azim-Khan, Partner, McDermott, Will & Emery

Contributor:

Ashley Winton, Partner, Pillsbury Winthrop

First published in 2003 by
Spiro Press
17–19 Rochester Row
London
SW1P 1LA
Telephone: +44 (0)870 400 1000

ISBN 1 904298 55 9

Reprinted 2004
Job Ref: 6489X8.2004

British Library Cataloguing-in-Publication Data.
A catalogue record for this book is available from the British Library.

Disclaimer: This publication is intended to assist you in identifying issues which you should know about and about which you may need to seek specific advice. It is not intended to be an exhaustive statement of the law or a substitute for seeking specific advice. The contents of this book including that provided by third parties are hopefully useful to the reader, they are intended to be general in nature and only provided for background information purposes. Neither this book nor any part of it consititutes, nor is a substitute for, legal advice which should still always be sought on any particular issue or in respect of any proposed activity or use and neither the author nor the contributors accept responsibility or liability for the accuracy of the same or any loss or damage howsoever sustained by any person acting or placing reliance on the same or otherwise arising therefrom.

Spiro Press USA
3 Front Street, Suite 331
PO Box 338
Rollinsford NH 03869, USA

Typeset by: Turn-Around Typesetting, UK
Printed in Great Britain by: Biddles, UK
Cover design by: REAL451

For Catherine, Chic, Clare, Ross and Kelpie – 'I told you I would finish it'.

Contents

Appendices

Acknowledgements

I wish to thank a number of people for their help in ensuring that the content is what it should be. Rafi Azim-Khan, partner heading the e-Business group at McDermott, Will & Emery, London, has provided the legal editing of the content of this book and his help has been invaluable. Ashley Winton, partner of Pillsbury Winthrop, worked diligently to provide precedents. I must also mention my colleagues at Dixons, in particular Ian Ditcham and Andy Gromniak who deserve thanks for their increase in my knowledge and Geoff Budd for his support. All errors and omissions are of course the author's own.

My family have had no end of patience with my progress of this book and have constantly provided the love and support which have allowed me to complete it. In particular my husband Ross has demonstrated the patience of a saint (almost).

About the author

Amanda C. Brock was born in Perth, Scotland, in 1969 and educated at Morrison's Academy, Crieff. She is an in-house solicitor and has spent the last few years working with Dixons Group Plc, where she was the first lawyer employed to work on Freeserve and has had responsibility for e-commerce issues in the UK and abroad. Prior to this she worked in private practice in a law firm acting for a number of clients including Vauxhall Motors whom she advised on IT and Internet matters. Amanda is dual qualified as a solicitor in Scotland and England & Wales.

On her way to this point in life Amanda managed to spend some time in a number of academic institutions and is LLB (Hons), University of Glasgow, Master of Comparative Jurisprudence, New York University and LLM (IP), Queen Mary and Westfield College, University of London. She was a member of the Association of Chief Police Officers Internet Crime Forum, is a member of the British Retail Consortium E-Commerce Task Force and of the editorial board of the Butterworths journal, *Electronic Business Law*. Amanda has written and lectured extensively in the area of e-commerce, as well as other areas of law.

Amanda is married to Ross, an architect. They live in Crouch End, London and they have one very contented cat.

To contact the author see Appendix 5.

Rafi Azim-Khan, Partner heading the e-Business Group at McDermott, Will & Emery, London, has advised clients ranging from major ISPs and technology companies to multinational manufacturers and media companies on a wide range of marketing, commercial, data protection and intellectual property issues and on all aspects of conducting business on the Internet. Rafi has co-authored numerous texts on such topics and is listed in *Legal Experts*, *Legal 500* and, as one of the world's leading e-commerce lawyers, in *Chambers Global Directory 2002–2003*.

CHAPTER 1

Introduction

1.1   Thoughts for this book

Over the last few years I have spent many a happy hour trying to understand the Internet, the technology that underlies e-commerce and the marketing/commercial needs which have dictated its structure. In my case this has been from the viewpoint of an ISP (Internet Service Provider) as well as from the view of e-commerce portals or businesses. This has allowed me an insight into some of the balances of power and the rationale behind the decisions and needs of these businesses.

My love of the Internet is not that of a technology lover, but rather that of a researcher and shopper. In the latter days of my schooling, computing was introduced as a subject and we were all obliged to sit in front of a screen clicking away in an attempt at programming. Without a doubt my contribution was a disaster for the poor teacher. At one point, having spent hours trying to fix the mess I had made, he came to the conclusion that there was no need for the computer to have reacted in the manner it had, and was reduced to telling me that in his opinion the computer just didn't like me. For some time I steered well clear of computers and when forced to use them found that I had a particular talent for finding the gremlins in systems – this has made me more popular with certain IT departments than others.

However, over the last few years of advising clients who have had a need for IT or the Internet in their business, I have been forced to learn something about IT. Recently I attended a talk by a very esteemed lawyer who said that there was a need to understand the technology in order to be able to apply the existing law to it. I couldn't agree more, and the intention of this book is to both try to explain a little of the technology from a non-technical perspective (enough to understand the issues) and then to explain some of the issues which are caused by this from a legal perspective. Largely these problems are ones where it is possible to apply existing law. However, in some instances new law has been required and recently made. Generally there is a resolution which is legal or at worst best practice.

At this point like every lawyer I must add my disclaimer. This book is not a substitute for proper technical or legal advice. It is intended to be no more than guidance for those who are new to the whole area or who need some general pointers on a particular topic. Many of the issues have reached a point of general acceptance, but have not had the benefit of case law or statute to confirm or disprove them. In the excitement of the dot com high we were frequently told that six weeks were a year in the world of the Internet. Those of us working in the area at the time certainly tried to carry a workload that would justify that statement! However, although life has now become calmer, there is still a constant change in the world of e-business and the applicable laws, and so I have delayed the publication of this book to allow it to incorporate the new E-Commerce (EC Directive) Regulations 2002. I have tried to be as up to date as possible, but must acknowledge and accept that e-business changes by the day and a line had to be drawn somewhere. For this book that line is November 2002.

1.2   Background (or the rise and fall of the Internet millionaire)

The days of spotty teenagers with no business experience being handed vast sums of money to create an Internet start-up with a questionable business plan may be over (and the money spent) but the Internet is most certainly not over. It has become an accepted part of our culture. For many businesses it is not yet the most profitable channel through which they do business and may not be for some time. However, PC and Internet penetration in the UK is high and as people become more comfortable with use of the Internet and its security this is likely to increase.

At the time of writing this book I am aware of a cost consciousness in business generally. I hope that the advice in the book will provide a good starting point for many businesses or at least flag the concerns raised by the Internet for them. It will never be a substitute for legal advice which needs to be tailored to the business itself.

Before we kick off you may be interested to know that the National Consumer Council (NCC) survey of September 2001 concluded that UK sites are either unaware of or are flouting laws and international guidelines (www.ncc.org.uk). In 2002 the Information Commissioner's survey also concluded that many businesses are unaware of the laws applicable to trading on-line. As many of these are intended to protect consumers and their privacy, the NCC and Office of the Information Commissioner are understandably upset and in the case of the NCC a recommendation was made to the Office of Fair Trading suggesting that new powers should be used to ensure that sites comply. As further enforcement may not be far away this appears to be a good time to ensure compliance – before sanctions bite!

1.3   What do you need to know?

When setting up an e-business it is necessary to consider what I will refer to as the front and back end of the site. The front end is the part of the business which a site user can see and which is 'customer-facing'. At the moment this can be a computer screen, a mobile phone or a TV, and through time who knows what it might be? The customer-facing part of the site will include the content, whether this is advertising, marketing materials, general content or product information, and the elements of the site which form the customer experience such as registration, purchasing of goods, services or information or perhaps games or some other interactive activity. This part of the site is clearly subject to legal restrictions as it involves customer relationships, and in the case of a consumer website, consumer relationships. As well as laws affecting advertising and sale it will also be subject to laws relating to personal data.

The front end and these consumer relationships will affect the site structure, e.g. the buying process which will involve a number of clicks, some of which are in place to make the site work legally, and the content which will need to comply with certain laws and codes. These are looked at in Chapter 6 which deals with the customer relationship and any impact this has on the site, and Chapter 5 which deals with content.

The second part of the e-business is what I will refer to as the back end, or all of the parts which the consumer is not necessarily aware of and certainly will not sec, but which are needed to make the site work. This will include the software platform and code on which the site structure is built, the software and systems which are put in place to allow for customer registration, order and stock management and any other systems which make the site perform its functions. These systems will vary from site to site but will ensure that when a customer places an order the site performs the functions it should. In a straightforward shopping site the customer will only be able to purchase those goods that are actually available and the back end will also ensure that the right goods are allocated to the customer. There will also be a system to deal with fulfilment or delivery and which will ensure that goods selected are then sent to the right person at the right time. Obviously, more sophisticated sites are more complicated.

As well as the purchase of various software which will possibly require licences (even if what is purchased is the simplest off-the-shelf site production software) granting the e-business the rights to use the software for its site there will probably be a need for other contracts. In very small simple sites software may come as a ready to use package, but in more complicated sites that software will be configured or set up on a unique or bespoke basis for the site in question. There may be a need for the various systems or software to communicate with each other and this will require interfaces (like software bridges and tunnels) to be built between the systems to allow this communication. Depending on how a business wishes to deal with its site design and build, a member of staff will need to be appointed, or alternatively, a consultancy or agency contracted to do this work. This may require both software licences and site design and build agreements to be put in place. These relationships are looked at in more detail in Chapter 9 on contracts.

The business will also need to consider whether it is able to manage all of the roles, e.g. fulfilment or delivery, itself or whether it will appoint third parties to do this. If it requires third parties then it may 'outsource' part of its business – such as management of its customer services or management of its fulfilment. The list of contracts is not exhaustive, but often when you have understood the business plan and technology behind something new an under-standing of these contracts will allow you to move forward with a contract in a new area or one which is not included in this book, in a sensible manner. Also you must remember that if one contract fitted all there would be no need for lawyers so don't be tied to the precedents too much. The precedents and templates contained in this book were kindly provided by law firms Pillsbury Winthrop and McDermott, Will & Emery both of whom specialise in Internet law. These may be used at will by readers (subject to the lawyers' disclaimers of course!). Freeserve, pubs247.co.uk and Dixons have also consented to use of their content by way of example and these are up to date at the time of going to press.

There are a number of legal obligations which may come into play such as providing the customer with certain information in a particular form by a particular stage in the relationship. Chapter 6 which deals with customer relationships and Chapter 8 which deals with customer data touch on these. They are particularly important as, although most of the rules which govern relationships with consumers in the 'real' world will apply, there are particular rules for sales at a distance (i.e. where customer and seller do not meet physically face to face before contracting) and the site must be set up and utilised in a way that respects these.

1.4   How can you use this book?

The book has been split into chapters, not necessarily by legal areas, but by areas as I perceive that they affect your business. Ideally you will have the time and the inclination to read all of the book (I accept not in one sitting!) and will have a fairly complete understanding of the issues. If not, then there is a danger that the book will not help you as you will not know what issues you should be looking out for. It may, however, also be helpful to pick particular topics and check these. I have tried to break these down into bite-sized chunks and have used headings which I hope will allow these to be found easily using the contents and index. To make sure that any related issues are flagged I have also used a fairly large number of cross-references between chapters. For those of you who find these irritating I apologise in advance, but believe that they are a necessary evil in my attempt to point users in the right direction.

I have included a jargon buster covering some of the terms which are relevant – I am sure that many of my readers will tell me where they could be better and can do this by contacting me through the publisher. This jargon buster owes a debt of gratitude to Rafi Azim-Khan of McDermott, Will & Emery.

At the end of appropriate chapters, and in the case of the contracts chapter at the end of sections, I have provided checklists of additional information. These are intentionally in a separate page format so that they can be photocopied and used practically for personal reference or as an aide memoire in meetings. Please feel free to copy these to your heart's content. I waive all rights in relation to these and hope that they help.

I have also included *Top Tips* which are useful nuggets of information (mostly not legal themselves) which may help with legal issues.

I hope that all in all this book will aid your understanding of law and the Internet and wish you every success with your e-business.

CHAPTER 2

ISPs

This book is not really intended as a guide for Internet Service Providers (ISPs) who have many and complicated issues to deal with and need specialist legal advice or a book of their own. However, for anyone who has an e-business or who deals with ISPs it is important to understand not only what an ISP does but also what restrictions or rights an ISP has in particular. Where an e-business site includes a bulletin board, community notice board or otherwise displays content which is provided by consumers and displayed without editing (e.g. book reviews on Amazon), the e-business is in a very similar position to an ISP and the risks, liabilities and benefits which apply to an ISP will apply similarly to the e-business.

2.1   What is an ISP?

Internet Service Providers or ISPs currently exist in three general forms: ISPs which provide Internet services to members of the public and also own and host their own network; ISPs which host networks but provide no services to the public; and ISPs which provide Internet services to the public but who rely on a third party ISP to host their services. It is generally of little concern to the public whether their ISP provides their own network or access to a third party's network so long as the service which is received by them is adequate and as a result of this when the mainstream press and public refer to an ISP they generally refer to public-facing ISPs (whether they self-host or have a third-party host) such as Freeserve.

The services which the public will generally receive from an ISP are e-mail, personal site hosting, domain name registration, portal content, promotions and updates. There may also be a host of worthwhile add-on services such as diary management. The home page of the ISP will generally allow the user to personalise this to the user's requirements and will certainly offer the user a number of channels of content and services – such as travel or beauty channels and services like traffic or sports updates. ISPs are very competitive and go to great lengths to gain competitive advantage over each other by providing users with more attractive or useful content. This often involves relationships with third parties who provide content on the portal or which can be linked to/from the portal. Over time more and more on the Internet appears to be the result of joint ventures between businesses.

2.2   Free ISPs

There are two types of customer-facing ISPs: free ISPs, of which Freeserve was the first, and ISPs which charge for Internet access. A free ISP does not necessarily mean that calls are free, but rather that there is no charge for the Internet account, and that the customer has unmetered access. There may still be a charge for use of the Internet which is the cost of the telephone connection. The Advertising Standards Authority (ASA) has recommended that ISPs which offer such a service make it clear that only access is free. Prior to Freeserve all UK ISPs' registered customers had to pay for monthly accounts when they registered on the Internet. It is fair to say that Freeserve revolutionised the Internet in the UK when it offered free access. Unsurprisingly, many other ISPs followed suit in what has become a very competitive market.

One of the consequences of the concept of a free ISP was that the Internet became more affordable to many people. Another consequence is that when customers register they provide details which may not be checked in great detail by ISPs as there is no financial or account relationship between the two. As a minimum the ISP will normally require CLI (Call Line Identification) to register a customer. Increasingly there are legislative and governmental proposals requesting that ISPs and mobile phone operators hold traffic data. The legitimate crime prevention reasons for doing this obviously need to be balanced against individual privacy.

These days, however, when one signs up to an ISP it is common to be offered a package for calls which allows unlimited telephone access and free Internet access for a set monthly charge and these packages now also may include access by way of ADSL (Asymmetrical Digital Subscriber Line).

2.3   Opening an account

Access to ISPs may be gained by logging on to a pre-loaded icon on a new PC, by searching out the ISP on the net using its Uniform Resource Locator (URL) or by loading a disk into a PC. Disks for ISPs are sent to individuals by ISPs as a form of direct marketing or can be picked up in shops such as Dixons which have an association with a particular ISP, such as in this case Freeserve. Different ISPs' disks are distributed by different shops.

Generally when a customer goes through the ISP's terms and Acceptable Use Policy (AUP) they will be asked to read these and click on an 'I accept' button. These terms will generally make clear to users what the code of practice of the ISP is and what is deemed to be acceptable or unacceptable behaviour. Where behaviour is deemed to be unacceptable – usually because it is in breach of an applicable law or regulation – the ISP will reserve the right to suspend the user's access to the ISP, or remove the user's content or site from the ISP. Actions which are not or at some stage have not been illegal, but have been generally accepted as a breach of netiquette (Internet etiquette), have also been included as grounds for removing content or suspending a user's account. A good example of this would be where a user was sending spam e-mail (see Chapter 8, section 8.8 and Appendix 4).

Where such an event occurred an ISP would generally suspend the account or content, inform the user of why this was the case and ask them to desist from this practice or remove the offending content. If this was not done in the specified time scale then the account would be terminated and the user would be obliged to find a new host ISP should they wish to continue with their account.

In terms of your e-business, if the relevant ISP has its own server on which to host your site, you will enter into an agreement with an ISP to host the site. Whether this will be on the standard ISP terms and AUP, a standard form contract provided by the ISP or on a tailored agreement will very much depend on the type and size of the e-business. In this context size will generally refer to the volume of traffic or use of bandwidth resulting from your e-business. Many small businesses will operate quite happily under the ISP's standard terms. The higher the volume of traffic or bandwidth use is, the more likely it will be that you will negotiate a full business agreement with the ISP. Of particular relevance in these agreements are the service levels as these reflect the service your ISP offers and in turn the service or availability which you are able to offer your users and customers. Chapter 9 reviews the content of hosting agreements.

Freeserve have kindly consented to the inclusion of their ISP terms of registration and AUP which are set out in Appendix 1.

2.4   Regulation of ISPs

There are no requirements for licences or other consents in the UK and anyone who wishes to and has the means can become an ISP.

ISPs do have self-regulatory bodies – ISPA, London Internet Exchange Limited and the Internet Watch Foundation – and most reputable ISPs are members of at least one of these. These have membership requirements and in some instances codes of conduct. They are not, however, able to exact a great deal of pressure on ISPs beyond removing their membership. Many ISPs also have representation on the Internet Crime Forum, run by the Association of Chief Police Officers.

2.5   Liability of an ISP

2.5.1   Potential liability for content?

ISPs provide access to a communications network through which third parties may display and make available information to the general community of Internet users. This can take the form of websites or contributions to newsgroups, bulletin boards and the like. The content of these sites and comments is not regulated by the ISP and is provided in an unedited form to any other Internet viewer who looks at it. ISPs claim to have neither knowledge of this content nor control over it.

The case of *Godfrey* v. *Demon* was the first and probably is still the best known case relating to ISPs. This occurred in 1999, when Mr Godfrey became aware of material which purported to be written by him and which he considered to be defamatory, on a news group hosted by the ISP Demon. Mr Godfrey informed the website of the existence and content of the material and asked them to remove it.

In the UK liability for defamation extends beyond the author to *publishers and editors*. There is also a statutory defence in the

Defamation Act 1996 for anyone who is not one of these three, and so the importance of whether an ISP (or other e-business) should be viewed as an editor or publisher is clear. This *defence* will, however, *be lost* if the party did not take reasonable care in its actions or alternatively became aware that what it was doing allowed the publication of a defamatory statement. By notifying Demon of his concern Mr Godfrey had made them aware of the potentially infringing materials. Demon, however, refused to remove the content from their website and the case hinged on this fact. Demon was, on this basis, held liable for the defamatory content.

As a result of this case ISPs have been put in a difficult position and their response is generally to remove content when they are made aware that this is potentially illegal or infringes third-party rights. An ISP is, however, a service provider and not a court of law and so should not really be in the position of making these decisions. It would be possible for the unscrupulous to demand content be removed when it is not actually illegal and for ISPs who are mindful of the outcome of the Demon case to remove perfectly legal content. The alternative therefore is not to simply remove content but suspend it, notifying the owner of the content of this fact and offering the owner an opportunity to prove its legality before removing it.

There is also a second aspect to this which is that should ISPs want to retain their status as a 'mere conduit' of information then they must not begin to review content placed on their networks by third parties. Should they begin to do so then they would run the risk of being found to be an editor and liable for the content of what is published.

This concept of 'mere conduit' has been taken further by the E-Commerce (EC Directive) Regulations 2002.

In a cross-border case decided in The Netherlands in June 2002, it was upheld on appeal that an ISP was liable for an indirect link to illegal content. The court's decision was based on its interpretation of the Dutch legislation implementing the E-Commerce Directive, which it believed makes ISPs liable for the removal of content which could be assumed to be illegal. This does not follow the concept of mere conduit and the UK's implementation of this aspect of the Directive is discussed further at section 2.8.

2.5.2   Similar issues for e-businesses

The same legal principles will apply to e-businesses which allow user contributions on their site whether these are through book reviews, chat rooms or bulletin boards.

It is important, however, to remember that this is not necessarily the same for every country. In July the German courts upheld a complaint about a notice board. Although the site owner had normally checked this at regular intervals it had not done so for some time and so was not aware that potentially illegal content had been added by a user. The German courts stated that there was a requirement on the owner to check such content at regular intervals. This may be particularly onerous for small businesses or businesses where the site is only a small part of the overall business and does not benefit from a huge amount of resource. It also seems to have been decided on a similar basis to the Dutch ISP case.

2.6 Requirement for disclosure

In the 2001 case of *Totalise* v. *Motley Fool* the ISP Totalise claimed to have been defamed by the content of two discussion groups operated by Motley Fool and Interactive Investor. When complaints were made both operators, having learned the lesson of *Godfrey* v. *Demon* and the potential for liability for third-party content, removed the allegedly defamatory content. Not happy with this Totalise demanded the name of the perpetrator of the comments. The comments had been added to the discussion forum by a web user under the alias of Zeddust.

The court ordered disclosure on a number of bases one of which was that the protection afforded to newspapers which are publishers would not extend to a website content. The site took no responsibility nor accepted liability for the content as they exercised no editorial control.

2.7 Data protection provisions

Although free ISPs require less information to register users, they do generally keep additional user data which can, in accordance with the UK data protection laws, be provided to the police or other third parties. ISPs do not generally provide data to third parties unless they provide the ISP with a court order or notice under the Data Protection Act.

The UK has called for the EU to require ISPs to hold more data through proposals for blanket data retention in order to assist in crime prevention, but the EU approach to date has been that data retention is only necessary for billing purposes. The data in question is traffic data which covers what has been done, e.g. e-mails sent rather than their content.

Data protection is discussed in more depth in Chapter 8, but it is worth noting that the laws of data protection in the UK cover dead people as well as live and also apply to e-mail addresses. This may all be applicable to ISPs and as they hold accounts for a large number of people dealing with the accounts of deccased customers is inevitable.

In 2002 there has been a great deal of coverage of new regulations which have resulted from the events of 11 September in New York. These relate to public bodies and which of these can obtain data, what data and for what purposes. They have been draped in controversy.

In July 2002, in a case involving NTL, the English High Court found that an ISP acting on a court order obtained by the police requiring it to intercept a customer's e-mails was not in breach of data protection laws. In this case, as a result of its technical infrastructure, in order to intercept that customer's e-mails it had to intercept all customers' e-mails without their consent. To achieve this the ISP had to hold on to the customers' e-mails for longer than was normal for billing purposes. This period of time is what is normally allowed under data protection laws. However, the Court believed that as the police needed a court order to achieve this enough checks were in place to allow this.

Freeserve's data collection notice is set out in Appendix 1.

2.8 E-Commerce Regulations 2002

The E-Commerce (EC Directive) Regulations 2002 ('Regulations') have been the source of some confusion for commercial people working in e-business. One of the reasons for the confusion is the Directive's terminology. The Directive refers to Information Society Service Providers – ISSPs – which are all of those individuals or companies which provide services via electronic means, and does not simply refer to ISPs but to a wider pool. Having established this to be the case and that the bulk of the Regulations do refer to all e-businesses, it is then important to consider the parts which do refer to ISPs. These relate to caching, the concept of mere conduit and hosting.

2.8.1 Mere conduit

This term has been used for some time to explain the situation of an ISP where it passes on third-party content via its network. This term of art has been further defined by the new Regulations.

The Regulations provide that where a service constitutes the transmission of information which is provided by a recipient of the service, in a communication network, or where the service constitutes the provision of access to a network, the service provider is not liable if it did not initiate the transmission (although may have done so from a technical point of view), did not select the recipient of the transmission and did not select or modify the information contained in that transmission.

This act of transmission/provision of access is specified to include the storage of the information so long as this was for the sole purpose of carrying out the transaction and also where the information was not stored for longer than is reasonably necessary for the transmission.

In the case of an ISP, examples of its application would include users accessing a site through its services or to e-mails being sent across its networks.

2.8.2   Hosting

The Regulations define this as the storage of information provided by the recipient of a service. The service provider is not liable for this content if the service provider does not have actual knowledge that the information is in breach of a law and it is not aware of facts or circumstances (i.e. has actual knowledge) which would make it apparent to the service provider that either the information or the activity was unlawful. On obtaining this knowledge the service provider must act expeditiously to remove the content or stop the activity. This is all subject to the information provider not acting under the control of the service provider.

In the case of an ISP this could, among other things, apply to the content or sites which it hosts on behalf of its users. This would range from chat rooms to websites.

This is not exactly the mere conduit type of defence which the UK ISPs were hoping for, and there may in fact be a duty for the ISPs (and other service providers) to monitor or take action in certain circumstances, which goes beyond what the ISPs currently do as a matter of practice and would have wanted the law to require. This can of course be seen from the German and Dutch cases discussed above. There is, however, currently no actual obligation to monitor in the UK.

2.8.3 *Caching*

In the same environment the Regulations remove liability for the transmission where this information is stored for the sole purpose of making more efficient onward transmission of it to other recipients at their request. Generally for an ISP this is where a website requested by a user is then cached or stored by the ISP to allow faster access for the next user who requests it. However, when the ISP does this it does not know if the site which it has cached contains illegal content.

The service provider can rely on this where it does not modify the information, complies with rules on access and updating of the information which are recognised by the industry, does not interfere with the lawful use of technology, and acts 'expeditiously' to disable or remove access to information stored by it on its becoming aware (having actual knowledge) that this information has at source (i.e. the actual site) been disabled, has had access to it removed or is subject to a court order requiring this.

In all three cases the exemption from liability is in respect of damages, other pecuniary remedies or criminal sanction.

The Regulations also deal specifically with notice for the purpose of actual knowledge. In determining whether a service provider had actual knowledge a court will consider all of the relevant circumstances including whether a service provider has received a notice and the extent to which any such notice included the details of its sender, details of the location of the information and details of the unlawful activity or information.

2.9   Unbundling the local loop

The move from traditional twisted copper pair or narrow-band telephone lines to broadband technology is occurring now in the UK. This phenomenon of moving from the old local telephone system to broadband technology has been a slow one and one which has been surrounded by controversy. BT's strong position in the local access network, having the majority of the existing standard lines, has generally meant that it has managed the conversion of local phone lines to the new digital and high capacity lines to its customers. Allowing third parties to have access to and to place their equipment in BT's exchanges in order to implement the change over is known as *unbundling the local loop*. These new broadband lines are necessary for both BT and third-party providers to provide the user with both new and better quality new media products. The slowness of this migration to the new lines has been greatly criticised and a source of discontent for ISPs and e-businesses.

Access to the Internet requires two elements of telephone technology. The first of these is network access and the second is the connection of customers to the Internet itself.

The new technology ADSL (Asymmetrical Digital Subscriber Line), which will allow users access to higher quality Internet services, will be faster. This means that load time and in turn call duration will be reduced by the new technology, saving the end user money or allowing the user to see or use more for the same cost.

The management of the changeover is monitored by OFTEL who are the regulators of the telecommunications industry.

ADDITIONAL INFORMATION

ISPA can be contacted on http://www.ispa.org.uk

LINX can be found at www.linx.net

Internet Watch Foundation can be contacted on http://www.iwf.org.uk/index.htm

The Internet Crime Forum website can be found at http://www.internetcrimeforum.org.uk

OFTEL can be contacted on www.oftel.org

The full details of the Demon case can be found at www.courtservice.gov.uk/godfrey2.htm, www.courtservice.gov.uk/godfrey3.htm

Freeserve can be found at www.freeserve.com

CHAPTER 3

Employees and e-business

3.1   Introduction

Whether you are a new world or an old world business the chances are that your employees will use e-mail and possibly the Internet in the course of their employment. When I first began working on Freeserve one of the people who came up with the idea of a free ISP told me that the concept would never have been developed if it had not been for Dixons' progressiveness in giving its staff access to the Internet (for business purposes) many years before most other businesses considered doing so. Giving your staff access to e-mail and the Internet may not have an effect which is as dramatic as their developing a major new business, but at the same time it will undoubtedly provide them with a useful business tool and access to a mass of information. For many people e-mail is now one of the main methods of communication in their business as it provides a fast, inexpensive and (generally) efficient route for communication anywhere in the world.

With these new tools come concerns – employees have the scope to waste time by spending their days 'playing' with these new tools rather than working, or cause an employer to incur liability for their inappropriate or illegal actions. An employer is generally liable for its employees' actions in the course of their business. These risks are not a reason to run scared from the effective use of these e-tools, but are the reason for becoming familiar with the potential risks and making employees aware both of the risks and the business policy you have decided to adopt in relation to their use. To do this first requires an understanding of the risks and issues.

3.2 Use of the Internet at work

3.2.1 Copyright

Employees may download information, music, etc. from the Internet and print or pass this on without first obtaining the right or licence to use such information in this way. When information is downloaded from the Internet onto a computer screen a transient copy is made, but when it is printed out or saved onto a hard drive then a true copy will be made. In such situations the download and the passing – transient and actual copies – of this information are both potential breaches of the Copyright, Designs and Patents Act 1988. It is arguable that there is an implied licence to do this which is created by the business including the information in the site and on the Web.

3.2.2   *Illegal information or content*

An employee may view or download illegal information online. This could be anything from a defamatory statement to pornography. If this information is in breach of UK laws and is accessed from a work PC or during the course of employment then the employer may be liable with his employee for the employee's accessing of the same.

3.3   E-mail use

E-mail is a fast and easy method of communication which may by its informal nature lull employees into saying things or saying them in a way which they would not normally put in writing. However, unlike a phone conversation e-mail creates a written record of conversations. As a business is 'vicariously liable' or responsible for the acts of its employees in the course of their employment an employer may find itself responsible for some of its employees' actions even where the action has been forbidden by the employer. An employer will not, however, be liable where an employee is considered to be 'off on a frolic of their own' or doing something which is not legitimately part of their employment.

I have set out below some of the main concerns associated with e-mail use in the workplace.

3.3.1   *Discrimination and harassment*

The use of e-mail as a method of harassing or discriminating against another employee or other third party could result in a claim based on discrimination. A company may be guilty of an offence where it fails to take action against sexual, racial and other discrimination. E-mails may provide a clear record of inappropriate conduct.

No right-thinking employer would want this type of conduct in the workplace but perhaps more important is that an employer may be found vicariously liable for its employees' acts of discrimination. However, it is a defence to such a claim for the employer to have taken steps to prevent the acts of harassment or discrimination. In the case of e-mail the employer should make its employees aware of the risks of harassment in the context of e-mail.

3.3.2   *Defamation*

Defamation is defined in legislation as the publication of a statement which would lower any right-thinking member of society's opinion of the victim of the defamation, unless this statement is true (the ultimate defence to defamation being truth). An individual may be defamed, but equally a company may be defamed.

In a now famous case as long ago as 1995, Norwich Union made a High Court apology and paid damages of more than £450,000 to Western Provident. This occurred as the result of one or more Norwich Union employees disseminating information which inferred that Western Provident was insolvent or otherwise in financial trouble and under investigation by the DTI. This information was circulated from Norwich Union's internal e-mail system.

The law of defamation is a complicated area and it is not the purpose of this book to explain it. However, it is possible that there is a risk on the part of an employer where its employee makes statements in e-mails which are read by third parties (whether internal or external third parties) and which are potentially defamatory of a third party. Not only a legal risk but a commercial risk might also occur where an employee makes such a statement which is potentially defamatory of their employer.

Deletion of e-mails does not remove an e-mail. It may still be recovered from the hard drive. In litigation it is possible that an employee's e-mail will be discoverable and that it will be recovered from the hard drive if it is pertinent.

Employees should be warned generally against making defamatory statements and the risk of these being made in e-mails explained to them. The seriousness of this should be clear in the Internet and e-mail policy.

3.3.3 Competition

As a cautionary note, e-mail documents are also 'discoverable' in European and UK investigations into anti-competitive practices. E-mails may therefore be used to provide evidence of such practices and again employees should be made aware of the risks.

3.3.4 Viruses

Viruses, as we have learned by experience of the likes of Melissa and the Love Bug, can bring a business to a standstill. Many viruses are imported into businesses through e-mail attachments. Obviously these can be attached to a business e-mail as easily as to a purely personal e-mail. However, they are probably more likely in personal e-mails.

Employees should generally be warned against opening attachments which are not clearly business attachments and this should be included in the Internet policy. If the policy is reasonably liberal then there will still be a risk of this happening and perhaps it would be wise to follow this up with a statement along the lines that any known viruses will be notified to all members of staff and when this occurs only attachments known to be business attachments will be opened. Perhaps in this situation even business attachments should not be opened.

This relies on businesses to make sure that they keep up to date with major virus problems and then notify their staff by e-mail or on their intranet site if they have one each time such a situation arises. This notification should give employees some indication of what they are looking for and absolutely prohibit the opening of such an attachment or any attachment that could reasonably be believed to be that.

3.3.5   Forming a binding contract

There are two main risks from this front. The first is that an employee makes a representation to a third party which is untrue or otherwise misleads them and which could in turn affect the validity of a contract. The second is that an employee may unwittingly commit its employer and form a contract on the employer's behalf with a third party. It would be very easy for a member of staff to send an e-mail saying 'yes I would like to buy this from you' without realising that they were accepting an offer and entering into a binding contractual relationship. That is fine if the employee has the authority to do this (and intended to) but is problematic where he acts beyond the scope of his authority.

Employers should make this risk clear to employees, explaining that they should not make any representations to third parties which are untrue and should not commit to anything beyond their remit/authority. Any restrictions on an employee's authority must be clear to them.

The Electronic Communications Act 2000 gives digital signatures the same validity as written signatures and is discussed in more detail in Chapter 7 on security. However, at this point it is worth noting that if an employee has a digital signature the implication is that they have authority to bind the company. The impression given to third parties and associated risks should be considered when deciding whether or not employees should have e-mail with such a signature.

3.4   Security and confidentiality

There are two sides to the risks to security and confidentiality – the outbound and the inbound.

3.4.1   Outbound risks

If we consider first the outbound aspect, there is an obvious risk that information which is confidential and sent through e-mail out to the rest of the world may fall into the hands of third parties who were not the intended recipients of the mail and/or the information that it contains. This is little different from the risks which attach to fax communication. Employees should be made aware of that risk and the importance of considering whether there is confidential information in what they are sending. If there is, then a decision as to what will be done to protect that information must be made. The means of protection are twofold: a robust security system which possibly includes encryption (as discussed in Chapter 7) and a policy applicable to the dissemination of confidential information by e-mail.

Although a very restrictive policy might on the face of it help, as the Internet has developed into an everyday method of business communication, so it has become more likely that employees will have little option but to send secure information. It is therefore perhaps more practical to require confidential information to be identified as such and for an appropriate disclaimer to be added. Such a disclaimer will bring the potentially confidential nature of the information to the attention of third parties. Most companies use this type of disclaimer and these are discussed in more detail below.

It is also worth bearing in mind that it is possible to innocently or accidentally send e-mail. Anyone going through the learning curve of using e-mail will have accidentally sent an e-mail – either to the correct recipient before it is ready or to the wrong recipient. Many systems will correct what they recognise as a wrong e-mail address to the one nearest in its address book. This type of issue can pose a risk where confidential information is sent to the wrong recipient as a result of it, e.g. where a business is considering sacking one of its employees and the system overrides the external adviser's name with that of the employee! This should be reviewed not only from a legal/policy but also from a technical/internal network point of view.

Another danger posed by e-mail is that of the disgruntled employee or ex-employee who disseminates company information which is confidential or untrue. This may be done not only by way of e-mail but also through bulletin boards or chat rooms. This may be difficult to prove and deal with.

3.4.2   *Inbound risks*

Inbound risks relate mainly to the downloading of viruses from e-mail attachments and it is important that employees are made aware of this and informed that they should not open attachments other than business attachments in an attempt to restrict this risk. Many businesses lost hours or days of business as a consequence of the 'Love Bug'. It can be difficult for an employee to distinguish potentially dangerous e-mails from other e-mail information or updates they may receive. A good firewall will limit the amount of spam an employee receives and make this simpler. Also, when a potential virus risk occurs, employees should be notified of this and instructed not to open suspicious e-mails.

Internally there is also a risk of either employees or third parties hacking into parts of the IT system to which they do not have access.

3.5   Examples of employee abuse

There have also been instances where employees have intentionally, and in some cases rather stupidly, forwarded e-mails.

I am sure that, due to the press reportage which arose from the following, you have heard of Claire Swires. Details of her sexual escapades were apparently sent by her through e-mail to her lawyer boyfriend. The boyfriend was more than a little pleased with the praise he received in the e-mail and rather unchivalrously forwarded it to a number of friends. In turn they forwarded it to a number of people and within a few hours millions of people are believed to have received the e-mail. The e-mail which was forward by the lawyer of course included his address at his law firm employer and in turn the law firm's name. Sadly for Miss Swires, the ability to create this volume of e-mail readership in an extremely short period of time has become commonly known as the Swires effect.

Although you might expect lawyers to be more aware of the laws and wary of the pitfalls, press reports have made clear that they are not exempt from this problem. In another report of this form of behaviour or e-mail abuse the effect occurred as a result of a lawyer based in the Hong Kong office of a UK law firm sending a hoax e-mail to a number of people claiming that a member of the Hong Kong office had been murdered. The hoax e-mail portrayed itself as a very callous internal memo from the law firm and the employee's actions represented that particular firm in a bad light.

3.6   E-mail and Internet policies

A policy should be written and provided to all employees. If it is to be enforced it should ideally be signed by the employee and made part of their contract of employment. If it is not then all employees should at least be provided with a copy of the policy. If it is not provided to all employees then, irrespective of the fact that it has been well drafted and is on the face of it legally enforceable, due to the fact that it has not been brought to certain employees' attention it may not be enforceable against those employees.

This policy should be consistent with any other policy that an employee has to comply with in their workplace, and so a total ban on e-mail may not sit well with a policy which allows reasonable phone calls for personal use. The significance of the cost of Internet use may be no more than the cost of a local phone call but may have legal implications depending on what is being viewed.

In international businesses local laws may mean that the same policy cannot be enforced in a uniform manner in each country.

If a business uses contractors or consultants, then should they be given access to the Internet and/or e-mail, the policy should also be brought to their attention. To the outside world they may seem like any other employee and potentially the risks of a contractor to a business are the same as those of an employee.

The employer's policy should cover:

1. What is proper use of e-mail and the Internet.

2. What, if any, use is expressly prohibited.

3. The risks of binding the company and the employee's role in this.

---

4. The fact that deletion of an e-mail will not remove it.

5. The consequences and potential risk of abuse of the policy.

6. The fact that the right to monitor is expressly reserved. (This should be read in conjunction with section 3.7 on monitoring.)

A sample policy, kindly provided by McDermott, Will & Emery, is presented in Appendix 1.

From a technical and practical point of view it is worth considering:

1. Whether an employee has a legitimate need for Internet or e-mail access. If they do not and they are provided with it then this access may send a mixed message. If a strict policy is to be put in place it may be wise to remove access from those who do not require it for business. It is also worth bearing in mind that even among those who do have access the need for that access may be different and a blanket policy may not work.

2. If access is a key or essential part of an individual's employment then it may be necessary for that individual to familiarise themselves with other websites and their ordering process. These may be the sites of competitors or sites which demonstrate good practice. A good example of this is my own role which (given the need to review websites from a legal point of view) has required me to surf to understand how various other businesses deal with issues, e.g. payment by cheque. This surfing was for a business purpose and would, even in a restricted environment, be quite legitimate. To some extent this legitimate need to surf is likely to apply to anyone working in a 'new world' economy. In such

circumstances an absolute ban on use or surfing may well not work and it is necessary to make the restriction on use one which is subject to reasonableness and to trust the employee's judgment to an extent.

3. Whether access is available for all or only those who need it, the use of technology can limit security risk and access to inappropriate sites.

A guideline for an e-commerce policy covering both Internet and e-mail usage is set out below. It is key that all employees are made aware of such a policy and that it is clear and easy for all employees to understand.

Employees should be given guidance along the following lines:

•   Never send e-mails at work which you would not want your employer or a third party to read.

•   Never send abusive, discriminatory or defamatory e-mails either internally within the company or to any external party.

•   Never send anything in an e-mail that you would not send in a letter.

•   Do not send e-mails which contain confidential information unless they are secure or make sure that these are marked confidential (depending on access to technology).

•   Be aware that you may bind the company using e-mail – do not commit to anything in an e-mail which your job does not authorise you to do. If you do not know what you have authority to do confirm this with your manager.

- Never give any passwords etc. to any third parties as you may compromise your or your employer's security.

- Remember that all e-mails sent at work are your employer's property and are subject to monitoring for business purposes.

- Internet use may also be monitored. (Use should be restricted to reasonable personal use and where possible personal use should be during breaks.)

- Do not open attachments to e-mails unless these are clearly for business purposes – attachments can spread viruses.

- Do not use the e-mail for non-work or personal purposes. Limit your personal use of the Internet to outside of your work hours. You may use e-mail and the Internet but only a reasonable amount, in line with the general policy on use of business equipment and not in a way which affects your ability to work.

- Digital signatures may be used by employees only with the consent of their manager.

- Be aware that deletion of e-mails will not remove them from the company's system and if necessary they can be rebuilt.

- Breach of these policies may result in liability on the part of your employer and may be treated as a disciplinary matter.

The Information Commissioner is in the process of providing more detailed guidelines on employees and the Internet including employee use of the latter. These will be in four parts and are currently being implemented on the website part by part. The first of these concerning recruitment was published in June 2002. The second part, monitoring at work and the extent to which this can be carried out for e-mail, telephone, etc. is currently being distributed for consultation by the Office of the Information Commissioner. The other two parts will cover employment records, their collection, storage, disclosure and deletion, and medical information.

3.7   Monitoring

The 'Big Brother' approach to employees may be intrusive and in some instances contrary to law. However, if an employee Internet policy is to be introduced and enforced it is necessary to have effective but legal monitoring in place. It is common practice to do this and can be done to an extent legitimately. This section must be read in the light of the Information Commissioner's guidance when it is finalised.

Subject to this, if an express right to monitor has been reserved, an employer may monitor its employees' e-mails subject to the restraints set out in the Human Rights Act 1998 (which incorporated the Human Rights Directive into English law) and the Regulation of Investigatory Powers Act 2000 (RIPA). RIPA created a new action of unlawful interception of communication which potentially impacts on the employer's ability to monitor both telephone calls and e-mail unless it has the employee's consent.

An employee must be made aware of the possible interception and the circumstances in which this may occur. This is why it is important to bring this to the employee's attention in the Internet policy. However, this will not inform the recipient of a mail who is effectively also being monitored and so it is also wise to ensure that they too are informed. This is often done through the addition of wording informing them of this in the e-mail disclaimer attached to the bottom of all mails sent by the employer's system. An example of such a disclaimer is set out in Appendix 1 (see also section 3.9 below).

It is also worth remembering that even if an employee does not use their e-mail access for business purposes, e-mail is an informal and friendly method of communication and may lead to business contacts forwarding jokes, attachments or other communication that an employer would not necessarily expect. The receipt of this would not mean that an employee was in breach of even the strictest e-mail policies and must be allowed for in the policy.

3.7.1 Regulation of Investigatory Powers Act 2000

This Act covers the confidentiality of communications on private networks which are connected to public networks. As almost all intranets are connected to a public network it is unlikely that a business will be exempt from this. An offence which makes it unlawful to intercept a communication on a private telephone network has been created. E-mails are sent through a telephone network and so fall into this category of communication. It will, however, not be unlawful to intercept communications where the consent of the sender has been obtained or it is reasonable to believe that this has been obtained. Also the Secretary of State has a power to make regulations setting out the circumstances where interception may be lawful and has done so through DTI Guidelines (October 2000). These set out when it is possible for an employer to intercept communications on its own network.

Employers may monitor employee communications for purposes relevant to the employer's business provided that it has made reasonable efforts to notify its employees and their correspondents that they may be monitored. Business purposes may include:

- prevention or detection of a crime;

- monitoring compliance with the business's e-mail policy;

- detecting unauthorised use of the e-mail system;

- monitoring whether the employee is using the system for personal use.

If an interception is to be made for any purpose other than one of these then it is necessary to have the individual's consent to it.

The Regulation of Investigating Powers Act 2000 was not greeted with a warm welcome. Many commentators have criticised it as a 'snooper's charter' and claimed that it may be in breach of the Human Rights Act 1998.

3.7.2   Human Rights Act 1998

This Act states that 'everyone has the right to respect for his private and family life, his home and his correspondence', at section 8(1). How this legislation may be enforced is unclear and in the light of recent high-profile cases it is certainly worth being aware of its existence. If the use of e-mail for purely personal matters is prohibited then it is unlikely that an employee would have a basis for a claim. However, this will often not be the case and as can be seen from this chapter e-mail usage may not be as clear-cut as this.

Over the summer of 2002 the Information Commissioner has challenged the validity of government proposals regarding access to personal data on the grounds that this would be a breach of the Human Rights Act.

3.7.3   Data Protection Act 1998

The Data Protection Act 1998 requires that processing of data should be done fairly and lawfully and applies to monitoring which involves the obtaining, recording or processing of personal data by means of automated equipment. The Act and complementary regulations seek to protect individuals and their data.

The Commissioner has recommended general standards to be applied to the monitoring of employee e-mail and these have been set out in the Telecommunication (Lawful Business Practice) (Interception of Communications) Regulations 2000. These advise employers as follows:

- Do not monitor content if a record of e-mail traffic alone is sufficient. Any further monitoring should be targeted and strictly limited.

- Only monitor e-mails retained and not deleted by employees.

- Do not monitor e-mails which are clearly personal.

- If there is a need to check the mail boxes of employees in their absence make sure that they are aware this might happen.

- A need for virus detection does not justify reading the contents of incoming e-mail and where possible a technological solution rather than monitoring should be utilised.

The Commissioner will consider whether an employer has taken account of these principles when reviewing any complaint brought by an employee.

Although not strictly relevant to e-mail it is also worth being aware that OFTEL (the Office of Telecommunications) has also issued guidelines which require employers to respect employee privacy and to make available private telephone lines.

TOP TIP

In the light of this confusing and sometimes contradictory legislation how can employee monitoring be dealt with? Suggestions are as follows:

- Provide employees with a clear and simple e-mail policy which informs them of the possibility of monitoring and interception, and makes them aware of the circumstances in which this might take place. Ideally this policy should be incorporated by reference into the employee's employment contract and should state that breach of the policy is a disciplinary matter.

- Make third parties aware of the possibility that e-mail correspondence may be intercepted in the disclaimer.

- When monitoring is viewed as necessary it should be conducted in a reasonable manner and those who do the monitoring should be made aware of any good practices put in place by the company. Monitoring should not be done in a heavy-handed manner.

- If there is a technical solution which could be used instead of monitoring, use that. These best practices should use the Information Commissioner's guidance as a reference.

3.8   Enforcement

If an e-policy is put in place and monitoring undertaken then it is essential that it is applied uniformly within a business and does not in any way appear to have been enforced in an arbitrary or discriminatory manner. An employee would have a good argument against the enforcement of the policy if it appeared that they were being singled out for punishment, and this would be evidenced by that employee doing neither more nor less than their fellow employees but being punished for it. At the same time when a disciplinary action is taken against an employee who is in breach this will be a deterrent to others who might stray down the same path and will set a precedent for future dealings.

Employers who breach the employment contract in England may find themselves guilty of constructive dismissal and subject to payment of damages of up to £50,000.

3.9   Disclaimers

Most e-mails received in a business context will have a disclaimer attached. The ability to enforce these will very much depend on how they are worded and some are obviously better than others. Ideally they should be as short as possible and be written in plain English.

A sample disclaimer kindly supplied by McDermott, Will & Emery is set out in Appendix 1.

3.10   Use of consultants

When a business contracts consultants to work on its e-business or at its premises generally there are a number of issues which should be considered. Many of these are raised in more depth in Chapter 9 on contracts.

3.10.1   Intellectual property

Copyright and other intellectual property (IP) rights which may arise in a 'work' (new creation) belong to the individual who creates (is the 'author' of) that work unless it is made in the course of employment when it will vest in (belong to) the employer. This is particularly important where an employee's employment involves actions which create new works such as website content.

If this role is undertaken by a consultant as opposed to an employee (or an employee of a consultant) then the intellectual property will not vest in you (as employer) as it would if this was created by your own employee, but will vest in the consultant.

To transfer in full or 'assign' the intellectual property there must be a written document which must be signed by the person making the assignment (the 'author' or owner of the work). If consultants work in your business in a role which might involve this then the terms of their consultancy contract should contain this written assignment, or there should be a separate document of assignment of this intellectual property and this should be signed.

3.10.2   Policies

Consultants should be made aware of all internal policies such as health and safety. These must also include any e-mail and Internet policies if they are provided with access to them on your business equipment or will be using them in the time when they are working for you.

ADDITIONAL INFORMATION

More information on employment law can be found on the following law firms' websites:

Berwin Leighton Paisner
http://www./berwinleighton.com

McDermott, Will & Emery
http://www.mwe.com

Telecommunications (Lawful Business Practice) (Interception of Communications) Regulations 2000 – DTI Guidance on when interception on an employer's own network may be permitted can be found at www.hmso.gov.uk under :Lawful Business Practice

Information Commissioner's Guidance is available at www.dataprotection.gov.uk, and part I of this is currently at www.dataprotection.gov.uk/dpr/dpdoc.nsf

CHAPTER 4

Brand protection

4.1   Names

Websites initially seek traffic and then hope that this traffic can be converted into sales or advertising or some other form of revenue stream. One way of encouraging this traffic is to choose a name which is easy to remember and which attracts people to that site. When a business is lucky or smart enough to find such a name then there is an obvious value to that name and this is something which should be protected. Protection comes in two ways. The first way is to use legal options such as registration of trade marks and domain names to make sure that ownership of the name lies with you and to stop third parties from using it or passing themselves off as you. The second protection in the Internet world is protection from abuses through technology. Obviously these develop with the technology and this list and discussion is not exhaustive, but they include such issues as metatags, domain name hijacking, deep linking and lemon and parody websites.

There are various forms of intellectual property which together will create the legal protection of one's name and restrict the use of a name by third parties.

4.2   Trade name and trade marks

Trade marks can be either unregistered, established by use or registered, established by an application to the Trade Marks Registrar in the appropriate location. As well as the option to register a mark in the UK, there is also the possibility of registering an EC trade mark (or 'CTM' – Community Trade Mark) which will apply across the 15 EU Member States. This can be substantially cheaper than registering a mark in each country. In the UK trade mark registration is governed by the Trade Marks Act 1994.

4.2.1   *What can be protected*

A trade mark can be applied for and obtained for anything capable of 'graphical representation' which distinguishes goods/services from other goods/services, e.g. words, designs, letters or numerals, graphic representations of a smell or a shape. The JIF lemon and glass Coca-Cola bottles are two good examples of this. However, recent case law has made it clear that this will not apply where the shape is inherent to the function of the product.

4.2.2 Making the application

Trade marks are registered in various classes and it is necessary to apply to register the mark in all relevant classes. It is possible for there to be more than one owner of the same mark each of which has a registration in a different class or classes. A good example of this is Apple where the mark is legitimately owned by both the computer company and the record company and is in each case protected by registration, but in different classes. As a result of this, a failure to register the mark in a relevant class will leave the mark open to a third party registering it in that class. There are now 45 classes of goods/services in which a mark can be registered in the UK (the existing 42 plus three new services classes as of 1 January 2002). If you believe that you are able to register your name as a mark the appropriate classes should be carefully considered.

In completing the application it is probably advisable to have specialist advice either from a trade mark agent or a lawyer. The registration process takes several months and not all words are registrable. For example, anything which is purely descriptive and/or not distinct will not be registrable. Also, if a pre-existing mark which is identical or substantially similar exists then your mark may not be registrable. As a result of this it is necessary to undertake trade mark searches to explore whether such a mark already exists before making an application. This can be done at the trade mark registry but is normally done through a specialist trade mark agent/lawyer who will use online search facilities.

4.2.3   Searches

In the case of an EC mark it is necessary to consider which countries should be searched for the mark. In obtaining the EC mark, the mark is checked by the registry for its inherent registrability; however, no detailed searches are undertaken in the various countries. This means that the CTM office in Alicante could allow the registration of an EC mark and then at a later date it might become apparent that there was a pre-existing similar or identical mark in another of the Member States. Ideally, to be sure that there is no other registration of the same mark in any of the Member States, each country should be searched. However, this can be an expensive process and it may be necessary to consider which countries you are likely to use the mark in where there is a genuine need for protection, then to protect in those countries. Doing this will save costs for searches and registration but does leave the brand with some exposure.

In the case of an EC mark, if the searches are not done in all 15 countries there is a risk that although the EC application is successful, there is a pre-existing mark in one of the countries and that mark has precedence due to the fact that it was pre-existing over the later EC mark in that particular country. A CTM registration is very much 'all or nothing' and if there is a problem with the mark in one territory the CTM will fail. There is a saving grace in the possibility of converting to national registrations; however, before going straight for a CTM application, if objections are a real risk in certain countries, it may be wiser to consider a 'Madrid Protocol' application through WIPO (World Intellectual

Property Organisation) which permits one to cherry-pick the countries of interest and proceed with one process for registration.

In the case of an e-business where the mark will be not only pan-European but truly international, the Madrid Protocol has the further advantage of including additional countries outside the EU.

4.2.4   Pre-existing marks

There is sometimes a misunderstanding around what a trade mark can do. It does protect the owner in the relevant territory from anyone else registering or using the brand in relation to the appropriate classes (remember someone else may use it in other classes), but only where such is used for the first time by the third party after the protection date (the date when protection begins). In the case of a UK trade mark this protection date is the date of the application being filed and is called the 'priority date'. In the case of an EC mark registration this protection begins on the date of publication in the Official Journal. If a third party is using the mark before that date then its use may be legitimate and there may be nothing that you can do – the registration will not protect the holder from pre-existing marks whether these are registered or not.

In the case of an unregistered mark it is protected by its course of usage rather than by registration. Obviously it is very difficult to check for such marks as, unlike registered marks, there is no register listing these (although one can undertake what are known as 'common law searches').

4.2.5   Objections to an application

When an application is made there is an opportunity for objections. Holders of major marks or companies with adequate resources will often check the applications made on a regular basis to ensure that nobody registers something which will infringe their mark or which will cause a risk to their brand. Where they find such an application they will make an objection to the new registration. If no objections are raised then the mark will proceed to registration. Objections may be raised in the UK either by the registry or by an individual. Currently the UK registry does check all new applications. This is not the case in the EU and marks will continue in the registration process unless an objection is made by an individual.

In the UK the application process takes around 6–9 months and in the EU the timing is a little longer at 12–15 months. In the case where there are objections the mark may not be registered, and even if it is then this will take substantially longer.

4.2.6   Duration and need to renew

A successful mark is registered in the case of both UK and EC marks for a renewable period of ten years. If a mark is not used within five years of its registration then it is possible for this to be attacked for non-use and set aside. If you are looking at an international strategy and considering what to do in Europe, it is possible that, despite having a registration which is successful on an EU basis now, if you do not then go on to use the mark in a particular country for that five-year period and a third party begins to use it then they may be able to challenge your right to the mark. Whether the fact that your website could be seen from that country is enough to show a course of use in a country is not clear. (It would be much better to be able to show some kind of trade via the web with customers in the country, even if there was no physical presence there.)

It is also now possible to register marks with their suffixes such as **.com** as part of the mark. If it is possible that you would wish to include this in your mark then the UK TM Registry has guidelines on this which should be consulted.

Making a registration protects not only the mark itself but may also be useful as it puts competitors on notice of the mark's existence and protection.

4.2.7   *International*

Outside of the EU there are a number of treaties which cover mutual recognition of marks and if any particular country is a concern the mark should be registered in that country or the reciprocity of an appropriate treaty confirmed. Be aware that this may be a costly exercise. As mentioned above, one more cost-effective route if one is seeking both pan-EU and extra-EU protection is to consider a single process such as the Madrid Protocol procedure which removes the need for multiple applications, fees, renewals and agents in different countries.

4.3   Database rights

These are relatively new intellectual property rights, having been introduced by the EU on 1 January 1998, which clarify the protection afforded to databases. They are granted to the 'maker' of a database (as opposed to the 'author' of a copyright work). The database will be protected by this whether it qualifies for copyright protection or not. The effect of this is that where a database may not, for example, be protected in some EU countries as a result of the lack of creative originality required to justify copyright protection, e.g. a telephone list, it will now have a form of intellectual property protection by way of the database right.

Database rights attach to original databases for 15 years from the end of the year of completion. It is also likely that where there is a substantial amendment or update of a database, a new 15-year term will run from that date. For a database to be 'original' there must be some selection or arrangement of the content such that the database constitutes the author's own intellectual creation.

It is necessary to prove that there has been a substantial expenditure on the database, e.g. by keeping a copy of relevant receipts or a record of employees' time spent on this.

In 2001 the UK had its first case on database rights in the William Hill case. The British Horseracing Board Ltd ('BHB') owned a substantial horse-racing database which listed information about meets, horses' form, jockeys, etc. BHB ran a commercial business licensing this data to bookmakers. William Hill allegedly helped itself to some of the data on this database without paying for a licence. William Hill argued that this was not an 'extraction' or 'utilisation' of a substantial part of the database, which would infringe the database right , as the amount or part which was used by them was not substantial. The first instance court held that repetitive extraction of a small part of a database could effectively amount to the extraction of a substantial part. On appeal, the Court of Appeal referred the issue to the ECJ (European Court) for a definitive view, the outcome of which is still pending at the time of writing.

4.4   Copyright

Copyright is a form of intellectual property right which protects certain 'works' and gives the owner or 'author' of the works various rights in it. These include the right to object to unauthorised copying (these terms are defined in the Copyright, Designs and Patents Act 1988, as amended). There is no requirement for registration in the UK, although as there is in other countries it may be helpful to add a copyright notice, e.g. '© Amanda C. Brock, All rights reserved'. The protection offered by copyright has not been harmonised within the EU, although the length of the protection has been and it is the life of the author plus seventy years. In addition to the legal right in copyright authors have certain moral rights, such as the right to object to false attribution of authorship of a work, e.g. content.

In the case of an e-business, copyright will not generally protect the business name but will protect the site content or its structure/ code. Protection of the name is dealt with at other points in this book. However, a logo may be in use as one's brand and that will likely attract copyright protection as an 'artistic' work.

It is also worth remembering that the source and object code which make up the site may also be subject to copyright protection.

4.5   Domain names

4.5.1   What is a domain name?

I doubt if there is anyone in the UK who has not heard of a domain name or who does not know what one is, but for the sake of clarity this seems to be the best place to start. A domain name is the consumer-facing name/address used by a website, and by which users will identify the site. This user-friendly front is backed by an IP address which is the technical – numerical – identifier or name of the site, which is used by other hardware and software to recognise a site.

A URL is the Uniform Resource Locator used to find a site on the Internet and follows a protocol which will include the www. reference to the World Wide Web and domain name including TLD (i.e. *.com* or *.fr*).

4.5.2   Primary domains (TLDs) and secondary domains

There is often confusion between primary and secondary-level domain names. A primary or top-level domain name (TLD) is one of the generic top-level domain names (GTLDs) which has a code assigned to it by ICANN (Internet Corporation for Assigned Names and Numbers) such as **.com** or one of the country codes such as **.es** assigned to each country. There are seven original TLDs and a further seven new TLDs which are in the process of being established. The secondary part of a name is the identifier of the unique owner of the name such as amanda@amandabrock.com. In some cases there may even be a tertiary domain name such as amanda.amandabrock.com.

There is also a sub-category of a primary domain name such as **.co.uk**, in the UK. If you are trading in a number of countries you may wish to register a number of these country codes or sub-categories of these rather than trade under a single TLD, or alternatively you may wish to trade under a TLD, or both.

There is some confusion as to what these secondary or sub-category country codes are and when they should be registered. Many people become confused and believe that **.com.es** is also a top-level country code. This confusion is not helped by the fact that many domain name agencies try to encourage registration of both the country code and the sub-categories. It is necessary to look at each country where the name is to be protected and decide whether there is real value in protecting the sub-categories before money is spent on doing so. Some less reputable registration agencies may try to encourage you to register secondary-level domains where this is not really necessary.

4.5.3   Sale of sub-category names

This is not a huge point, but a number of scams trying to sell businesses secondary domain names or sub-categories of country codes as if they are TLDs (always at exorbitant prices) have occurred in the last couple of years. If an individual does not understand the difference between what is really used in a country and appropriate to register and what the TLDs are then they may be duped into paying a lot of money for a name which does not carry any true benefit for them. If you are offered a domain incorporating your brand then make careful investigations into what the name actually is and what the local registrar will do about this before you hand over any cash.

4.5.4. *What should you register*

On this basis it is worth looking at a list of the primary TLDs and country codes and using these to establish which names should be registered to provide adequate protection for your business where it operates. In doing this you need to consider what your e-business aims to achieve and what your likely markets will be. It is also worth considering if you have any ambitions in other countries and whether you plan to realise these by cross-border sales or by setting up websites with separate domains in each country.

Remember that not all TLDs are applicable to your business. For example, **.org** applies to organisations, **.net** to network providers and **.biz** to businesses. If a business or organisation registers its name under one of these three it is likely that the other two will not be relevant to it.

I have set out below a checklist of TLDs and a checklist of European country codes to assist you in this. Beware that these have changed fairly frequently over the last couple of years and in some cases the rules are still in development.

The new names are generally being allocated around certain dates, with trade mark owners being given a limited time to make an advance registration. This will allow early registration where only one legitimate trade mark owner exists but not where there is more

CHECKLIST 4.1 TLDs

Existing TLDs

Code	Prerequisites for registration (as at August 2002)
.com	none – commercial organisations – used internationally
.org	none – organisations
.net	none – networks, e.g. ISPs
.edu	accreditation of NSI – US educational
.int	accreditation of NSI – international organisations
.gov	accreditation of NSI – US governmental
.mil	accreditation of NSI – US military

New TLDs

Code	Prerequisites for registration (as at August 2002)
	(The first seven are ICANN accredited.)
.biz	none – ICANN accredited
.name	individuals – ICANN accredited
.info	none – ICANN accredited
.pro	professional – ICANN accredited
.aero	none – ICANN accredited
.coop	co-operatives – ICANN accredited
.mus	museums – ICANN accredited
.firm	none – likely to be used by those who missed .coms (not ICANN accredited)
.nom	personal name (not ICANN accredited)
.shop	none (not ICANN accredited)
.web	businesses focusing on Web (not ICANN accredited)
.arts	alternative to .org – none (not ICANN accredited)
.rec	not ICANN accredited
.eu	European Union but not necessarily governmental – approved by the EU in April 2002 but not yet available as a registry has not been assigned

CHECKLIST 4.2 EUROPEAN COUNTRY CODES

Each country has a two-letter code

Code	Country	Prerequisites for registration (as at December 2000)
.uk	United Kingdom	(.co.uk the secondary name is generally used) none unless right to name challenged
.fr	France	French company with this as trading name or European trademark holder. Restrictions recently relaxed
.es	Spain	Spanish company or resident (currently under review) only – maximum of one name
.it	Italy	none – recently changed
.de	Germany	German company only
.au	Austria	none
.ch	Switzerland	none
.be	Belgium	none
.nl	Netherlands	Dutch company only
.lu	Luxembourg	company in Luxembourg
.no	Norway	none – recently changed
.dk	Denmark	none
.se	Sweden	registered company in Sweden with same name or trading name
.fl	Finland	registered company in Finland with same name or trading name
.is	Iceland	company in Iceland

than one. In the case of multiple legitimate owners this is not so straightforward and in most cases this is dealt with on a first-come first-served basis or a lottery.

In the last couple of years many domain names have been registered. I have been told that every combination of four letters which can be made has been registered as a .com, although this may not be true. However, I tend to believe it and think that it is probably the case for five or possibly six letters too. If it is not then it is certain that few names are left with less than six letters.

4.5.5 New TLDs

There are seven new TLDs which have been approved by ICANN. These are **.biz**, **.info**, **.name**, **.pro**, **.aero**, **.coop**, and **.mu**. The first two of these are now available for registration. In the case of **.biz** and **.info**, in an attempt to avoid cybersquatting and trade mark conflicts, ICANN opened the registrations initially to those who could establish their right to the name through a trade mark registration or the like.

It is difficult to know whether or not it will be worth paying for the registration of these new TLDs, as nobody can be sure how popular they will be or whether they will in fact catch on. However, it is probably worth registering where possible and if they do not prove successful then not going to the expense of renewing any unpopular names.

However, it is clearly possible that there will be more than one company which can prove a legitimate right to the name. In these circumstances the allocation is to be done by way of a random assignment. How many names this will apply to is not yet clear as the closing date for applications on this pre-assignment basis was in late summer 2001 for the main bulk of the names and is being set up on an ongoing basis for other new names.

4.5.6   Cases

There have been a number of disputes over names which have hit the headlines. The most famous are probably the 'one in a million' and 'Harrods' cases which are discussed in a little detail below. You are also likely to have seen press reports of names involving celebrities. In many of these cases a celebrity's name has been registered as a domain name by someone else. Legally it is possible for a personal name to acquire a secondary meaning and to be registrable as a trade mark. This would only be the case where someone is very well known and their name brings certain connotations to mind, such as Monica Lewinski.

Recently, as well as cybersquatting, typosquatting where a third party registers a common mistype of a domain name, has come to light. There has been at least one US case where such bad faith intentional misspelling of trade marks has been found to be illegal.

4.5.7   How do you register a domain name?

A domain name is registered through an allocated registry. In the case of the GTLDs they can be purchased from a company which is accredited by ICANN. Registration can last up to ten years depending on the option purchased. Country codes are registered by national naming authorities. In the UK this is Nominet UK –

www.nominet.org. Names registered in the UK are valid for an initial period of two years.

The registries do not generally vet registrations but allow applications on a first-come first-served basis. If a name is available and someone applies for it then they will, on payment of the appropriate fee, become the owner of the name. Country codes, however, may be subject to national restrictions and some of these for Europe are set out in Checklist 4.2 on p. 62.

Individuals who want to buy a name may do so through the registry direct, or may buy it through one of the companies which specialises in this such as Net Names – www.netnames.com. These companies charge a fee which is more than the actual cost of registration and includes a mark-up for administration. It is worth shopping around as these costs can vary hugely. When a name is registered it needs to be allocated to an IP address. Very simply, this is an address which attaches to a server and from which the server can be identified. As most individuals do not have a server the provision of this through a registration company is part of the service paid for.

If you use any of these companies I would recommend that you consider not only their price for registration but also look at the terms on which they offer the registration. Most of these look to exclude liability for lost names.

4.5.8   *Length of ownership and renewal*

Domain names are registered for a period of time which may be optional or may be fixed – in some countries you can pay for one year or two. This depends on the suffix which is registered, e.g.

.com is for ten years and **.co.uk** can be for two. It is important once you have a domain name or a portfolio of domain names that the renewal dates are noted and that someone ensures that the renewal takes place.

A renewal notice will be sent to the holder of a name, and will be marked for the attention of an individual within the holder's business who is noted at the registry as the administrative contact. If, for example, that person has left the business and the notice is not passed to the appropriate person, there is a risk that the renewal will not happen. This is particularly relevant in an international portfolio of names where the renewal notice may be in a language which the recipients do not understand. There is nothing to stop a third party registering a name where a renewal has not taken place. In fact, on one occasion I was able to retrieve a name from a cybersquatter without paying anything to them as they forgot to renew the name on the renewal data and I applied for it.

4.5.9   The registration decision

Deciding what to register can be difficult. It is necessary to first work out what countries you wish the name to be registered in, whether your main trading will be under a GTLD, e.g. a **.com**, or each country's own code or both. When this has been established it is then necessary to review each country's legal requirements and to establish whether there are particular restrictions such as having a company in a particular country or holding an applicable trade mark. This sounds like and used to be a huge task. However, most companies which provide registration services can provide a list of the countries where there are no registration requirements (and which are therefore at high risk from cybersquatters) and arrange a swift registration of all such names which are available. They will also provide details of the requirements of each of the other countries. This can then be reviewed in the light of the costs of these registrations and where protection may be necessary.

Having decided which TLDs and country codes to register the next step is to decide what word or words will be registered. This again is a very commercial decision. Some unscrupulous individuals have made a practice of registering similar names or names with something such as 'sucks' added to the end. In the case of the typo (or typosquatter) it is possible that their use of this name carries a risk of diverting your customers. This needs to be balanced against the cost of the registrations.

4.5.10 Domain name disputes and cybersquatting

ICANN has adopted a dispute resolution process called the Uniform Dispute Resolution Procedure (UDRP). This is not a government-regulated procedure but is run privately. This now requires certain terms to be included by the various registries in their contracts with their customers. One of these includes a term stating that the person registering the name is not breaching anyone else's intellectual property rights. This will cover registered and unregistered trade marks. It does not resolve any problems where more than one person has a legitimate right to a name, but the aim is to help reduce cybersquatting. The process, however, has come under a great deal of criticism with ICANN itself acknowledging that it may not be adequate and this year instigating a review of the procedure. It is worth bearing in mind for the future that this will change.

In the UK Nominet has announced its first decision under the AUDP (its UDRP equivalent) in July 2002. In a dispute involving Seiko, the expert's decision was upheld.

Tracking the owner

One additional problem is finding out who owns a domain. Although it is possible to find out what is on the application form, the registries have generally not required applicants to provide accurate details and there is no way of checking this. It has, however, been very easy for unscrupulous individuals not to provide accurate details and then not to respond.

In some cases it may be possible to contact the holder through the ISP which holds the name if the customer has an account. However, free ISPs require only CLI (Call Line Identification) – which may be a mobile phone or any number – when the customer registers, and if they chose to be Mickey Mouse who lives in Never Never Land then there is little that the ISP can do.

Arbitration

It is not mandatory for all registries to have an arbitration or dispute resolution process and some do not. Where they do then it is often necessary (precise requirements depend upon the relevant policy) to prove that the domain name is identical to the trade mark and that any third party who has registered the name does not have any legitimate rights to have the name. It is also often necessary to prove that the name has been used in bad faith at the time of registration (such as a proposal to sell the name at an exorbitant price to the rightful holder of the name). The issue of passive holding, where a third party buys a name and does nothing with it nor tries to sell it, was clarified recently by the case of *Telstro* v. *Nuclear Marshmallow*. In this case it was held that passive holding can amount to bad faith.

Remedies for breach of rules

The remedy where a breach is found is to cancel the domain name. Note that this does not mean that the name is automatically transferred to the claimant. If they wish to have the name they must register it after the cancellation. There are no monetary penalties.

The process typically takes around 45–60 days and an administration fee is payable to the registry. The process is done without personal representation by way of completing a form. As there is no second bite at this particular cherry it is extremely important to make sure that the form is correct.

It is worth noting that, aside from such a dispute procedure, one always has the more expensive option of pursuing a wrongful registrant through the courts.

4.5.11   Other legitimate owners

One of the most difficult problems faced by a legitimate owner of a trade mark is where another third party also has a legitimate right to that mark. Costly litigation could be undertaken but there is generally little that you can do.

Practically, if you are looking at a new brand, check the availability of the name and try to register domains before you begin trading. Unlike trade marks, if the name is available this may be relatively easy. You might also take advantage of the new TLDs, registering these if the other party does not or has not. The risk with these is that none of us can be sure just how effective and widely used they will be.

TOP TIP

If you want to find out who is the owner of a domain name then you can do this by looking on the 'Who is' website at www.whois.com or www.betterwhois.com.

4.6   Software patents

There is not a huge amount to be said about these now as it is a very new area of the law. However, there are moves afoot as a result of a new EU consultation which would allow new forms of protection of them and if this could be relevant to you then you should look for information on this. There has perhaps been more press than this really justifies as a result of the BT claims on hypertext links and Amazon's one click. Given the risk of losing the ability to obtain patent protection through disclosure to the public it is essential to seek specialist legal advice at an early stage.

4.7   Web-related brand issues

With the technology of the Internet we have gained not only a fantastic tool but a means for the unscrupulous to take advantage in many ways. This is not just the possibility of taking advantage of insecure sites, but the possibility of a third party obtaining a competitive advantage through the use of a meta tags, hypertext links, etc.

The Web therefore threw some difficulties at the feet of the legal profession. What exactly were these actions and how could the established legal rules and regulations be adapted to protect against the unscrupulous? Although to date there has been a limited amount of case law, a body of good practice has established itself and in the worst case scenario where there is no direct legislation and no appropriate test case, following this is the best one can do.

I have tried to give a brief understanding of the technology.

4.8   Search engines

A search engine is a massive index of the Internet. You may be familiar with these through your ISP or through Google or Yahoo! When a user looks for a site they can do this either by inserting the URL and going to a site, like phoning a telephone number you know to speak to the person you expect, or by putting some words which they believe to be relevant or key into the search box on a search engine site. These key words may be the name of the company or business which the user is trying to locate, the products sold or some similar but relevant words.

The search engine then searches through its indices to provide a list of relevant results, a bit like 192 searching for a telephone number when it has the benefit of a surname, but no initial or street name. The engine will then show the results in the order which it believes to be most relevant – starting with the words closest to those searched for or the site which includes those words the greatest number of times.

When you open a new site part of the process of doing this will involve contacting search engines.

4.9   Meta tags

A meta tag is a piece of HTML including key words which are embodied in a website and from which a site can be identified by a search engine. The information in the meta tag will be used by the owner to identify the website to a search engine, although they are invisible to the site user. Meta tags generally include the site name, the business name or some related information with which a user might associate a brand such as the main product type or an event for which it sells tickets. When one registers with a search engine it is important to consider words which may be relevant to one's trade. For example, a computer retailer would generally include the words computer and PC in his metatags. It is important to spend some time thinking through what should be used as a metatag as this is very relevant to the traffic which may be able to locate your site and be passed through the search engine to it. Obviously some sites need to update their meta tags on a regular basis. It is worth also running searches on various engines to see what happens when you input your meta tag.

In theory, therefore, there is nothing wrong with a metatag from a legal point of view, and they are in fact essential in ensuring that search engines function and the 'Web world' goes round. However, they have been very controversial and problems arise where the words used as a meta tag have been trade marks, unregistered or registered, owned by a third party.

I came across one situation where a manufacturer sold directly to the public and also through certain agents. When one of those agent's relationship with that manufacturer came to an end the agent set up his own website selling similar products from another source. However, when registering his own website, the agent unscrupulously used the name of the manufacturer, which was a protected brand, as one of its meta tags. The outcome of this was that whenever the manufacturer's brand was searched for the agent's own site also came up on the list of search results.

In deciding the order in which the results will be shown, the search engine uses a number of methods of categorisation and one of these methods is the number of times that the keywords searched for appear in the text. In this case the agent used these a large number of times and was actually ranked ahead of the manufacturer in the search results.

Understandably the manufacturer was more than a little unhappy and believed that his business was being affected by the potential diversion of its customers to a third party by the agent's use of the manufacturer's name. The manufacturer considered this practice to be unscrupulous and an abuse of its name which was protected by a registered trade mark. The manufacturer therefore instructed lawyers to issue what is often called a 'cease and desist letter' to both the agent and the ISP hosting its website. This letter alleged a breach of trade mark rights and requested that the agent stop or cease its use of the name and undertake not to do so in the future. The letter to the ISP was similar but put the ISP on notice (remember the *Godfrey* v. *Demon* case) requesting that the site be removed until such time as the infringement was stopped.

At this stage it is worth noting that one should not issue third parties with cease and desist letters without careful consideration and that there may be legal consequences (it can be an offence in itself) to their wrongful use.

This reaction is, however, fairly understandable. The manufacturer views a brand which he has spent a lot of time, energy and money developing to be an asset which deserves respect and not to be something which should be open to abuse by a third party.

Not surprisingly a number of situations like this have arisen and some have ended up in court. Most of the case law has been in America, but there has been a UK case: *Road Tech Computer Systems Limited* v. *Mandata*. Mandata used the words 'road runner' and 'road tech' in its meta tags. These were marks which had been registered as trade marks by its competitor, Road Tech. Understandably Road Tech was unhappy with this practice and wrote to Mandata requesting that it remove these meta tags and also that it publish an apology on its website, with a redirection by way of a link to Mandata's site. When Mandata failed to do this Road

Tech sued. Mandata in turn admitted having infringed Road Tech's trade marks and removed them. The court found Mandata guilty of both trade mark infringement and passing off and awarded damages of £15,000 and expenses of £28,000 to Road Tech.

This was an expensive lesson for Mandata's IT staff, but also provides a useful case in terms of UK law as it has supplied a little certainty as to when a meta tag may infringe.

There is currently legal debate at a level beyond which a commercial person really needs to be aware over whether a trade mark can actually be used as an indication of origin. This may affect the ability of a trade mark owner to enforce its rights, and in some situations specialist legal advice will need to be taken. However, as a general rule it is fair to assume that third parties should not use your trade marks as a meta tag and you should not use theirs.

Case law has not always followed the same line in other countries, and there are cases which have allowed the use of a trade mark as a meta tag. Perhaps the most well known of these is the Terri Wells case. Terri Wells was a Playboy 'Playmate' in 1981. On her website she used the word 'Playmate' as a meta tag and was sued by Playboy. In this instance the American court found that she was using the mark in a descriptive way and in good faith as she had in fact been a Playmate. This was mainly upheld on appeal in 2002. Bear in mind that had she not been a Playmate then the outcome would probably not have been the same.

In 2002 the press was full of reports relating to meta tags. In Germany the Dusseldorf regional court decided that the use of words not directly related to the website as meta tags was an infringement of the German Unfair Competition Act, while in

England, the High Court held in June 2002, in the Totaljobs case, that a trade mark may be infringed by use of metatags which are invisible, but which are visible in the search engine results.

TOP TIP

When on a website, if one clicks view, then source and then meta tag, one is able to display the meta tags which have been set up for that particular site/URL. This can be an interesting exercise generally, but can also allow you to see what approach your competitors have taken when registering with a search engine. If you have any suspicions regarding an unscrupulous use of a trade mark as a meta tag, then this may also be a useful investigative tool.

There is also an interesting play on the meta tag concept. It is possible to buy banner advertising on many search engines and some clever advertisers have purchased this in particular categories. For example, when someone searches for a fashion retailer, whether by name or category, it is possible that a competing fashion retailer who has purchased the advertising space can have their advert displayed. Although this can appear confusing the ads are generally sold on the basis of a category.

TOP TIP

....

Lawyers may be keen to issue cease and desist letters in this and other circumstances when there is an apparent abuse of trade mark rights. However, these should be used with care and some caution. In the UK the Trade Marks Act 1994 sets out the limited circumstances in which you can threaten another person with legal proceedings for infringement of a trade mark and certain other intellectual property. This extends beyond what is put in writing to what is said to that third party also. Cease and desist letters should be handled with care.

....

4.10   Spiders and bots/comparative shopping

One of the things I love about the Web is the jargon. Really, it was inevitable that with a web there would be a spider!

Unsurprisingly a spider crawls around the Web. It is a program which automatically searches the Web to find information. From a very simplistic point of view it will gather information and bring it together. For some time search engines have used spiders as a method of collating information. This use of spiders is fairly uncontroversial. More controversy has been caused by a more recent use of spiders by aggregators in comparative shopping sites. These sites use their spiders or bots to go out into the Web and to bring together information about products and prices sold on particular sites. The information is then collated and used to show price differences.

Many businesses are not happy with this use and have looked to both technology and the law to stop the practice. This is a difficult issue, as although there are justifications for banning this activity, it is at the same time argued that these actions when used in other ways are responsible for the collation of information on the Web and much of the Web's value.

4.11 Domain name hijacking

A hijack is where the details of a website's IP address are changed by a third party which then has the effect that a query for www.amandabrock.com results in a person connecting to a different place or site on the Internet. When this is done by a true fraudster the different place may not be obviously different from the user and they may be duped into thinking that they are where they intended to be and thus part with their personal and credit card details. Generally these sites are referred to as clone or look-alike sites.

The fraudster attempting to create this must have access to the site's Domain Name Server (DNS). This of course raises issues of DNS security and also of third-party liability where there is a third-party DNS host.

4.12 Lemon and parody websites

4.12.1 Lemon sites

Lemon websites are set up with the purpose of criticising or poking fun at other websites or businesses. They may use metatags or divert the domain name from a legitimate site to direct the user who is looking for a legitimate site to the lemon site. A number of these sites will show in the results of a search engine. These are as visible to you undertaking a search as they are to your customers or users and can be monitored by you simply by undertaking searches on a search engine. Some of these sites even use 'sucks' or similar as part of a derogatory domain name, e.g. Amandasucks.com, to lead users to the lemon sites.

Obviously they are set up for a number of reasons and one of these is where a legitimate customer complaint has been dealt with so poorly that the customer feels the need to use this tactic.

There are a number of legal solutions to this type of site. One of these is to issue a 'cease and desist' letter where a trade mark is used by a third party. The use of this should be restricted to circumstances where it is legal and also where its use may practically result in the end of the problem. Volkswagen apparently overreacted to the use of their VW symbol on a website and sent letters of this nature to the owners of a fan site. Apparently as a reaction to VW's behaviour the site simply turned the logo around, to allow for its continued use, but perhaps more importantly turned the site into an anti-Volkswagen site.

This serves as a good example for anyone considering how to deal with apparent abuses of their site. The reaction to these sites should never involve a purely legal solution. However, in terms of the legal solution it may also be possible to require the site to break links to yours or also to ask an ISP to remove a site which it hosts where that site contains potentially illegal content.

4.12.2 Parody sites

A parody site is one which actually pretends to be another site, duping customers in some instances into making purchases and paying the fraudulent site. This type of site effectively hijacks a legitimate site and its business. There are various technical ways in which this can occur and as it is unlikely that you will be able to trace the protagonist it is also unlikely that you will be able to have the site removed through legal channels. Contacting the ISP if that is clear may be the best route. Avoiding such a situation is realistically more of a security than a legal issue. Where your site faces these problems then I would suggest a security overhaul is required.

In June 2002 it was reported that Radio Shack sent a cease and desist order to the owners of a website Radio Slack, a site parodying Radio Shack. In response to this Radio Slack displayed the facts and details of the cease and desist order, with unflattering commentary on what to do next. This is a good example of the problems which can be caused if a heavy-handed approach is taken.

4.13 Linking and deep linking

Linking is where a user moves from a page or a site to another page or site directly without the use of a URL. The Internet is a mass of links between websites, many of which are legitimate but some of which may not be. In Chapter 6, restricting third-party links by terms of use is considered and this should work with the provision of a linking agreement as discussed in Chapter 9.

Your site may have links to or from its home page and may also have links to and from other pages. These links to and from pages other than the home page are called deep links. As well as a policy on linking generally you should also consider whether you wish to have deep links as these can have certain risks attached. It is possible that deep links to a page in your site may bypass security or advertising and have an adverse effect on your site. It is also common that when a user follows a deep link from one part of the Internet to the other, the URL at the top of the page they view will not change and they may well be confused or duped into thinking that they are still on the other site or page. One of the first UK cases on deep linking involved this very issue. In the Shetland Times case one newspaper linked directly into the content of its rival with, importantly, the content being 'framed' by the masthead and viewer of the infringing paper. The court struggled to fit the new issues into an existing category of copyright infringement (persuaded by the free loading aspect of the activity) but came to the view that this did amount to copyright infringement. Care obviously needs to be taken. However, on the other hand, if structured and carefully managed such links can be a useful revenue stream in certain circumstances. This is looked at in more detail in the review of linking agreements in Chapter 9.

The question with links really splits between links which you know about and have chosen to have and linking without consent. In this latter case structuring the legal relationships on and with your site may allow you the facility to remove these links.

It is also worth being aware that some sites do not allow links out from their site, but only into their site. This is generally for commercial and competition reasons, but can also serve to avoid some of the abuses, such as links to lemon sites, which sites face.

TOP TIP

....

Who links to a site?

It is possible to obtain the information as to who is linking to a website from the following URL: http://www.bookmarklets.com/tools/categor.html

....

4.14   Framing

Framing occurs where a site or business's content is displayed as a header or footer or otherwise around your content, acting like a picture frame. In many instances framing is agreed to and is legitimate. In other cases unscrupulous e-businesses have tried to take advantage of content or a third party's brand by using their frame on that content or brand. This may result either in an untrue association between the framer and the brand it frames, or even a situation of unfair competition where the content framed is believed to be that of the framer rather than its legitimate owner. This may leave the framer open to accusations of passing off if all of the elements of this, including loss of profit, can be proven or to claims of copyright infringement.

Aside from the Shetland Times injunction hearing referred to above, a recent German case involved a UK recruitment agency –

Stepstone. Again, content from one party was appearing to be content of another.

In coming to its decision on this the German court also considered database rights, and the fact that two-thirds of the jobs on the framer's site were actually from the Stepstone site.

4.15   Terms of use

It is common for websites to display a set of terms of use on the home page. These and the requirements for acceptance are discussed in Chapter 6.

The terms of use should display a copyright notice. This is not a legal requirement in the UK, but as it is required to protect copyright in some jurisdictions where the site may be accessed, it is useful to display this. It is also useful to state the purpose for which the site is to be used and, if you do not want third parties to create links for commercial purposes without your agreement, to state this.

It may also be wise if you do not wish to be subjected to shopping bots, which are not a link, to state that there should be no 'electronic trespassing' or that spiders and bots should access the site only with consent. This at least would be helpful in providing some basis for asserting that third parties were put on notice of the site owner's desire to exclude that practice and that prior consents was required.

The terms of use displayed on Dixons.co.uk and pubs247.co.uk sites are set out in Appendix 1.

4.16 Monitoring and enforcement

In deciding what monitoring and enforcement activity is to take place a decision weighing up the level of risk and exposure versus the cost of monitoring and enforcement must be made. A number of companies will undertake monitoring and analysis of site use and abuse.

It is also possible to undertake some internal monitoring by running your brand name through search engines, checking who is linking to your site and what shopping bots are visiting your site. When you have done this you can then decide what if any action is relevant bearing in mind that being too heavy handed can in fact backfire and that to turn a third-party complaint into a satisfied customer or user would be more useful.

If you wish to use any of the information you find to stop any particular activity then you should make sure that you keep copies of this and a note of the time at which it was found – remember that third parties can easily move or change their sites. The legal methods of enforcement will be dependent on what action they are intended to prohibit and in the case of most of these I would recommend that you involve a lawyer.

ADDITIONAL INFORMATION

The UK Trade Mark Registry can be contacted at www.patentoffice.gov.uk

The Community Trade Mark Registry in Alicante can be contacted at http://oami.eu.int/

EU Guidelines on domain name issues: see http://www.europa.eu.int/ISPO/legal/en/lab/991216/brochure.doc

Nominet UK can be contacted at www.nominet.co.uk

NSI can be contacted at www.nsi.com

The UDRP can be found at www.icann.org/udrp/udrp.htm

The following Law firms have additional information available on many of the areas touched on in this chapter:

McDermott, Will & Emery at www.mwe.com

Pillsbury Winthrop at www.pilsburywinthrop.com

Kemp Little's Shortlines publications at www.comlegal.com

Olswang at www.olswang.com

CHAPTER 5

Content, advertising and trading

The structure of a website will be governed partially by various legal requirements such as customer registration, acceptance of terms and conditions and the like. This is dealt with in Chapter 6 on customer relationships. The content of a site relating to customer relationships is also dealt with in that chapter. This chapter deals more generally with the content which may be displayed on a website to attract customers and encourage sales.

5.1   UK regulators

Any high-street shop in the UK is subject to a number of trading laws and laws which protect consumer rights. This is the same for an e-business and its trading channels. Some allowance has to be made for the method of compliance which may not be as straightforward as it is for a high-street store.

This is a relatively short book and if these rules were to be set out in detail the book would be a guide to trading law. However, a short summary of some of the appropriate legislation may be helpful and this is set out below.

It is important to remember that these laws need to be applied to the content included on your site. A simple example is where products may only be sold to people over a certain age. However, on a website it is not possible to check proof of age. It may even be the case that the site does not collect its users' ages, as this data is not generally necessary. Unlike the owner of an off-licence or pub there would not be a possibility of the user's appearance alerting the vendor to the fact that the user may be under age. This type of scenario needs to be dealt with as well as it possibly can be within the technology or the site content.

The Chivas Regal website requires users to register and confirm that they are over 18 before they are able to enter the site. Amazon UK includes a statement on age-restricted products to the effect that the product is age restricted and may only be purchased by someone who is over that age, and when buying these goods a statement that the buyer confirms that they are over this age appears. Dixons has a general statement to this effect in its terms of sale. All of these are possible solutions but none of them are complete solutions as none of them leave the vendor certain that they have sold to someone who meets any age criteria. This and similar problems create a quandary for the enforcement authorities.

The UK's trading standards authorities understand that this is a problem and are working on best practice for websites through the Local Authorities Co-ordinating Office on Regulatory Services

(LACORS) which is apparently aiming to create a centre of excellence. Trading Standards is the enforcement authority and is divided on a regional basis. In the past major retailers with a number of outlets have had a single authority appointed 'the Home Authority' to deal with all of the problems faced by that retailer in its stores whether these are within the physical locality of that authority or not. This principle is now being applied to websites and a home authority selected for each site, which will then be responsible for the investigation of complaints about that site and enforcement of the applicable laws.

A new website on behalf of the Trading Standards Authority will provide information about Trading Standards' approach to websites and will apparently also allow consumers to complain about UK websites.

The powers of enforcement against websites are currently the same as those which apply to other retailers. However, as is mentioned elsewhere, calls are being made for stricter penalties to apply to websites.

5.1.1 Advertising Standards Authority/British Codes of Advertising and Sales Promotion

The Advertising Standards Authority (ASA) administers the British Codes of Advertising and Sales Promotion (BCASP or Code), written by the Committee of Advertising Practice. The Code covers all advertising which is non-broadcast. In the early days of e-business it was unclear what exactly this code covered online and in particular whether all content was to be considered to be an advertisement and so subject to the Code.

There are two important aspects to the Code. The first is that if you breach it you may be subject to an investigation; and the second is that if you are aware of one of your competitors breaching it you may make a complaint to stop them continuing with their advertising or promotion in breach of the Code.

I have made and won complaints against competitors who have not respected the Code in their online business. These complaints related to both advertising and content displayed by e-businesses.

In September 2000 the ASA clarified what the Code should apply to in the online world and stated that this would be:

1. online advertising in space that was paid for, such as banner and button ads;

2. advertisements in commercial e-mails; and

3. sales promotions online including both websites and e-mails.

This means that although a particular promotion on a website such as '3 for 2' would be covered by the Code, any claims in the website by the e-business would arguably not be covered. The difference between these may be a little difficult to understand and whether the Code will apply depends on whether the content is advertising (as set out above). If there is any danger that the terms of the Code are not being followed then it is essential to be clear that this is in the case of content (not advertising) only.

There is a very important general point to make in relation to Code compliance. The fact that the Code does not apply does not mean that other consumer legislation will not apply and the claims on the website will be subject to this despite not being governed by the Code. In short, everything from the way one describes one's goods/services to the pricing indications will be governed by a variety of, often criminal, laws which must be noted and complied with, notwithstanding the Code.

The Code itself requires that advertising is decent, legal, honest and truthful, and that advertising is prepared with a sense of responsibility to consumers and society. Advertising should also be in line with the principles of fair competition.

More information can be found at http://www.asa.org.uk and a copy of the Code can be obtained from the ASA on request. The fifth version of this will be available in March 2003.

It is also possible to have an advance, informal, pre-approval of advertising by sending this directly to the Committee – this can be obtained from copy advice on 020 7580 4100 or copyadvice@ cap.org.uk. Any such advice is confidential.

The new E-Commerce Regulations (EC Directive) 2002 also include requirements of online advertising, which may fall under the category of information society services or may be a commercial communication. These relate to information to be provided to the user and are dealt with in Chapter 6.

5.1.2   ITC Code

The Independent Television Commission is the broadcast equivalent of the ASA (although with added statutory remit). It has jurisdiction for the ITC Code which regulates broadcasts and broadcast advertising. This will not apply to Internet sites, but will be applicable to iTV sites. A copy of the ITC Code can be obtained from the ITC.

Although the ITC Code is in many respects similar to the ASA Code there are definite differences and because a site has complied with the ASA Code does not necessarily mean that it will comply with the ITC Code. Each code has been written with a different medium in mind and looking at a site from a distance on a TV or from a few inches or feet on a website are very different experiences. Also the ITC has not restricted what content it will apply to in the way that the ASA has and there is no clear distinction between advertising and content, but rather all is subject to the ITC Code.

In light of this it is important to ensure that any re-purposed content or iTV site is reviewed from this perspective. It is also wise to involve the person who is doing the compliance check at an early stage, as the last thing you would want to have to do would be to make major changes, e.g. to the size of text, at the last minute. Alterations of this kind could easily require changes to a page format.

It is also worth being aware that the ITC Code only applies to the broadcast side of iTV and should the site involve a combination of broadcast and Internet, as soon as the user moves outside of the pure broadcast walled garden, then the ITC Code ceases to apply.

5.1.3   New regulator

The Office of Communications Act 2002 has been passed and this requires the establishment of a new regulator to regulate the telecommunications and broadcasting sectors in place of the Broadcasting Standards Council, the Radio Authority, OFTEL and the ITC. The new regulator will be knows as the Office of Communications (OFCOM) and will have an obvious impact on new technologies.

This new authority will come into place as a result of the convergence of technologies evident to all involved in this sector.

5.2   Third-party content

A site will often be made up of content provided by you and by third parties. In Chapter 9, there is a discussion of both web design and build and content provision contracts. These cover many of the legal implications of content provision. However, it is also probably worth summarising these at this point.

5.2.1   *Web designer*

A web designer will often build a site using standard building blocks of code and some new or bespoke code. Ideally you will own the bespoke code and will receive this by way of an assignment from the designer/agency. However, it is extremely unlikely that you will ever receive more than a licence to use the building blocks and it is possible that you will only receive a licence to use the site. The recommended terms for such a licence are set out in the contract discussion. If only a licence is obtained then this should be backed by an escrow agreement.

The design will often include not only the structure of the site but content, in particular relating to the look and feel, which is coded into the site. This content will be provided by you to the site designer and ideally the designer should not acquire any rights in this.

5.2.2 Content provider

It is possible if not likely that you will obtain some of the content from a third-party content provider or that you will allow a third party to advertise on your site and to provide content in this way. These relationships should be covered by content provision and advertising agreements. The terms of such agreements are set out in Chapter 9, but again it is worth highlighting a few points. You must be clear that the party who provides the content or advertising to you provides content that is both legal and not in breach of any third party's intellectual property. If the content is illegal or is in breach of a third party's IP you will be legally responsible for this content as it is transmitted from your site. It is necessary to require this in the contract, but as you will be responsible it is also necessary for you to check commercially supplied content and advertising yourself. An indemnity against costs incurred for breach of this will do what it says and will reimburse you. You may even be able to negotiate some form of damages. However, it is unlikely that this would or could ever compensate for the bad publicity and future loss of users.

Taking each of these elements in turn, first, the content should not be obscene or defamatory and if appropriate should comply with the trading and advertising laws described above. The editor of your site should be provided with guidance on what to look out for and if in doubt legal advice should be taken. This also highlights the potential need to have a right to edit and remove third-party commercial content. Secondly, the content should be the content provider's to give you. Either it should be the original work of the content provider or he should have an assignment or licence from a third party. There is little that can be done practically to check this, but the contract should contain provisions to this effect and an indemnity. There is an obvious inherent risk.

5.3　Links

A second way that third-party content may be associated with your site is through links in or out of your site. Of greater concern are links out of your site. Some sites do not in fact allow these. If a customer is not aware that they have left your site they may hold you responsible for content which they link to. Currently this area is a legal minefield and there is no straightforward answer as to whether you will have liability. There is certainly more risk attached to deep links that to links to a home page.

In some instances links are incorporated into a site on a commercial basis, such as from a review site to the supplier of the product reviewed. The potential endorsement may also affect what liability will apply.

Again, a contract should be put in place and the terms for this are set out in Chapter 9. Again, an indemnity is useful but may not be enough to protect a reputation and careful consideration should be given to what if any sites your site will link to. A policy should be put in place and made known to anyone within your business who might have the authority to create links.

5.4   Customers

Another category of third party who may provide your site content and who may in turn cause problems are customers. It is not uncommon to have customer reviews, notice boards or discussion forums. The site owner has little control over what will be included in this although he may be able to use technology such as nanny software to remove some of the inherent risk. The site runs the risk of being held liable for its content including that provided by its customers. However, in such circumstances a site could argue that, like an ISP, it is a mere conduit (see Chapter 2) and try to rely on the provisions of the E-Commerce (EC Directive) Regulations 2002 relating to mere conduit and hosting.

If a site wants to rely on this then it will need to behave in a similar manner to an ISP and not become involved in checking or editing the content.

Sites have, however, been forced to disclose the identity of contributors in both the Line One and Totalise cases.

5.5   Worldwide risks

As a site can potentially be viewed in any country in the world then potentially it would appear that the site would also be subject to the laws of any country from which it is viewed. In contrast, the Internet has also been described as the 'Wild West' in terms of regulation – so which is true?

To have a better understanding of the risks it is necessary to understand the legal regulations on applicable laws and jurisdiction which are set out below.

5.5.1 Applicable laws and jurisdiction

The new Brussels and Rome regulations in conjunction with the E-Commerce Regulations give the regulatory basis for this.

If a site falls foul of the laws of a country other than the country in which it is based there is potentially a risk that the operators of the site will be liable for prosecution or open to litigation by a party in such country. This has been a major problem in the development of the Internet and has led many businesses to restrict the countries in which they actually do business to ensure that their risks are limited. Other companies have tried to deal with the possible legal outcomes in a number of countries and the terms and conditions on the eBay site are a good example of this.

Courts in certain countries have been happy to exercise jurisdiction, and Yahoo! was the victim of this in 2001, when the French courts applied French law to a US site. Over the last few years there have been a number of other cases like this.

The Regulations have tried to deal with this in a way which allows the trader to trade in other countries. A concept known as the 'country of origin' has been developed. In essence this states that the laws of the country in which the site has its domicile or place of establishment should apply, i.e. the trader complies with his 'home' laws and does not have to try to comply with all the laws of the 15 EU Member States.

The concept of place of establishment has itself caused problems and the Regulations have clarified that where a business is spread over a number of places the service should be regarded as being provided from the place of establishment considered to be where the centre of the activities involved in the service is located.

The Regulations set out that for a UK business the legal requirements of the UK (i.e. the part of it in which the business is based) will apply to the provision of goods or services by it whether in the UK or another Member State. The UK enforcement agencies will also have jurisdiction over such provision whether in the UK or another Member State.

The above is subject to certain exclusions where the law of the country in which the service is delivered will apply. These generally apply to the areas of public health and consumer interests, with a general but important exclusion ensuring that the country of origin principle doesn't deprive consumers of the protection of their home country's consumer laws (with which they will be familiar if the trader's local original laws have a lower standard).

The jurisdiction which applies to a consumer transaction should be stated in the terms of sale.

5.5.2   EEJ NET

Dispute resolution may be viewed as more difficult where the consumer and retailer are not in the same country and various proposals to allow the consumer to obtain justice without resorting to court action have been made. Currently the European Commission is working on a proposal for a clearing house system known as EEJ NET which will assist with this.

5.6   Avoiding liability

5.6.1   Disclaimers

It is possible to fill your site with disclaimers in an attempt to remove liability. However, whether there is any point in this depends on whether a court would uphold those disclaimers.

Limitation clauses restrict the amount of liability which a site will have. Such clauses may state that a site is governed by a particular law and that this country's courts will have jurisdiction over disputes. This type of clause must be clear and unambiguous if it is to bc enforceable. As these may not be enforceable in consumer transactions it may then be necessary to back this legal statement with a practical solution by delivering the goods or services only in that country. In this case the law of the place of origin and the place of delivery will be the same.

It may also be possible to exclude liability and statements such as 'X takes no liability for errors or omissions in its site'. However, any exclusion will only be upheld if it has a reasonable balance and is fair. In deciding whether this is the case or not it is necessary to consider what is being excluded to establish whether the exclusion meets these standards.

The enforceability of such a clause in the UK will be subject to the Unfair Contract Terms Act 1977 (UCTA) and the Unfair Terms in Consumer Contracts Regulations 1999. Generally speaking UCTA prohibits exclusions of death or personal injury in consumer contracts and restricts other exclusions in these contract to those which are reasonable. The rules are slightly less restrictive in contracts between two businesses, but the courts have in recent times refused to enforce certain exclusion clauses in standard term contracts depending on the circumstances. This is an important but complicated area and one which, if relevant to you, I would recommend you take legal advice on. The Regulations relate to the balance in standard form contracts and have a requirement of good faith.

5.7   Protecting the site

5.7.1   Intellectual property

Various intellectual property rights may be used to legally protect the content of your site. Where trade marks are used they can be flagged by using the small TM logo and where these are registered by marking these as TM®. Note that it is an offence to use this where the trade name is not registered. Also the terms of use can flag up trade mark rights. There are various other intellectual property rights which can be used.

5.7.2   Copyright notice

As is discussed in Chapter 6 a site should include terms of use. As a minimum this should include a copyright notice, making clear to the world that you own the copyright in the site and that this is going to be protected by you. A notice would include the name of the owner and the date, e.g. © Amanda C. Brock 2003.

5.7.3   Database rights

See section 4.3 in Chapter 4.

5.7.4   Use of legal terms

The terms of use, registration and sale are discussed in Chapter 6.

5.7.5   Music and film

This high-profile area owes much to the famous (or infamous) Napster cases. The use of MP3 and other methods of download for software and film are among the most natural uses of the Net, and could potentially be the providers of very large revenue streams. However, as we all know illegal use of downloaded material has become a major problem. Legally it has been made clear that this is not tolerated, but at the end of the day it may be difficult to enforce such laws. A possible solution to this will be digital rights management (DRM).

5.7.6   Digital rights management

DRM is fast being hailed as potentially the best protection against copying of content. By use of technology a site can be protected in various ways against copying of its content. This technology can be used to ensure that third-party copying is restricted or where allowed that the copies have a limited use or life expectancy. Not only will this protect a site but if it proves robust and easy to use it could increase the value of the site and its content.

5.8   Laws applicable to trading in the UK

This area of law is huge and cannot be covered in any depth in a book of this length. However, to give you a head start I have set out below some of the laws which apply to trading in England and have where appropriate looked at certain aspects of e-business and how these apply. To a large extent these laws are the same for e-business as for any other business but it is necessary to consider how they apply to a site bearing in mind the inescapable background of the site's technology. It is not the purpose of this book to provide a detailed analysis of these or an exhaustive list, but further information can be obtained from a number of sources.

5.8.1   *Terms of any agreement with a customer*

Unfair Contract Terms Act 1977

The terms and conditions must be reasonable and there are certain rights and liabilities which the retailer cannot exclude.

Unfair Terms in Consumer Contracts Regulations 1999

These apply to standard terms not specifically negotiated with a party, which create a significant imbalance in the parties' rights and obligations to the detriment of the consumer. These regulations state that such unfair terms will not be binding on a consumer.

The Consumer Protection (Distance Selling) Regulations 2000 and the E-Commerce (EC Directive) Regulations 2002

Both of these regulations apply to content displayed by an e-business and information which must be provided. Their requirements are dealt with at length in Chapter 6.

Terms which affect the quality or safety of the product supplied

The Sale of Goods Act 1979 (as amended) and the Sale and Supply of Services Act 1986 apply here. The European Directive on Certain Aspects of the Sale of Consumer Goods and Associated Guarantees was implemented in the UK in December 2002. This new law is in the main similar to the existing sale of goods law but makes some small changes, in particular with regard to the length of time for which a consumer's rights apply.

Generally goods purchased must be 'fit for purpose' and of 'satisfactory quality'. The Directive will also require that they conform to the contract at the time of delivery which means much the same. In layman's terms this means that the goods must do what they were supposed to do and be as they would reasonably have been expected to be, particularly given any description which will include the labelling and advertising of the product and any statements made by sales people regarding the goods. The Directive required that the law apply to defects which arise in a minimum period of two years from the date of delivery. However, in England there is a longer six-year limitation period, and in Scotland a five-year period, which will continue to apply.

Also any installation service will be considered to form part of the contract and failure of this or, where the customer has to self install, failure to provide clear instructions will also be considered to be non-compliance.

Services provided must be provided using reasonable skill and care.

5.8.2   Product-specific provisions

There are various other pieces of legislation which apply to specific products and these must be complied with. A check of what applies to any goods or services which you intend to sell should be made before launch or the addition of new categories. The laws will generally be the same for distance sales and high-street sales, although in some instances the technology may need to be adapted to accommodate this.

5.8.3   Pricing and product description

Although in general I have really only pointed you towards the correct law, it is important to consider some aspects of content in a little more description and so I have tried to summarise below the laws most relevant to content that you may display when trading. This should be read along with the provisions of the Distance Selling and E-Commerce Regulations set out in Chapter 6.

In the event of a wrong price an English retailer would traditionally rely on the invitation to treat sale structure and remove such goods from sale on the site. Whether this would be legally possible would be dependent on the site structure. Even if the site is set up on an invitation to treat basis, if the customer's order has been accepted, the money paid and the contract formed, then the point in time at which the retailer can withdraw the goods will have passed.

The Distance Selling Regulations may make product withdrawal on an invitation to treat basis a little more difficult as they require the product price and description to be made clear to the customer prior to the sale contract being formed. If these are wrong then the consumer may argue that they are entitled to rely on this. However, it is not clear if this would hold water.

The Price Marking Order 1999 and the Consumer Protection Act 1987 provide for this area. It is an offence to give a consumer a misleading price indication. A price indication is not simply the price itself but might include a reference to a price, a promotion or even a site's pricing policy, e.g. if the policy said all prices include delivery and then there was a separate delivery charge then this might be misleading. The E-Commerce Regulations also require that pricing is clear and indicates whether prices are inclusive or exclusive of VAT. In this light beware marketing information. This is often viewed as the fluffy part of the product content but may actually be viewed as being part of the price indication and wording which implies low prices or the value of the goods or services sold must not mislead.

In terms of clarity, all information which forms part of the price indication must be clear and should not be stuck in the small print. It is important to consider how some of the more detailed information will be displayed on a site. Having this accessed by requiring a customer to drill down through a link or click may mean that it is not clear and that this is viewed as the equivalent of putting the information in the small print.

Information about the goods or services gives an indication of what the consumer may expect for the price and so may also be relevant to it.

If a promotion, offer or price is being provided in a limited way, either due to limited stock or being on offer only for a limited period of time, then this should also be stated clearly. There is a risk that if it is not and customers order goods or services which the site does not have it could be forced to supply them (somehow and at its cost and effort) to the consumer. Where stock is limited some sites, such as the Boden clothes catalogues at www.boden.co.uk during its sale, offer a clear indication of whether there is stock at all and how much or flag limited stock. From a legal point of view, assuming it works, this is an extremely useful tool. However, if this is not an option prudent stock checks are strongly suggested as are appropriately drafted disclaimers and terms and conditions.

Note that it is not legal to offer the same goods or services for different prices depending on method of payment.

5.8.4   Stock availability

There is a requirement that where a customer's order is accepted then the goods should be available for supply. Although the penalties for failure to comply with this imposed under the Distance Selling Regulations are not high, it is also an offence to advertise for sale goods at a price (particularly when this is a low price) when these are not available for sale. This would be viewed to be misleading advertising. Ideally the order management system should make clear when stock is low and add a low or out of stock sign to a website. As consumers are realistically only likely to pursue a sale when they believe that they are getting a good price, it is the case, almost without exception, that goods ordered which are out of stock and are demanded by the consumer will be low priced goods.

5.8.5 Price changes

Where a site wants to show a saving from a previous price it may do so by using what is commonly known as the 'was' price. Where this is done the previous price must be obscured or struck out. To claim a saving the 'was' price must be the price at which the goods or services were advertised and available for a consecutive period of 28 days. There are also restrictions on what can be called a saving and reductions have to meet either minimum amounts or percentages to fall into this. Also any claim must be accurate and something like a final saving must really be a final saving.

Price changes, whether these include a 'was' price or simply an amendment to an existing price, must be done carefully. A number of retailers have been caught out when their sites have shown incorrect prices. UK legislation makes non-compliance on such pricing issues a criminal offence, so it is important to get it right.

Comparisons with other retailers are possible but again must comply with the laws on comparative advertising and should be handled carefully. The one certainty of comparative advertising is a very unhappy competitor who may well want to retaliate and a good way of doing so is to complain where any legal requirement of comparative advertising has been breached.

5.8.6 Baskets and storing goods

Most sites use a basket like a high-street shopping basket. The consumer can place goods in the basket and then review the contents of the basket before they take the goods to the till or proceed with the order process (generally by way of a proceed to order button).

However, it is worth bearing in mind that if the basket is capable of retaining the customer's goods between visits then it is necessary for the prices in the basket to reflect the prices for the goods or services on the day and time when the customer looks at them and not the time when the customer put the goods in the basket. This means that the site structure must link the storage of these goods with the price management system on the site. Amazon provide a good example of this and in my experience, if you store goods in your basket and return to the site to purchase at a later date, if the goods have decreased in price that decrease can be clearly seen.

5.8.7 Financial services

Financial Services are subject to separate laws some of which are based on the E-Commerce Directive in Financial Services. These are at the consultation stage in the UK and will shortly be made law. This area is also subject to the provisions of the Financial Services and Markets Act 2000 as amended.

5.9 After-sales/consumer complaints and disputes

Ideally the website should include an area of frequently asked questions (FAQs) or a customer help section. This should be clear from the home page and if possible linked to or easily accessible from each page.

The content of this will to some extent depend on the site but it would be advisable to cover:

- who owns the site;

- how the customer can contact the site;

- what to do in the event of a complaint or problem;

- what the site privacy policy and data protection rules are, how to obtain your data and how to change this;

- what to do if you forget your password and rules on passwords.

The Distance Selling Regulations require that the consumer is made aware of how they can complain to a website and the E-Commerce Regulations require contact details to allow rapid communication. Some sites also make the customer aware of how they can complain about that website if the site does not respond to their complaint and this would meet some of the new requirements.

As well as supplying the information, ideally an e-business will provide a back-end system which allows for complaint logging and have some form of internal service level to ensure that customer queries and complaints are responded to. The internal logging system will allow an operative to see what the customer or complaint history is and can avoid the complaint resolution itself becoming a cause for complaint.

5.10   Codes of conduct

Over the last few years a number of organisations have created codes of conduct for websites. These have come from organisations like the Consumers' Association with its *Which? Web Trader* (which it has announced will be withdrawn in 2003 due to lack of funding) and IMRG (the Interactive Media Retail Group), as well as trade organisations.

Generally the code of conduct will set out guidelines and practical guidance for the retailer and will require that it complies with these. Where the retailer holds itself out to be compliant with these then the retailer may display a logo or crest on its site to demonstrate this. The idea of these is that the consumer will be inspired by confidence when it sees the logo which effectively endorses the site as compliant with that code and will therefore be more willing to trade with that site.

However, although there have been a proliferation of these codes, their effectiveness is variable. In some cases the owners of the codes have not been particularly vigorous in checking compliance with their codes before authorising the display of their logo on a site. In other cases the initial audit requirements are met by the code owner, but should you have a problem with the site in question and it is clearly in breach of such a code with which it claims to comply, then it is difficult for the code owner to enforce the code. I have in fact come across one such situation where the code owner was wholly ineffectual in dealing with a complaint as it had no real teeth to bite with and its member was not in any way punished for the breach.

Which? Web Trader notably removed its accreditation of Jungle.com, albeit for a day or so until they brought their site into compliance with that particular code. This implies that *Which?* are an effective policeman of their code and perhaps lends it additional credibility. More information can be obtained from www. whichwebtrader.co.uk.

If you wish to sign up to such codes then it is important to consider what the terms of the code are, whether you can actually comply with it (and if you can't do you really think that all of the other members do?), who the other members are, do they actually comply with it and what happens if you or another member fail to comply? It is also worth considering how you become an accredited user of the code – is it bought and if so at what price, and what of any public perception there is of this? It may also be worth looking at who the other members are – if their sites are trustworthy then this may add some credibility to the code/accreditation and in turn to your site. This may be of particular relevance to pureplay e-businesses which do not have the benefit of a high-street presence to add to their consumer confidence.

Remember any codes which relate to the provision of information society services and which you subscribe to must be referenced on your site with information on the means of access. This requirement was created by the E-Commerce Regulations (EC Directive) 2002. Although it is a little confusing this does not mean that all codes to which your business signs up must be displayed but only those which deal with the part of the business which is an information society service (i.e. the part provided online). However, there is no obligation to sign up to any e-commerce or information society service codes.

If a code is referenced it is necessary to provide details of how any such code can be accessed electronically.

5.10.1 *Trust UK*

Launched in 2000, Trust UK is an initiative of the Direct Marketing Association (DMA) and is backed by the DTI. Further information on Trust UK and those who have obtained accreditation can be obtained from www.trustuk.org.uk.

Although it is often mistaken for a code of conduct, Trust UK is in fact a 'code for codes of conduct'. It sets out requirements which a code must comply with to have the potential to be endorsed by Trust UK. It is applicable to organisations and not to individual retailers. By this I mean that a trade association can sign up to it but a retailer cannot. If an association or code holder wishes to obtain the accreditation of Trust UK then it must provide a code of conduct which complies with the Trust UK terms and all of its members must be subject to this.

Accredited codes may display the Trust UK Hallmark. Accreditation comes at a price of between £1,000 and £5,000 per annum, as well as compliance with its terms. To date there appears to be little take-up of Trust UK. This must in turn beg the question whether it has really achieved its goal of becoming recognisable to consumers and associated with secure sites and transparency in consumer dealings.

A European equivalent of this – TrustE – is currently in development.

5.11   Issues relating to minors

5.11.1   *Contracts*

Under English law a contract with an individual who is less than 18 years of age is voidable, as the age of capacity for entering into a contract is 18. The contract will be valid unless it is repudiated by that minor. When a customer registers on a site it is possible to ask them for their age or date of birth. However, realistically there is no practical way at present of checking that this is what is stated. If the contract is for necessaries then it can be enforced against the minor, but most e-business contracts will not be and will be for luxuries such as software or CDs. If a minor obtains goods or services by fraudulent misrepresentation then the retailer can require the return of the goods. In the light of this it may be wise to state in the terms and conditions that only people aged 18 or over may purchase from the site. If this is done and a minor accepts these before he purchases then he has committed a fraudulent misrepresentation, and the retailer will have the opportunity to have the goods returned.

The addition of this age requirement is not something which happens often on the Internet. It may well be that sites have taken a view as to the age of their customers versus the risk of being exposed to repudiated (or cancelled) contracts from minors and found this to be slim.

5.11.2   Age restricted goods

If goods or services sold from a site are in any way age restricted then this should be made clear in the product description. However, as the retailer will sell to an individual in reliance on the information provided by that individual it will not know when to question age. A site selling alcohol may not know that it is trading with a 15-year-old if the 15-year-old claims to be 18. Unlike a pub, the owner cannot guess an age from appearance nor can it know when to refuse to sell.

The best the retailer can do is to both make clear on the site that the product is age restricted and to flag in its terms and conditions that the consumer declares where any goods purchased are age restricted that it meets that age requirement.

5.11.3   Means of payment: cards

I have often heard people say that a minor cannot shop on the Internet as they will not have a card with which to pay. Assuming that an e-business does not accept cheques this is not strictly true as although debit and credit cards cannot be issued by banks to minors on their own account, they may have access to their parents' cards. I believe that some banks will actually issue second cards on accounts to minors, but these cards are used with their parents' consent. If the card is used without parental consent then in any event the parent is liable for the minor's action and for payment as if they were the contracting party. There is in reality no more risk in accepting a card payment from a minor than from any other customer.

5.11.4   The US

It is also worth noting that in the US at least there are strict rules on collection of data from minors, and that this is generally prohibited for anyone under 13. If you are working with a US business or have servers in the US then this could be an issue and you ought to take advice from an American lawyer who specialises in this area.

ADDITIONAL INFORMATION

The European Commission has launched a website www.safeinternet. org, known as the 'awareness exchange', to provide advice to individuals with concerns about site content. This includes reference to a hotline for reporting of illegal content and information on filtering, site ratings and the like.

Trust UK can be found at: http://www.trustuk.org.uk

The Consumer Protection Regulations and guidance can be found at: http://dti.gov.uk/regulatory_guidance.html

The DTI has recently published research on Internet and cross-border shopping at: www.dti.gov.uk/ccp/topics1/ecomm.htm

CHAPTER 6

Customer relationships

6.1   Business to consumer relationships

Most e-commerce consists of the combination of a number of elements – marketing, legal and regulatory, technology and selling or retail. What each of these means and requires in terms of a particular business needs to be established and then considered collectively before making decisions about a website. How the site will work, what technology is needed to facilitate it, what the technology has to achieve, how the site will be structured and what the content can or will be must all be established by consideration of these elements collectively. Essentially, these impact on what the site user will see and what their dealings or impressions of the business are. This will affect that person's desire to use and buy from your business/site.

A high-street store can rebrand or redesign and when a passing customer sees this, despite a previous bad impression, the customer may be tempted back in. Websites are only seen when they are searched for, linked to or otherwise purposely visited by an Internet user. If a customer has a bad experience with the site and decides not to actively return then it is unlikely that they will stumble across the site again – they will not simply pass by it on the way to somewhere else as they would in the high street. As you are not face to face with your customer but dealing with them at a distance it is also less likely that you will be aware of the quality of your customer's experience. Customers or visitors are the inevitable revenue stream of a website, as many e-commerce entrepreneurs found to their cost when the Internet 'bubble' burst in 2000. It is essential that the experience they have is the best that you can possibly provide and leaves them with no or as little cause for complaint as possible.

When Amanda Brock walks into a shop, for example a Currys store, to purchase a fridge, she knows that she is dealing with a reputable company, can easily check who that company is and how she can contact them, can ask the sales assistants questions about the products on offer and their availability and can see the goods she is considering buying. Having made her selection she can pay knowing that she has the goods or will receive them shortly, and has a receipt for the money paid. None of this is news. It adds up to the elements of a retail experience. Often we do not consider what these elements are but feel comfortable with a retail experience because of them.

In the same scenario, when Amanda Brock visits an online store, whether that store is a well-known name or not, she is in a different position. The store is not real and can only be seen on a PC, and only when it is called up like a genie from a bottle. If she wants to deal with the site she has to rely on the fact that the site is legitimate, but may have little proof of this. As there is no assistant to talk to it may seem hard to get the information she wants or to ask questions. She cannot see the goods and so has to rely on the description of the goods and the site's representation that it has the goods it purports to sell. If despite all of these uncertainties she decides to trade with the site, then having made her payment and passed her credit card details into the apparent ether of the Internet (worrying about where these may end up and who might intercept or use them) she then has to rely on the fact that having taken her money this store she has never visited will deliver.

These are the uncertainties of the retail experience which occur when trading at a distance. At this juncture it is worth pointing out that many of these are no different from the issues or experiences which have occurred for many years when trading through catalogues and telesales. Perhaps the swift arrival of so many sites with such a high profile (or the failure of many of them) and the apparently increased security risks have been catalysts, but it is probably fair to say that customers have not in the old world of catalogues and telesales been as aware of these uncertainties as they might have been and now obviously are in e-commerce. The press has delighted in emphasising these concerns and the UK government and EU have reacted by attempting to put legislation in place which allows the consumer to have more certainty and which attempts to provide transparency in online sales and Internet use.

Some of this legislation has been helpful and has removed problems which detracted from the online experience. Some of the issues raised do not merit new legislation but still need to be addressed and technical or practical solutions utilised to further improve the customer experience – increasing clarity and removing uncertainty. Through the course of this chapter I have tried to provide short explanations of what the issues are/have been and what, if any, legislation exists or has been developed to react to these issues, what their resolutions actually mean to a website and finally, where possible, have flagged up technical or practical measures which may protect the site from legal issues when there is no legislative solution.

One aspect of the Internet which must be considered in tandem with this is the site's security and I would suggest that you also review Chapter 7 before making any decisions.

6.2   Legal relationships with consumers

The relationship with site users and customers can really be split into three:

- site use – becoming a visitor to the site;

- customer registration – becoming a registered user;

- purchasing – becoming a site customer.

Each of these is different and as the relationship is different so are the terms which should govern it. I suggest that, rather than overwhelming the customer with all three sets at once, effectively jumbling them together in a way that may not make clear which parts of the terms are applicable to which of the relationships, that you instead split them up on your site. Many sites do use a single set of terms and this is not necessarily wrong.

In a way the additional volume of legal terms may raise commercial and marketing concerns (believe me I have heard them) but this method also means that the customer is faced with three, more edible chunks of legal terms. These smaller chunks can also be more tailored to the relationship in question and if written in clear and plain English should also make more sense to the consumer. Within the actual body of the terms it is possible to make this into a more customer-facing and user-friendly guide as opposed to traditional legal terms.

6.3   Making terms and conditions binding

The terms you choose to apply to your customer relationship need to be binding on the customer. To form a binding contract there must be an offer, acceptance and consideration. These are dealt with in more detail at section 6.8. To be binding the content of these terms should be legal and also the customer should be made aware of them and then accept them (whether expressly or through conduct or implication as discussed below).

To make terms and conditions binding:

- The customer should ideally be forced through the terms each time (scroll).

- The terms should, if possible, also be accepted or agreed to by the customer (click).

- If the customer is not forced through every time they must be at least once and should replicate this when there are changes.

- Whether the customer has scrolled or is simply offered a link to the terms there should be no way forward without clicking 'I accept' (whether the customer is forced through or not).

- You should have some method of demonstrating that this has occurred, to prove acceptance of your terms.

To be sure that the contract terms are binding there needs to be positive 'assent' on the customer's part. This means that the customer must have had the opportunity to see the terms and conditions and agree to them. The only way to be sure of this is to incorporate the terms into each transaction. When this is done there is no doubt that the terms have been seen. Some sites only show their terms the first time the customer deals with them, but in these circumstances there is room for a customer to argue that they have forgotten what they are, or that he did not know that the terms applied. How important this is depends on the contents of the terms – whether the customer's expectations are in any way restricted – and whether any of the legally required advance information is shown only in these terms. If this is the case then the importance of forcing the customer through is increased.

Ideally, in order to be clear that the customer has accepted the terms, the customer should be invited to read the terms but then be forced to scroll through them (move down the page to the bottom of them). At the end of the terms the customer should be faced with an 'I accept' button. Whether the consumer reads the terms or not is really up to them, but the fact that you have forced them to see the terms and have obtained their positive affirmation that they have read and agreed the terms should be adequate proof of this. This is generally referred to as scroll and click. The alternative (less watertight route) to these is to have a link to the terms and to offer the customer the opportunity to read the terms but not force the customer through them.

If the customer does not accept then they should not be able to proceed with the transaction. There are two possible ways of dealing with this. A button stating 'I do not accept' can be added next to the accept button. If this is clicked the customer should be returned to the previous page and should be unable to proceed until they click on accept. The second alternative is to have only an accept button but again bar the customer from moving forward until they click on this. If a customer does not accept the terms the consequence must be that the transaction or process is abandoned and the technology must match the legal intention of barring the transaction. If a customer who does not accept the terms was able to move forward then this would defeat the purpose of scroll and click. This would remove your ability to prove that a customer had assented and put your site in the risky position of having customers or users who had not agreed to its terms.

It is sensible to force the customer through the terms and conditions on each sale. If this is not done then there may be instances where customers who do not go through them claim that they have never seen them and that they cannot be applied to their transaction with the site. Also where the terms change the customer can argue that they were not aware of any change and insist that the pre-change terms apply. If the customer is not forced through the terms then the business may be required to show how and when the customer was shown these and provided his or her assent. It is simpler to be sure that all customers see the terms each time as a consequence of the structure of the site and to keep a record of the initial terms and then each amended version and the date and time at which it was implemented.

Although your marketing team may not like the fact that you have scroll and click terms and conditions, when this is compared with the possible alternative of, say, e-mail notification to all customers of changes, they may understand that it really is the best alternative. I have actually seen a situation where scroll and click terms were not used. As a result of this, when a legal change was required, every customer had to be sent an e-mail with the change in it. There was then the ensuing debate as to what to send and how to make it more user friendly without defeating the purpose of making the change clear to the customer. In these circumstances it is necessary to rely on the customer's ongoing use following their receipt of the e-mail to prove their agreement to the change. It is possible, of course, that the customer had not read it.

However, it is increasingly common to see sites which do not scroll and click. Instead they refer to the terms and require the customer to click on 'I accept the terms and conditions'. Many lawyers are of the opinion also that this has become the generally accepted method of the customer accepting the terms and is adequate. Whether they will change their view as a result of the E-Commerce Regulations which require additional information to be provided to the customer prior to contracting remains to be seen. The use of a scroll and click would ensure that the needs of the regulation are and are seen to be achieved.

If a change is not notified to customers, or they do not scroll and click, a business may find it difficult to rely on a change. The importance of this depends on the nature of the change. If a business has taken time up front to establish appropriate terms and conditions it is unlikely that it will change them on a whim. A change is likely to be the result of an error, a change in commercial policy, e.g. cost of delivery, or a legal requirement. In these circumstances having the customer agree to the change is important. If this is not forthcoming, a potential cost exposure to the business may be created.

The terms should ideally be accessible from every page and on many sites, e.g. at www.amazon.co.uk, the terms are listed with a number of options (customer services and the like) which can be linked to from any page. This means that at any point in time before or after they contract with the site a customer can find the terms and check what they say. If it is possible to build this into a site then this is the ideal. Other sites make the terms and conditions available from a link on the home page and this is also good.

TOP TIP

Even if you 'scroll and click every trip', if the customer can somehow close the terms and conditions page or move forward in their transaction without clicking on the 'I accept' button, the site structure is no longer conclusive of the fact that the customer has accepted the terms. This defeats one of the main purposes of forcing the customer through the terms! Make sure the technology matches your requirements and progress is barred unless customers click 'I accept'.

6.4   Terms of use

When any Internet user visits the site they will be brought to a page on the site. Ideally this will be the home page, but if the site has or allows deep links then it may be any page on the site. I would recommend legally that the user sees the terms of use of the site and is required to scroll and click on 'I accept' before being able to surf further. However, I understand that for most sites this is commercially unacceptable. As a result of this a practice has evolved where a user will see the terms on each page of the site and this is generally viewed as a notification. The argument then runs that when a user, having seen these terms, continues to use the site, they have acquiesced. To accommodate the terms on every page they are generally kept short. If this is not the case then there will at least be a link to the full terms on every page and the full terms will be given on the home page.

There have not been any cases to date on whether this form of acceptance of the terms of use by continued use is satisfactory, and the matter is not covered in any Internet-related legislation. Site owners who rely on this do so on the basis that the use of the site takes the place of clicking on an 'I accept' box, but it is not clear whether this would hold up in court. In the absence of scroll and click, it is, however, good commercial practice to include the terms on every page and this is better than not doing so at all.

Sample terms of use

The terms of use from www.dixons.co.uk, which are fairly short and can be seen on every page of the website, and its terms of sale are set out in Appendix 1. For information pubs247.co.uk's and Freeserve's terms of use are also included.

6.4.1   *Who owns the site?*

You can see that the terms inform the customer of who the site belongs to. This is a legal requirement. To keep the terms short the full company details are in many cases accessible by clicking on the highlighted company name. This is useful in limiting the wording but it is essential, where this practice is adopted, that the links to this work, that the information is kept up to date and that the links are regularly tested. The information which is displayed or linked to should set out the company:

- name;

- registered number;

- address;

- contact details – geographical address and means of contacting rapidly;

- VAT number if applicable.

6.4.2   *Intellectual property*

As well as notifying the customer who they are dealing with, it is normal to have a copyright notice, as virtually all sites will include copyright material. Although this notice is not legally required in the UK, it is in some countries in which the site may be viewed and therefore may add some protection in these countries. It also makes clear to third parties that the site contains original material which they cannot copy without consent. If such a notice is included it may also be wise to inform the site user of how and where they can obtain permission to copy the whole or part of it.

If the site includes trade marks, whether registered or not, the site should draw this fact to its users' attention. The trade marks and other rights in the content will also be referred to in an effort to put third parties on notice that they are not up for grabs simply because they are on a site. This may be particularly useful where a third party has unauthorised links to your site or copies parts of it. After all, with such a notice on your site third parties are certainly made aware of the restrictions on them.

6.4.3   Links

There is a legal debate over what putting content onto a website means. Is the fact that content is there an implied licence to use it or is it an implied licence to use it only for certain purposes? This is relevant to linking and is looked at in more detail in Chapter 4. However, debate aside, it is wise to try to protect your site from unauthorised linking by placing third parties on notice of the fact that you require them to have consent to link and how they can contact you to get this.

6.4.4   Cookies

As explained later at section 8.7, there will shortly be a need to make the consumer aware in advance if the site uses cookies and also how they may remove them or that if the site is to be used cookies must be accepted by the user. Most sites already deal with this as a matter of good practice.

6.4.5   Other terms

The terms of use often link to the other terms of the site and perhaps the data protection provisions or privacy policy.

In deciding what the terms of use should be you should consider what users of your site do and adapt the terms to the circumstances. Examples of this may occur if the site offers information for free or perhaps free software. There then may be a need to disclaim liability.

Some of the most common problems for businesses operating on the Internet arise from inappropriate terms (often put together in a cut 'n' paste fashion from 'real-world' trading terms) that have not been properly tailored. Resist the temptation to recycle those old trading terms at all costs.

6.5 Registration

When a customer registers to use your site it is the equivalent of them having a customer account with you although that may not involve any element of credit. They enter into a relationship with you and provide you with data necessary for you to communicate with them. Some sites, particularly information providers, will require customers to register to use the site. This is partly because these sites need customer details to function and partly due to the fact that these sites may not sell anything but rely on their registered user numbers to attract advertisers and their source of revenue stream. Many sites, particularly retail sites, do not require registration from surfers, and individuals can use the site without registering. In such sites it is normal to be required to register prior to purchasing and this will be built into the first order.

Ordinarily there are few more terms on registration than are contained in the terms of use with the exception of a data collection notice. Obviously there is a need to have a data collection notice as the customer's personal data is being collected and more information on this is set out in Chapter 8.

6.5.1 Sample collection notice

The collection notice used by Freeserve is set out in Appendix 1. Freeserve's privacy policy is also included.

6.5.2 Password

Most sites provide the customer with a password or the facility to use one and this should be dealt with on registration. Passwords provide both sites and users with certainty. The user should be more certain that third parties cannot access their account and the site will be clearer that the person they are dealing with is in fact the user with whom they believe that they are dealing. This can provide some comfort from Internet fraud and charge-backs from banks. It is no guarantee – should a customer leave the site open with their password access entered, in theory any third party could use the account. Also, although we would like to assume that individuals register as themselves, the number of Joe Bloggs, Mickey Mouses and Tony Blairs who register on sites and can be found on many databases shoot a hole through that belief.

I would suggest that the registration page should tell the customer that their password is confidential to them, how it can be changed or where they can get that information, and that they should not provide it to anyone else. This last point is particularly important and although your site or customer services may have a security check which involves providing some detail from the password, it should not involve actually providing the password. In this way the customer can be reassured against internal fraud and this extra check will in reality limit the number of members of staff who have the ability to access the password and in turn the customer account. It is reasonable to confirm this term in the terms of sale.

If a site allows users to amend and update their data using their password then this should be explained in the registration page. Most of what is contained in this page will be an explanation rather than formal terms and on this basis there is not really a need for a scroll and click. If the site actually sells something, such as a subscription-based new service, then the story is different and there is a need to incorporate the registration with the terms of sale and to use a scroll and click.

6.6   Terms of sale

In order to tackle what is probably the most important relationship you will have with your customer I have broken the terms of sale into three main sections:

- selling and contract formation;

- requirements of a sale at a distance/e-commerce regulations; and

- what the terms of sale should say.

6.7   Selling and contract formation

6.7.1   Invitation to treat

The law of sale in England is different from that in many other European countries. When goods are put on display this can be regarded as an 'invitation to treat' as opposed to a direct offer to sell. Over the years that I have been in the legal profession I have heard many different versions of these three words from commercial people. On occasion the understanding is that there is a 'treat' which means that retailers can withdraw goods from sale. In simple terms what it actually means is that when a retailer displays its goods on a shelf it is showing the customer what it has available and allowing the customer to make an offer (normally the marked asking price) should the customer wish to purchase the goods. The customer normally makes that offer by taking the goods to the till and if the retailer wishes to accept the offer this will occur when the money offered for the goods is accepted. In other jurisdictions in Europe the concept is alien and it is the seller who would be deemed to be making an 'offer to the world' capable of acceptance by anyone coming across it.

Offer and acceptance are also legal terms and both are essential if a contract is to be created. Until the contract is created the goods are not sold. The legal process in England means that there are three stages in the sale contract which is not actually complete until the price has been paid to and accepted by the retailer. Perhaps more importantly, as the retailer has not made an offer itself but is considering an offer made by its customer, the retailer is able to

---

reject the customer's offer. This means that, provided the offer/ acceptance procedure has been properly constructed to present the goods by way of invitation to treat only, the retailer should be able to withdraw the goods from sale at any point before the contract is formed, i.e. any time prior to its accepting the customer's money as payment for the goods. You may well have come across this where a retailer has mispriced goods or somehow the wrong price tag has been placed on them. Unless you have actually paid for the goods the retailer is able to refuse your money and withdraw the goods from sale. Sometimes as a gesture of goodwill or because the error is not noticed by the sales assistant, this does not happen.

6.7.2   Offer and acceptance

As mentioned above, in many countries the legal process of offer and acceptance does not work in this way. Instead, when a retailer displays goods for sale this is deemed to be an offer to customers and when the customer selects the goods, such as clicking 'I accept' or 'proceed with purchase', this amounts to the customer's 'acceptance' (mechanics will vary as to the point in time the contract is actually formed). Unlike the bricks and mortar environment, there is one major difference online, the retailer cannot withdraw goods from sale when a customer has accepted them. In the case of a website, the site needs to be structured to allow for this withdrawal to replicate the English bricks and mortar legal position, i.e. to allow this last-gasp ability to avoid being bound.

6.7.3   True story: Argos

Almost three years ago the retailer Argos notoriously became a victim of a pricing error on its website. At some point in most retail processes prices are manually input and errors are easy to make. Add to this the risk of software errors (apparently the problem Argos had) and most retailers will admit that it is almost impossible to be sure that no price errors will occur on their site. This emphasises the need for websites to replicate the invitation to treat principle and to ensure if possible that they have the ability to withdraw goods from sale.

If you are sitting comfortably then I will begin the Argos story. Over a weekend in September 1999, Sony televisions which should have retailed at £299 were displayed on the web site at £2.99. Over the course of the weekend, more than £1,000,000 worth of TVs were ordered by customers. One shrewd customer who undoubtedly knew that there was a mistake on the site apparently ordered 1,700 £2.99 TVs in one transaction. It is unlikely that this individual was unaware of the error and probable that he expected to make a healthy profit!

The fact that this problem happened over a weekend is interesting. If this had happened in a store I am sure that Argos' till system would have picked up the error, or if it didn't it is a fair bet (given the huge price discrepancy) that the majority of sales assistants could not have failed to. The error would have been noted, other stores would have been informed immediately and a decision on the one customer insisting that they were entitled to a £2.99 TV made.

But this was not the real world, this was the virtual world. This makes two differences. First, the site is likely to have effectively been left unattended – operating unless there were any technical problems and downtime which alerted its owners to a problem. Secondly, as another consequence of the technological medium, many customers could have found the e-mail error and within seconds informed their friends. As we have already seen, this can spiral in numbers in a very short period of time. Perhaps this explains why Argos took orders for more than 300,000 TVs at £2.99 in such a short space of time. Certainly if that had been a normal weekend's trading at normal prices I am sure the bubble would not have burst.

The dilemma faced by Argos when it apparently discovered the error on Monday morning was whether it was obliged to honour the sales which had been made or whether it could simply tell customers that there had been a mistake in price and the goods were being withdrawn from sale. The true legal answer to this is that it depends. This is not a lawyer's cop out! Whether Argos could legitimately have withdrawn the TVs from sale or not depends almost entirely on how the sale process was structured. An analysis of whether the site had been structured on a basis which (with appropriate content) made its sales based on an invitation to treat would be necessary. A major complication was the use of an automated e-mail response which (rather than highlight the mistake) thanked the purchasers for their custom! This nicely highlights the fact that where e-mails are sent to customers as part of the order process, their content must be as carefully considered as that of the website.

Although in Internet terms Argos may be assigned to the annals of history, in 2002 a similar problem was faced by Kodak whose website wrongly advertised cameras which retailed at £300 for £100. This was resolved by Kodak honouring the orders at the lower price.

By its notoriety the Argos case serves to highlight a problem: the lack of clarity of the contract process and how and when a contract is formed online. This problem has been tackled by the EU in the E-Commerce Directive implemented in the UK by the E-Commerce (EC Directive) Regulations 2002. Although these do not set out a particular way in which a contract should be formed, they do require that the steps which are to be followed to form a contract are made clear in advance to a recipient of services.

The regulations also require that the consumer is provided with an acknowledgement of the order in electronic form. This could be built into the structure of the site so that the page/e-mail confirmation following the order is triggered on receipt of the order. If this is before the stock check has occurred, it would be wise to make clear that this is an acknowledgement and not acceptance – this is done on the Tesco site www.tesco.co.uk. However, if the stock check has already occurred and you are ready to accept the order and commit to supply, then it is possible to also make this acceptance. If it is not acceptance then you must remember to communicate acceptance to the customer. If the acknowledgement is not part of the site then it should be sent by e-mail and a strict system must be put in place to ensure that this occurs promptly. The same considerations between acknowledgement and acceptance exist.

The terms and conditions applicable to the contract should be provided to the recipient and be available in a form which is capable of being stored and reproduced by the recipient. A large number of sites are structured in such a way that it is not possible to either print the terms or to copy them. My general advice is that the terms should be included on the back of the receipt and in this way there can be no doubt that the customer has received these in a durable or permanent form. However, the risk of this is that the terms should reflect the website terms, and as these are amended, the terms on the back of the receipt must also be amended.

A risk of cancellation exists where the recipient is not given the requisite opportunity to identify and amend input errors before the order is sent. The information provided must allow an appropriate, effective and accessible means for the user to amend the error. In simple terms, once the customer has inputted all of their order and personal data and the price is displayed they must have a chance to change anything. This is often done by asking the consumer to confirm all the details of the order on an additional page which restates all the details and gives the consumer an opportunity to change any detail of the order or even whether they wish to process the order. Often the order is not sent to the site until this additional page is seen and the customer clicks a box confirming their desire to order. This is the ideal in the light of the regulations.

6.7.4   E-mails or communications from the seller

E-mails sent to the customer as part of the sale process may obviously also have an effect. The content of these e-mails can impact on the sale process. It is a different thing to receive an e-mail saying 'your order has been accepted' from one saying 'we have received your order'. This was highlighted by the Argos case. The E-Commerce Regulations' requirement that a customer is informed of the stages in a contract being made with a website may not only be of help to the customer but also to a retailer whose staff may now achieve a clarity of understanding which they did not have previously. This must be made clear to the customer and I would suggest that it is best to include this in the scroll and click terms of sale if these are used.

At this point, as I do not want to be accused of picking on Argos who at the time had enough trouble, I will leave their story. Instead I have set out below some sample pages from a website. These are examples of how a site may be structured to offer its goods for sale on an invitation to treat basis.

6.7.5   Stages of contract formation

In accordance with the E-Commerce Regulations it is necessary to make clear to the customer what the stages of contract formation are. It is wise not to simply include this information in the terms and conditions of sale, but to make this clear to the customer on the pages in the ordering process.

This is only a suggestion and may not be the only way to achieve this result. Depending on the nature of the goods sold and the purchase made you may not want to have the point of acceptance until the goods are delivered. I believe that this is the case with a major food retailer where customers order goods but do not have the order accepted until the goods are delivered.

However, there is one small question mark over this, as the final Regulations varied from the consultation draft and made changes to the requirement for a technical method of changing input errors prior to the placing of the order. The implication of this is that the site will be structured on an invitation to treat basis and customer orders will always be offers. Unless there is a good reason, such as in the food retailer's case, it may be wise to avoid the use of any other structure and to ensure that the customer order is always the contractual offer.

The nature of this food business approach is that when an on-line customer buys on a Monday using the website they in fact pay the prices charged on the day that the goods are delivered. Prices may go up as well as down and the price that the consumer will pay for the goods may change between the day they order and the day they receive the goods – this is made very clear to the consumer. In effect they are pre-ordering, and pay the price on the day of order. The retailer will not accept the order if the customer is unwilling to make an offer of the amount that the goods retail at on the day they are delivered. In such a scenario the goods are brought to the customer's door on an invitation to treat basis. The customer is told what the retail price is and is then free to offer this or not. If they do not then the retailer may exercise their right not to accept the offer and withdraw the goods. In this situation the response received by the customer acknowledging the order, in order to comply with the E-Commerce Regulations, would definitely not be acceptance but only an acknowledgement of receipt of the order.

By explaining this I hope to highlight the fact that every site's needs are not exactly the same and that the commercial aspects need to be considered at the same time to allow the right decision to be made. However, the legal principles are generally the same and need to be taken into consideration. Don't be glued to my example but consider it, look at adapting it to your business needs and consider the ramifications of any changes you make.

6.7.6   *When is the contract formed?*

The Regulations state that in the case of the order and the acknowledgement of receipt, these will be deemed to be received by the parties to whom they are addressed and are able to access them. This creates a potential minefield when things go wrong and either the order or the acknowledgement are not received. In such a case, the recipient is unlikely to be able to access them and a potential gap arises. It would of course be possible for the sender to prove when they were sent, but for the recipient who does not receive them it is not possible to show when, if ever, they were accessible. Whether this will really be an issue remains to be seen and the gravity of it will be assessed only when the Regulations come to be applied.

However, in the world of e-commerce, when would the contract be deemed to be formed? This will, as we have seen, depend on the structure of the site. The contract will be formed when acceptance occurs – a very simple lesson to learn. Make sure that your site is clearly structured on an invitation to treat basis and that the terms of sale state this, and make clear to the customer in advance of the transaction what the stages in this are and when a binding contract will be formed.

6.8 The requirements of distance selling

6.8.1 Sale at a distance

The Consumer Protection (Distance Selling) Regulations 2000 and the E-Commerce (EC Directive) Regulations 2002 both govern sales at a distance. In the case of the Distance Selling Regulations these cover not only a sale from a website but almost all sales at a distance. A sale at a distance occurs where the customer and the retailer are not face to face or physically present, e.g. catalogue sales or sales by fax are also covered. This means that the provisions apply to all new technologies considered in this book and not just to the Internet.

Exempt transactions

There are a number of exceptions to the rules set out in the Distance Selling Regulations where the rules do not apply at all or apply only in part. Included in these exceptions are where the goods or services sold fall into certain categories, including flowers and food, sales of land, sales by way of auction and sales through automated vending machines. In particular it should be noted that financial services are dealt with by way of separate similar legislation and are not subject to the provisions of the Distance Selling Regulations. A full list of the exceptions can be found in the Regulations and the full text can be viewed free of charge at www.hmso.gov.uk.

6.8.2   The E-Commerce Regulations

The E-Commerce (EC Directive) Regulations 2002 came into force on 21 August 2002 (compliance deadline of three weeks from this date). These are accompanied by two guidance notes from the DTI, one general and the other for small businesses.

The Regulations apply to information society services, which are defined in the Regulations as being a service (or goods) normally provided for remuneration which is provided at a distance and which is provided by means of electronic equipment. The Directive itself referred to a coordinated field which made clear that the Directive and in turn the Regulations apply only to the activity which is the information society service and not to the goods or service themselves or to their delivery if this is not supplied electronically. If it was supplied electronically, for example a software download, then the delivery and the goods both being supplied by electronic means would also be subject to the Regulations. Where the same piece of software was delivered to a customer on a disk, neither the software not its delivery would fall into this coordinated field and the Directive and so the Regulations would not apply. This is more than a little confusing and I understand that the DTI intend to explain this in simple terms in the guidance documents.

The Regulations look at the place of establishment of the information society service provider and make clear that this is the location where the business takes place. Where the supplier has its place of establishment in the UK then the goods or services supplied by it, to the extent that their supply falls within this coordinated field, must comply with UK law. Where the business effectively has multiple places of establishment it will be the centre of the information services activity which will apply.

However, this does not mean that the e-tailer who sells from a place of establishment in the UK may not also be subject to the consumer laws in other Member States (see section 5.8). National courts have shown a willingness to apply their local laws to e-businesses based overseas.

6.8.3   Information requirements pre-sale

Information to consumers

The Regulations require that retailers or other businesses or professionals provide certain information to a consumer in advance of a sale taking place and the contract being formed.

It is worth noting that a consumer may include a business. Although this statement may seem contradictory, businesses which purchase goods or services where such transactions are not in the course of their business may be deemed consumers. They do not apply to sales between two businesses dealing in the course of their business. If you have any doubt whether you are dealing with a business as a consumer or as a business you should consider whether any of your actions would be different for a consumer, and if you have any concerns take further legal advice.

What information?

It is necessary to provide the following information prior to a sale taking place:

1. The name and address of the supplier. This should include the company name, registration number, VAT number, registered address and a contact name. The customer should also be provided with the details of a means of contact such as e-mail, phone or postal address. A post box number is not adequate.

2. The main characteristics of the goods or services to be supplied. This amounts to a product description from which the products or services can clearly be identified and which does not mislead the customer but makes clear the characteristics attributable to what is purchased.

3. The cost of the goods or services – including not only the price to be charged for the goods but also any additional costs for tax and delivery and the total cost payable. This means that there should be no hidden charges and any additional delivery or other costs should be notified to the customer, in order to create certainty, in advance of their agreeing to form a binding contract with you.

4. The cost of using the means of distance selling where it is other than the basic rate.

5. What the arrangements for payment are – i.e. when the payment is to be made and how this can be made, e.g. Switch, credit card and provisions for cheques etc.

6. The period for which the offer or price will remain valid – this is so where the price is a special offer or simply the normal cost of the goods. All prices must be clear and should show whether they are inclusive or exclusive of VAT.

7. The right of cancellation or withdrawal – the process for the exercise of these rights – should be clearly set out. This should also explain how the goods are to be returned to the retailer and what will be refunded and when. The retailer appears to have to refund not only the cost of the goods but also the cost of delivery. However, if it is specifically stated that the cost of return will be borne by the purchaser then this may be deducted from the sum refunded.

8. If the supplier wants to reserve the right to provide substitute goods where the goods are not available then this must be specifically reserved.

This information must all be supplied to the consumer prior to the sale in a form which is clear and comprehensible. On the whole it should be sufficient to put the general information in the terms and conditions and to ensure that the product-specific information and price are available in the order process.

Additional information under the E-Commerce Regulations

The E-Commerce Regulations have added to the original list of information requirements and where directly relevant these requirements have been added to the above list. They also require the following:

1. Where the provision of the information society service is subject to an authorisation scheme, details of that scheme.

2. Where the information society service exercises a regulated profession then particular details.

3. Before an order is placed the consumer must also be provided with the language in which the contract may be concluded.

4. Before an order is placed the consumer must also be informed whether or not the concluded contract will be filed by the service provider and whether it will be accessible. What this actually means is difficult to know, but it is likely that this is a hangover from the Directive and other European legal systems which do on occasion require that contracts are registered or filed.

5. There is also a need to provide details of any relevant codes of conduct which are subscribed to and a means of consulting them electronically.

6. If the service provider is registered in a trade register or similar register available to the public details of how that register can be consulted and the registration number or similar.

7. Where subject to an authorisation scheme details of this.

8. Details of any applicable regulated profession.

9. In addition to the provisions of the Distance Selling Regulations, geographical address, e-mail or other contact details to allow rapid access, and VAT number.

CHECKLIST 6.1 INFORMATION TO BE PROVIDED

Distance Selling Regulations

The information to be provided pre-sale:

General in the terms and conditions:

- name and contact details; ☐
- how the goods can be paid for and when; ☐
- what the cancellation right is, how this will happen; ☐
- how to return the goods; ☐
- what will be refunded and when; ☐
- how long the advertised price will remain valid; ☐
- the cost of the use of the means of access if this is not standard. ☐

Specific to the goods or services:

- the main characteristics of the goods or services; ☐
- the total price including delivery and taxes; ☐
- how long the advertised price will remain valid – may be in general terms. ☐

CHECKLIST 6.1 Contd

E-Commerce Regulations

The information to be provided prior to the contract being formed where concluded by electronic means:

- the language(s) in which the contract may be concluded; ☐
- the stages which form the contract; ☐
- a technical means to correct any input errors; ☐
- whether the contract will be filed and whether it will be accessible. ☐

Codes of conduct:

- any codes of conduct to which the vendor subscribes and how the codes can be consulted electronically. ☐

The information to be provided in a form directly and permanently accessible:

- the geographical address, e-mail address or a means of communicating rapidly, and VAT number if applicable; ☐
- details of trade registers applicable to the information society service; ☐
- details of authorisation schemes applicable to the information society service; ☐
- details of regulated profession. ☐

6.8.4 Provision in a durable medium or permanently accessible form

The distance selling legislation has made it necessary for certain terms to be provided to the customer in writing or a durable medium which is available and accessible to the consumer, no later than the time at which the goods are delivered or the service is being performed. This issue of what is a durable medium has come to the fore as part of the distance selling legislation and now the new e-commerce legislation raises the question of what is a permanently accessible form. The distance selling legislation did not make a decision on what amounts to a durable form, but the DTI indicated that where the transaction took place by e-mail this may be acceptable in e-mail form. In the past the EU has raised doubts as to whether e-mail is a permanent form and have suggested that only something which could be saved on the customer's hard drive would be considered either a durable medium or permanently accessible.

The DTI has suggested that fax or e-mail are acceptable, but I have set out below my suggestion for the provision of this with the receipt which puts this beyond doubt.

Distance selling

The Distance Selling Regulations require that some of the pre-sale information and the following additional information is supplied by the seller in a durable form:

- conditions of cancellation and return of goods;

- contact details for complaints;

- after-sales and guarantee information.

The E-Commerce Regulations require that some of the information be provided in a permanently accessible form. This includes much of the information already listed and:

- the geographical address, e-mail address or a means of communicating rapidly, and VAT number if applicable;

- details of trade registers applicable to the information society service;

- details of authorisation schemes applicable to the information society service;

- details of regulated profession.

How to provide this in writing or a durable form/permanently accessible manner

Many sites state in their terms and conditions that customers should print out their terms and conditions. This may be a wise provision and inclusion of it certainly does no harm. If you decide to include this then be aware that some sites or parts of them cannot be printed, so make sure that your web designers are aware of this and that they accommodate the need to print in the right place. However, it is possible that a customer may order at a time or in a place where they do not have access to a printer and with the increase in new technologies I believe that the risk of this is becoming increasingly higher. In these circumstances it is certainly

CHECKLIST 6.2 DISTANCE SELLING

The information to be provided in writing or a durable form:

General in the terms and conditions (back of receipt):

- name and contact details; ☐
- how the goods can be paid for and when; ☐
- what the cancellation right is, how this will happen; ☐
- how to return the goods; ☐
- what will be refunded and when; ☐
- information regarding aftersales and guarantees; ☐
- contact details (including physical address) for complaints. ☐

Specific to the goods or services (front of receipt):

- the main characteristics of the goods or services; ☐
- the total price including delivery and taxes; ☐
- cancellation form. ☐

E-Commerce Regulation additions – permanently accessible form:

- the geographical address, e-mail address or a means of communicating rapidly, and VAT number if applicable; ☐
- details of trade registers applicable to the information society service; ☐
- details of authorisation schemes applicable to the information society service; ☐
- details of regulated profession. ☐

arguable that asking a customer to print the terms does not amount to the terms being provided in a permanent form. An alternative might be to ask the customer to save the terms and conditions to the hard drive. Again it is possible to imagine situations where this would not be possible and may not be ideal.

I would suggest a fairly simple solution to this problem. Most sites provide some form of receipt or delivery note with the goods or services when they are actually delivered. I would suggest that the appropriate terms and conditions and any pre-sale information be printed onto the back of this and the provision of a hard copy be referred to in the terms and conditions themselves. If this is done then it is again important to make sure that these are the same as the terms on the site. If any changes are made to the site then these will also need to be made to the printed copy. Obviously there is a cost impact to re-printing (which might be a good deterrent of frivolous changes). Small changes could be made on existing terms by way of stickers if there is a large number of copies of printed terms in stock – but be careful to ensure that this actually happens.

If a business has a number of services or different provisions depending on what is purchased, e.g. warranties as well as the product sold, there may be a variety of applicable terms. To avoid confusion I would suggest that these are all included and it is made clear that the additional terms only apply 'if you have also purchased x … then …' An alternative to this would be to provide the customer with links within the terms, e.g. 'if you have also purchased x … then additional terms apply and can be read by clicking here'. This, however, is not as ideal as incorporating all of the terms. In either case the hard copy must include all terms. To avoid confusion or the wrong customer receiving the wrong terms I would again recommend that you take the most straightforward route available and only print one set of terms. There should be no risk of the wrong terms being sent if this is done.

The Distance Selling and E-Commerce Regulations require certain information to be included in this durable or permanently accessible form and this is looked at in section 6.7 and Checklist 6.2 above. Ideally, to make life simple, this information should be included in the terms and conditions and where it is variable, e.g. the price, on the front of that document in the receipt.

6.8.5 *Failure to provide this information*

Failure to provide the information required by the Distance Selling Regulations means the customer's right to reject the goods or cancel the contract/reject the goods (usually seven working days from the day after delivery) is extended further by up to three months. If one rectifies the situation by supplying the information within the three months' window, the seven-working-day period runs from the consumer's receipt of the information. In respect of the information required under the E-Commerce Regulations, failure to provide this may result in damages being awarded to the consumer or the issuance of a 'stop now' order by a regulator.

6.8.6 *Gift sales*

Many sites allow for goods to be ordered by one person as a gift for or on behalf of another. This can be a particularly lucrative business at certain times of the year such as Christmas. Where this occurs then the terms need to be provided in a durable form to the person who ordered the goods and not the recipient no later than the date on which the goods are delivered to the third party.

If this is the case then should you provide the information with the receipt as I have suggested, and this should then be sent to the person who has ordered the goods and not the recipient. A system to ensure this should be put in place.

In any event it is commercially good practice to send the purchaser and not the recipient of the goods the receipt, although a gift receipt may also be included with the goods as delivered.

6.8.7   *Duty to supply the goods or services*

As well as the information which is to be provided to the consumer prior to the sale the Distance Selling Regulations add a couple of additional requirements on the retailer. The first of these is the duty to supply within a specified timescale. The general rule is that unless the parties have agreed to the contrary (terms and conditions) the goods must be supplied by the retailer within 30 days. This period of 30 days is to run from the day following the day on which the consumer sends his order to the supplier.

If the retailer is unable to do this then he must refund all sums paid for the transaction by the consumer within 60 days of the date on which the original order was placed (i.e. a further 30 days). Alternatively there may be a provision for substituted goods.

6.8.8 Substitute goods

There is the alternative of supplying the consumer with substitute or alternative goods of an equivalent price and quality. However, this can only be exercised where the terms of sale specifically provide for this in advance of the transaction being made. There is one further condition to this – this can only be specified with a commitment to return the full cost of delivery as well as the goods if the consumer rejects them, i.e. a retailer cannot charge a consumer the cost of returning substitute goods.

6.8.9 Cooling off periods/cancellation rights

1. The second consequence of the Distance Selling Regulations is the creation of a seven-day cooling off period for customers who purchase at a distance. This right is exercisable within 'seven working days'. The Regulations state that a working day is any day other than Saturday, Sunday or a public holiday. For the sake of clarity for your customers it may also be wise to state what a working day is in your terms and conditions. This rejection right is actually similar to the change of mind type of provision offered by many businesses as opposed to the consumer's right to reject the goods as faulty.

2. This period of seven days begins to run on the day following the day on which the goods have been delivered or the contract for services is concluded. However, it is possible that this seven working days will not begin to run until much later. If the information required by the Distance Selling Regulations is not

supplied and confirmed in a durable form within the timescales set out in the Regulations (i.e. supplied before the contract is formed and confirmed in a durable form no later than the date of delivery of the goods or in the course of supply of the services) then the period of seven days will not commence until the information is supplied and confirmed. This can happen any time up to three months after the transaction has taken place and leaves a business potentially exposed to the cancellation of orders and return of possibly dated goods for over three months. It is important to note the goods also do not have to be returned in perfect condition! (See below.) It is obviously to your business's advantage to ensure that you have complied with the information requirements and avoid this risk and cost exposure.

3. There are certain exceptions to the consumer's ability to withdraw from the transaction:

- where the goods have been tailored to the customer's needs/specification or customised such as a build-to-order computer, the customer may not withdraw once the contract is formed;

- where the contract is for services and the customer has been told in writing or a durable form before the conclusion of the contract that there is no ability to cancel once the performance of the services is commenced;

- the supply of audio visual recordings or computer software if the consumer has broken the seal on the packaging;

- newspapers, periodicals or magazines;

- gaming, betting or lottery services.

4. The E-Commerce Regulations also allow the consumer the right to cancel or, as it describes it, rescind the contract, but there are no restrictions to the duration of this or exceptions as in the Distance Selling Regulations. This right was, until the stage of the draft regulations, going to apply in three circumstances but as a result of a great deal of lobbying by industry this was reduced to a single circumstance. The right to cancel applies where a service provider has not made available a technical means of identifying and correcting input errors.

6.8.10   Return of the goods

If the consumer cancels a contract your business will generally want the goods to be returned. Perhaps surprisingly this is not an automatic consequence of the Regulations and the right to cancel must specify the requirement for the consumer to return any goods rejected prior to the formation of the contract of sale – in the terms and conditions. This clause should explain how the return can be made and to be valid this should not be unduly onerous to the consumer.

If you have specified that the consumer must return the goods and explained how to do this and the consumer fails to return the goods then you are able to charge the consumer for the direct costs you have incurred in the recovery of the goods. This is obviously not an ideal situation. You may instead prefer to offer the consumer a specific route of return such as the same method by which the goods were delivered.

The right to charge the consumer for this will not apply if the consumer has a right other than under the Distance Selling Regulations to reject the goods – such as the goods being faulty.

Cancellation notice

I would suggest that, when using the receipt method of communicating the necessary information to the consumer in a durable medium, the actual cancellation notice be attached as a tear-off part of the form and/or an e-mail address to which notice of cancellation should be sent be provided. The form and method of the cancellation notice must be provided to the consumer as part of the information required in a durable medium and this method will ensure compliance.

Condition of returned goods

At this point it is worth noting that most goods (other than the list of audio visual goods and software) may be returned where the packaging is opened. This may present retailers with the problem of goods being returned in a condition which is not new. The strict requirements are only that they be handled with reasonable care and this less than perfect state throws up some potentially difficult scenarios (the classic debate concerns a five-day-old car returned with five hundred miles on the clock – see further below). Where packaging has been opened/goods are not perfect, the goods should not be sold as new but instead as second-hand goods. This again may create a cost consequence which cannot be avoided. It may, however, be permissible to request that consumers provide returned goods in a complete form, unopened and where possible in new condition. This could not, however, be an absolute obligation and needs to be carefully worded.

There is also a potential issue with software and audio visual downloads. Although there is no clear decision on this, I would suggest that the 'seal is broken' at the point where the clickwrap licence is clicked on.

Consumer's obligation of care

Under the Distance Selling Regulations the consumer is obliged to take reasonable care of the goods until they are returned to or collected by the retailer and must, on the retailer's request, make the goods available at the consumer's premises for 21 days from the date of cancellation if there is no clause requiring the consumer to return the goods and a period of six months where such a clause is included. Retailers should not only ensure that such a clause is included in their terms but also that the process covering consumer rejection and a process for collection is put in place.

6.8.11   Refund on rejection

The consumer is entitled to a refund of the cost of the goods and any other charges paid for the goods such as delivery for goods or services which are rejected. This refund should be made as soon as possible and in any event within 30 days of the date on which the goods were cancelled. Cancellation occurs when the notice of cancellation is served. The consumer may be charged for the cost of return (which can be deducted from the refund if the consumer does not actually pay this) only where the requirement for return is specified as in section 6.8.7, above.

For information, any credit agreement which runs with the goods will be cancelled by this and the supplier is responsible for notifying the creditor of this fact.

The E-Commerce Regulations fail to provide this detail with respect to the right to rescind.

TOP TIP

....

Your systems must not only be able to track sales but also cancellation, refunds and collection of cancelled goods. It is important to ensure that order and stock management systems as well as accounting systems can interface and swap relevant information.

....

6.8.12   Cancellation of fraudulent transactions

Consumers are also given a right to cancel payments which they believe have been made fraudulently on their credit cards. Previously the Consumer Credit Act stated that the consumer would be liable for the first £50 of their losses when the card was out of their possession. The effect of this provision is removed for sales at a distance.

There is a potential consequence of this for retailers as the whole of a fraudulent transaction (proven to be such) may now be included in any chargeback applied by a credit card supplier.

This also applies to Switch and other debit cards. For these cards in particular this may give the consumer an additional layer of protection which was not previously provided by their banks.

6.8.13   Contracting out

It is not possible for a retailer to contract out of the terms of the Distance Selling Regulations or, in respect of transactions with a consumer, the E-Commerce Regulations. As a consequence of this anyone who supplies goods or services in a professional capacity to a consumer who is a UK resident is subject to the terms of these Regulations and, importantly, they cannot be contracted out of by applying the laws of another country. This means that, for example, an American website which is not subject to similar regulations in its home jurisdiction will in fact be subject to these.

6.8.14   Failure to comply with these provisions

Failure to provide the various pieces of information required by the Distance Selling Regulations before and after the order has taken place will result in the consumer having up to three additional months to cancel the order and reject the goods. Failure to comply with the information required by the E-Commerce Regulations before the contract has taken place will allow an unlimited right to cancel.

CHECKLIST 6.3 DISTANCE SELLING REGULATIONS: SUMMARY

- Applicable to all sites trading with consumers in the UK. ☐

- Information to be given prior to sale contract. ☐

- Further information to be provided in a durable medium by no later than delivery of goods or supply of service. ☐

- Strict provisions regarding substitution. ☐

- Customer has a defined period to cancel most agreements and receive a refund of all charges. ☐

- Return can only be charged for in certain circumstances. ☐

- Set timescales for performance. ☐

- Extra protection for consumers where fraudulent payment by credit and debit cards. ☐

- No ability to contract out of the requirements. ☐

CHECKLIST 6.4 E-COMMERCE REGULATIONS: SUMMARY

- Applies to the provision of information society services where the place of establishment is in the UK. ☐

- Explain stages of contract formation in advance. ☐

- Send acknowledgement of order in electronic form. ☐

- Geographical address and also e-mail or means of contacting promptly. ☐

- Information: VAT number, registers available to the public and any codes of conduct which are subscribed to. ☐

- Prices clear and indicate inclusive or exclusive of VAT. ☐

- Other provisions regarding identification of commercial communication. ☐

CHECKLIST 6.5 CONTRACT OF SALE

Distance Selling and E-Commerce Regulations requirements:

- who the customer is contracting with; ☐
- how the contract is formed – what the steps are and when the contract will occur; ☐
- invitation to treat; ☐
- how payment is to be made and when this will occur; ☐
- when delivery will be made; ☐
- right to substitute; ☐
- right to return without cause; ☐
- right to refund; ☐
- cost of return borne by the customer; ☐
- information on any warranties and guarantees; ☐
- fight to reject for change of mind; ☐
- what to do to reject the goods. ☐

Other terms:

- password; ☐
- age restrictions if applicable; ☐
- rights regarding faulty goods and refunds; ☐
- if any software is provided, licence terms; ☐
- governing law and jurisdiction; ☐
- provisions for dispute resolution; ☐
- reference to any arbitration or equivalent procedure; ☐
- codes of conduct or other industry bodies which are subscribed to. ☐

In its initial draft of the Regulations the government proposed to apply criminal sanctions where the Regulations were not complied with. This provision was met with a general outcry from the retail industry and partly as a result of this the sanctions were watered down.

The Director General of Fair Trading acting through Trading Standards has a right to invoke injunctions (interdicts in Scotland) against the owners of non-compliant websites (or other distance sellers). In the case of both sets of regulations 'stop now orders' may be applied by a regulator.

At this point it may be worth noting that in May 2002 the Office of Fair Trading's 2001 annual report reviewed the first year of the Distance Selling Regulations. Three hundred and sixty-nine cases were reviewed under the Regulations. When the OFT reviewed more than six hundred UK websites it found that half of them failed to comply with the Directive's requirements. It was reported that the OFT planned to undertake further work in this area so beware.

6.9   Terms of sale: content

Having seen how the contract is formed and what the Distance Selling and E-Commerce Regulations require, I think that it is useful to bring these together by looking at what a set of terms of sale should contain as a minimum.

The content of these will depend on your business, in part on the legal requirements set out above and in part on general UK consumer protection laws. To give you an idea of what may be required a sample from the Dixons.co.uk's website is set out in Appendix 1.

6.10   Methods of payment for goods and services

6.10.1   *Card payments*

Almost all consumer transactions on the Internet in the UK will be paid for by cards, whether these are debit, credit or store cards. The site should make clear which of these is accepted and should ensure that the card number when provided on the site is not readable. The need for encryption and other security relating to card payments is explored in more depth in Chapter 7.

The customer should be made aware of the point in time at which their card will be debited.

6.10.2   *Credit*

Currently consumer credit transactions cannot be completed online as they are required to be signed by the consumer.

If any information regarding a consumer is passed to a credit reference agency then the fact that this occurs and what it will be used for should be made clear to the consumer. The consumer will then have the opportunity to contact that reference agency should they wish to see what information is being held by them.

Information may be passed not only in a credit card purchase but in a normal credit card transaction if the reference agency is providing card authentication services.

6.10.3 *Cheques*

Some sites do in fact accept cheques although this does beg the question why, when someone wishes to pay by cheque, they would order from a website, removing one of the key advantages of e-business sales – its speed!

Where payment by cheque is accepted it is necessary to modify the contract process or applicable terms to be sure that the cheque is cleared before the goods are sent to the customer. This may mean that goods need to be ring-fenced from stock for a customer who wants to pay by this method. In order to regulate the time for which this will occur, which is particularly relevant for high-demand items, there should be a specified reasonable time period for receipt of the cheque and a disclaimer of all liabilities and losses if the cheque is not received in that time.

6.11   VAT: a competitive disadvantage?

Currently the rates of VAT or equivalent charged throughout Europe vary from country to country. For example, books are zero rated in the UK but subject to 5 per cent TVA in France. This has created a question of whether the VAT or equivalent should be charged in the country where the goods are sold and at that rate, or should be charged in the country where the consumer receives the goods. This is obviously not a problem where the retailer and the consumer are in the same country.

Traditionally businesses charge local tax to consumers and so they pay the tax in the country in which the goods are sold. This is the case for high-street businesses.

In February 2002, the EU agreed a change so that the VAT or equivalent charged on digital products will in fact be charged in the country in which the consumer is resident when there is a sale of goods or services online to a customer in the EU. This is to be implemented in Member States by July 2003. This will mean that non-EU suppliers will be liable to levy VAT when selling their products into the EU at the local rate, and that this will be the same rate as those selling digital goods into other Member States where they must charge the VAT of the Member State of the recipient, thus creating a level playing field. The country of registration for VAT will reallocate the VAT collected to the country of the customer.

Most Member States appeared to be happy with this but the UK government opposed it. The UK was not, however, successful in this. Its opposition was on the basis that this new system creates unnecessary complication and make e-businesses subject to an additional layer of administration which their high-street counterparts are not.

6.11.1   The US problem

The crux of the problem is not, however, the EU but the perceived unfair competitive advantage which is obtained by foreign, in particular US, companies. As in the EU there is no harmonisation in state taxes between US states. The Federal Trade Commission are aware of this and have currently declared a moratorium on this issue. The effect of this is that where a server is located in the US but the business sells in other countries no local tax is paid. Where the US business sells into the EU and therefore competes with an EU site the US site will not be subject to any local tax but the local sites will be. As VAT equivalents can be as much as almost 20 per cent this can create a cost advantage to retailers from outside of the EU. Reportedly AOL has saved in the region of £100 million as a result of its legal non-payment of VAT in the UK. In September Freeserve was granted the court's consent to challenge Customs and Excise's earlier decision in an attempt to stop this allegedly 'unfair advantage'.

In July Freeserve announced that it would move the provision of its Internet any time service to Madeira and would by doing so save a reported £4.5 million in tax. Virgin.net already runs its service from there.

6.12   Other customer relationships

Generally this chapter has looked at the sale of tangible goods to consumers. It is also worth considering the sale of services or intangible goods.

6.12.1   *Services*

Services may be sold alone or in conjunction with goods. The Supply of Goods and Services Act 1982 (as amended) and the provisions of the distance selling legislation relevant to services will be applicable. Where goods and services are both sold, or are sold together, then both sets of legislation or provisions should be borne in mind.

6.12.2 Downloads

Increasingly the downloading of software and audio/visual 'goods' is part and parcel of e-business. In Chapter 9 contracts for third parties to provide these services through your site are considered and this inevitably raises a number of issues.

It is worth considering that there may be a need for a licence, how this licence will be made binding and how returns will be dealt with.

6.12.3 Commercial communications

This is covered in Chapter 8.

6.13 Business to business

The Distance Selling Regulations and their requirements do not apply to business-to-business (B2B) transactions, only to business-to-consumer (B2C) transactions. Generally consumer legislation in the UK may be excluded in business transactions and the terms of sale will be upheld where these are reasonable. Increasingly courts are turning over standard business terms which are not negotiated if these are not reasonable and it is therefore important to keep this reasonableness test in your head when considering the terms you wish to place on business dealings.

Registration of a business will generally be more important than registration of a consumer on a B2B site, and this is particularly so where any credit or account facilities are offered to a business.

Remember that a business may deal as a consumer and that if this is the case the consumer's statutory rights will apply and should not be excluded in your terms.

Also remember that, although you are dealing with a business, if you collect data from individuals this is still personal data and the data protection provisions and requirements looked at in Chapter 8 must be complied with.

ADDITIONAL INFORMATION

The OFT has produced a guide to the Distance Selling Regulations. This is aimed at business and can be obtained by calling 0207 211 8000 / 0845 722 4499 or accessed at www.oft.gov.uk

The full text of the Distance Selling Regulations and all other UK legislation can be found free of charge at www.hmso.gov.uk

The E-Commerce Regulations, guidance note and small business guidance *Complying with the E-Commerce Regulations* can be found on the DTI website at www.dti.gov.uk or by telephoning 0207 251 5000

Which? Web Trader can be found at www.which.co.uk

Useful legal information relating to some of the matters set out above can be found on the websites of the following law firms:

McDermott Will & Emery (UK and US) – www.mwe.com/ebusiness

Olswang – www.olswang.com

Pillsbury Winthrop – www.pillsburywinthrop.com

Wright Johnson and Mackenzie (Scottish) – www.wjm.co.uk

CHAPTER 7

Security

7.1   Security and fraud

Security has, like a nasty virus crawling through the Internet invading networks and computers, spread through almost every chapter of this book. Whatever you do, whether you transact with customers, buy from third-party suppliers, offer a service, allow access to the Net for your employees or simply go online for a chat or a surf, security and fraud will be of concern to you. How real that concern is remains to be seen, but the press has made all of us aware of the 'security threat' that is the Internet and e-business.

So what are those concerns and how can they be avoided? The first part of this question I can answer, the second part I can guide you through from a legal point of view and try to give you some high-level technical advice too. If you need technical advice on protecting your business from the risks of the Internet then I would recommend a technical audit and the introduction of security software/protection which these days includes more than virus scanning. This can be undertaken by a number of companies and in Appendix 5 I have included details of a couple of security providers which may help you as a starting point. I would also recommend a review of your internal procedures and dealings and this could also be provided by a security company.

In order to put the law on this area into context I have split the chapter into sections based on the areas of business or your relationships that it is going to affect. These are:

- your business and third parties;

- employees;

- your customers;

- terrorism and cybercrimes.

7.2   Your business and third parties

All businesses that access the Internet run some basic risks. These can be seen to exist in businesses that use IT as part of their means of operation as well as those that actually run an e-business. The risk here can be measured as being both internal and external. The cost to business can be huge and a number of surveys carried out over the last couple of years has shown the cost to be hundreds of millions of pounds.

7.2.1   Viruses

There is the risk that third-party outsiders will do something to affect the business's IT infrastructure either intentionally or unintentionally. This could occur in a number of ways. The introduction of a virus into the IT system can have a number of adverse effects, possibly deleting information stored on that system and bringing down the system in the case of a 'worm' virus eating its way through the data, or through a Trojan Horse which, as the name suggests, appears to be innocent on entry but which carries a hidden enemy within.

Most business people will not necessarily understand the way that a virus works and generally do not need to. They do, however, know that the effect of a virus to their business will be adverse. Viruses such as Melissa and the Love Bug, which have such a huge impact on business and business's capacity to function that they are reported on the 10 o'clock news, have made viruses – and software protecting organisations against them – big business.

Historically many businesses introduced policies requiring that employees do not use software that has not been virus checked on their employer's equipment. These days the majority of viruses are introduced through the Internet, via e-mail, accessing a website or within a document. Such document-borne viruses are often referred to as 'macro viruses'. Although not always introduced by attachments to e-mails, this is often the case and has led to Employee Internet Policies requiring that attachments which are not of a business nature are not opened or in some cases that the Internet and e-mail may not be available for personal use. A full explanation of the contents of these policies and making them enforceable can be found in Chapter 3. Remember that any policy should not only apply to employees but also to any third parties such as consultants who also have access to your system.

Fighting such an enemy from within is possible through internal policies and virus checking software. The use of devices such as firewalls that check all incoming e-mail as it goes through the server will also assist in the fight against viruses. From a legal point of view there is little that can be done unless the perpetrator of a virus can be found and I am sure that we have all seen press reports where those who have intentionally created viruses have been subject to criminal liability and brought to justice. The search for the perpetrators of such crimes is often international and involves a number of intelligence agencies and law enforcement bodies.

In the case of individuals sending viruses to your business, the chances are that they will not on the whole be the creator of the virus and in many cases will have innocently passed the virus on to you or may even be the victim of the virus themselves. The recent 'Bug Bear' virus is a good example of a virus that, once it enters a PC, will replicate itself and then send copies to everyone in the PC's address book. When it arrives at the recipients' PCs it will repeat this action until it has spread to many many PCs. In these circumstances only those with adequate technical protection will escape the problems a virus brings.

Another business nuisance which is directly related but which may be even harder to stop is the hoax virus. In this instance rather than send a virus the perpetrator will send a mail warning of a fictitious virus and perhaps giving specific instructions as to actions to be taken to avoid the hoax virus, some of which, if carried out, result in damaging the PC's operating system. As the recipients will not be aware of the false nature of this apparently friendly warning they are likely to waste time calling friends and forwarding the mail itself as well as undertaking the required actions to protect the business.

These are all costly to business and a waste of business time. To an extent they can be protected against by a combination of a technical means – virus protection tools – and legal means – codes of conduct – but neither is one hundred per cent effective.

7.2.2   DNS attacks – denial of service

Domain Name Service (DNS) is a system of mapping meaningful names to computers. When someone types in www.mybusiness. com a DNS server will translate that to an address that is used by the PC to connect to the site.

Denial of service (DOS) and distributed denial of service (DDOS)

By exploiting weaknesses in the DNS application a DNS service can be stopped. This results in a site's customers not getting to the site and can stop your business.

Similarly attempts to overload a DNS might result in it no longer responding to queries.

Cache poisoning

Here the object of the exercise is to subvert the DNS such that it no longer points to the correct site but to another, which may or may not look like the correct site.

In recent weeks ICANN itself has been a victim of such attacks and a number of its DNS servers actually collapsed under the pressure. However, with a farm of ten servers, the servers which were able to withstand the attack were able to continue providing ICANN's services.

This type of attack is a malicious attempt to affect a business. Although no specific crimes currently exist, the EU has for some time been looking at a possible Cyber Crime Directive which would create a number of new offences relating directly to the use of the Internet. Although and rightly child pornography and the like would be covered by this Directive, most of the offences that would actually have the most impact would be those protecting business from such attacks.

Hacking is a crime and is covered by the Computer Misuse Act 1990, but the way that Act defines hacking requires accessing a computer (which is not defined) which may not apply to the form of attack on the Internet. The potential new offences which will cover this are still at relatively early stages and further information may be obtained from the Home Office.

7.2.3 Encryption and digital signatures

As well as situations where a business's systems as a whole may be attacked its daily dealings may be subject to security risks. As we know business which was once conducted face to face or through the postal service, where documents can be signed for, is often conducted over the Internet with the parties never meeting. This creates the question of who is one dealing with? 'Nobody knows I'm a dog' has probably become the first Internet cliché. So who are you doing business with? Do you really know? This raises a question of authentication.

The next question is, if you do know who you are dealing with, how do you know that what you receive from them online has really come from them (a further question of authentication), and also that what has been sent to you is in the form that it was sent, that it hasn't been tampered with and that it has not been read by anyone else on the way? These are questions of confidentiality and security of communication.

The EU has created legislation through the Digital Signatures Directive, implemented in the UK by the Electronic Communications Act 2000 which came into force in July 2000. In brief the Act introduced a law which allowed the legal recognition of electronic signatures in the same way as hard copy signatures, created a mechanism for the removal of obstacles in existing or other legislation which would block or inhibit the use of such signatures, and also created a scheme for the approval of businesses which provide cryptography services.

The aim of this is to provide verification that the sender of an electronic communication is who they say they are, confirmation that the communication has come from that source, reassurance that it has not been interfered with or altered in transfer and comfort that it has remained confidential. Another side to this is that the sender will not be able to deny that they are in fact the sender and repudiate what has been sent.

Certification Authorities (CAs) are defined in the Act which also makes provision for the approval of CAs and a register of approved CAs. CAs issue digital signatures, create public and private keys and certify that each individual is granted a unique certificate. They also verify through more traditional means that each individual to whom a certificate is granted is in fact who they say they are. CAs also renew and may revoke a certificate. They are a form of trusted third party.

The Act does not prohibit those who are not approved from providing services but does set out standards for approved CAs and requires that the register of approved CAs be made available to the public. However, the government has taken the view that if self-regulation can be seen to work it will not actually enforce this part of the Act.

At the present time the Alliance for Electronic Business administers 'tScheme' which is an industry approval scheme and is not statutory. It sets out standards to which its members should adhere. The government has allowed a five-year trial period following which it will review whether there is a need to enforce the Act and set up a register.

A Digital Certificate is issued by a CA to confirm the identity of the certificate holder.

Encryption is a way of encoding information and turning (or locking) normal readable text into something which is unreadable (a coded series of numbers and/or letters) which can only be unlocked by the holder of the relevant key (decoding device) which will then transfer it back into normal readable form. Encryption may take a number of forms. Symmetric encryption allows both parties to know the secret key.

Keys which are used for this take the form of public and private keys. A public key is one which is available to a number of individuals whereas a private key is available only to one. They may be used in differing ways.

Where encryption is used to create a digital signature this will be done by the holder of a private key signing a document. Only the holder of that key will have access to it and will be the only 'individual' who can do this. However, it is likely that the signatory will want to send the signature to a number of others and so when the private key is used to lock the signature there will be the possibility of it being unlocked and recognised by multiple recipients all of whom hold the public key. In this example the private key is the lock and the public key the unlock.

In other examples where a number of 'individuals' may want to keep communications to a single recipient secret or confidential the public key may be provided to all of those individuals. This will allow each of them to send the information in a public key encrypted form to a single holder of a private key but as only the private key can unlock the information and only one 'individual' holds and has access to this the information can be kept confidential to the specific recipient.

It can be seen how important encryption is to business from the point of view of commercial security as a result of digital signatures, and the verification and certainty created in terms of proof from a legal point of view. This should obviously encourage the use of encryption in communication where there is a need for security or confidentiality or where it is vital to have an absolute guarantee as to who the sender is.

Secure systems

Much of the corruption or crime which exists in B2B relationships is made simpler or possible by the use of the new technologies themselves which create e-business. Data which is not securely stored may be vulnerable to hacking thus allowing access by unscrupulous employees and third parties. The speed at which data is transferred also permits corruption. For example, in e-procurement it would be possible for a corrupt employee to provide one tendering party with information from the other tendering parties so quickly that they might modify their tender and yet still submit it prior to the deadline. Some of these potential risks may easily be eradicated by use of existing technology to ensure that data is held securely.

VPN

I have a mental block on this and always raise a smile in meetings by referring to VPL. However, this abbreviation has nothing to do with a seamless appearance under a pair of trousers but in fact refers to Virtual Private Networks. These are secure systems put in place between organisations to ensure that data which is passed between then is adequately secure.

There are two variants of VPN:

- gateway (hardware) based – firewall to firewall, firewall to VPN device and combinations thereof;

- client-based VPN – gateway to software running on a PC.

The former is typically used to connect two businesses directly via a uniquely encrypted network tunnel running via the Internet. The latter works similarly but tends to be used for mobile and home workers.

It is common for payment authorisations and transactions to be conducted through such networks, where the VPN is used to transfer a customer's details from the Internet site to the credit card authorisation provider.

Where your business considers passing payment details or similarly sensitive/confidential information to a third party it would be wise to consider whether there is a genuine business security need to justify the creation of a VPN. If there is then it will be necessary to look at who will build and maintain it and, if this is to be carried out by a third party, to consider whether the VPN actually meets your standards and what is to happen if they fail to keep data in the VPN secure.

EDI (electronic data interchange) is a closed environment set up between various businesses which, if secure, cannot be accessed by the rest of the world. Many businesses use such systems for ordering and in some cases payment. Although EDI has been around for some time and is not exclusive to e-business it is still worth highlighting the need for security within it, which is the same as for any other network or business tool which carries extremely sensitive data.

Duty of confidentiality

Although there are many and interesting technical areas to be considered we shouldn't forget the existing law. There is to an extent an existing common law right of confidentiality, something which can be lost if the information is provided to a third party on a basis which is not confidential. So, although you may consider having an e-mail disclaimer largely to protect you from your staff and their actions, it may also be wise to ensure that this includes a confidentiality notice and makes clear to the world that while there will be content which is not confidential included in your business's e-mails, it is also possible that these will include confidential information and should be treated appropriately. Such a confidentiality notice may also help to protect your business from information going astray or falling into the hands of third parties. In the same way most businesses will also use a fax cover sheet which alerts both the intended and any incorrect recipient to the confidential nature of the information and any associated duties.

Despite the common law provisions in this area I would also recommend that at the outset of any relationship with a third-party business or individual to whom any confidential information may be provided that a confidentiality or non-disclosure agreement (NDA) is signed. It may then be wise to ensure that all e-mails also include a notice to the effect that they may contain confidential information.

7.3 Employees

As has been referred to above and in Chapter 3, it is essential that employees' use of the Internet and e-mail is subject to a policy, and that this policy is made clear to all employees and properly enforced. An aspect of the ability to enforce the policy is the requirement for proof of contravention. For many businesses this will involve the ability to monitor employee communications.

7.3.1 Monitoring

The Regulation of Investigatory Powers Act 2000 (RIPA) must be complied with if there is to be any monitoring of e-mails and Internet usage. This allows for the internal communications systems of a business to be monitored by its owner in certain circumstances. This must be read in conjunction with the Telecommunications (Lawful Business Practices) (Interception of Communications) Regulations 2000 and allow an employer to intercept e-mails or calls of an employee, customer or supplier without first obtaining their consent where this is for one of the stated purposes, which include (among other things):

- compliance with regulatory or self-regulatory practices; and

- the prevention or detection of a crime.

In these instances it is possible to monitor and record the communications. In other circumstances, while it may be possible to monitor, it is not permitted to record the communications. Again the circumstances are clearly set out in the Regulations.

If this interception is to include personal data then it is necessary that the interception also complies with the Data Protection Act 1998 and the Human Rights Act 1998. The Data Protection Act is discussed in more depth at other points in this book, and the Information Commissioner has also issued guidance as part of the Code of Practice under this Act (still at the consultation stage) which should be complied with. All of this can be found in Chapters 3 and 8. In short it creates principles as to the collection and treatment/processing of personal data and protects the confidentiality of communications by means of public telecommunications systems.

The Human Rights Act 1998 also creates a guarantee of privacy by which everyone has the right (as against private bodies) to respect for their private and family life, home and correspondence. It is not clear if the Act can be enforced against a private sector employer, although it may be viewed as good practice to comply.

If you could believe everything that you read it would appear that the UK's Information Commissioner has considered challenging the legality of RIPA. The draft Code states that the intrusion of privacy necessitated must be proportionate to the benefits and that there should be consent to monitoring unless it is necessary to a vital interest. If it is possible to use a method which would have a less adverse impact then this should be used and monitoring should be proportionate and targeted.

However, it may be that there is a need for covert monitoring under RIPA. If this is the case due to the sensitivity of this area I would suggest you obtain specific legal advice before embarking on such a course of action. If a specific criminal activity has already been identified and there is a need for covert monitoring (i.e. without consent) to establish evidence, then: (1) there should be an assessment of what monitoring will be needed; (2) the employee cannot be told; and (3) there should be an assessment of the length of time the monitoring should last. In the light of this, if an employee is to be restricted in their use of the e-mail system in certain ways then this should be made clear to the employee and also to any third party to whom they communicate.

The Information Commissioner has also indicated that where there is a potential intrusion into personal information this should be limited to traffic data and not content, that spot checks should be undertaken rather than continuous monitoring and that monitoring should be targeted.

From the potential contradictions in the above it is clear that this is a complicated area of law. It is further complicated by the fact that a court may also grant an order against a third party who is unwittingly involved in a fraud, such as an ISP whose systems pass on a mail, and that this may be accompanied by a 'gagging order' prohibiting the third party to whom the order applies from notifying the fraudster. Breach of these orders could amount to contempt of court.

7.3.2   Confidentiality

Third-party requirements are discussed above and the same confidentiality requirements are necessary in employee relationships. It is always wise to highlight these duties to employees and to make sure that anything which is confidential is clearly marked as such.

Further, as well as being provided with an e-mail use policy, employees should be made aware of the risks which are created by the Internet and e-mail. All e-mails which an employee sends should be subject to a confidentiality provision and internal policies as to e-mail retention should be put in place and adhered to by employees.

7.4 Customers

7.4.1 Data

Customer data should be kept secure online. This is discussed at Chapter 8.

7.4.2 Secure payment systems

Although I am sure that the incidence of exposure to security breaches involving payment is no more frequent than with the divulgence of personal data, the biggest concern most customers have is not simply that their personal data will be exposed to the world on the Internet (although that in itself is unacceptable) but, even worse, that it is possible for a third party to access payment details and in turn to use the customer's payment tokens.

From a practical point of view, giving one's card details to a website is little different from reading them out over the telephone to a telesales representative, or perhaps even more surprisingly is little different to handing a card to a waiter to pay for a meal. In my personal acquaintance I know more individuals who have been the victim of credit card fraud where their card details have been misappropriated by a waiter than who have suffered credit card or other payment fraud on the Internet.

Despite this I know few people who panic at the thought of giving their credit card to a waiter but a number who are at best distinctly uncomfortable when inputting their payment details on-line. I have been surprised to find that in some countries it is not uncommon for customers to want to be invoiced on delivery or to pay by cheque. These may give a customer confidence that they are not putting the secrecy and security of their payment methods at risk, but they are extremely impractical for an e-business. The use of cheques involves ring-fencing stock until such time as the cheque is received and the payment has cleared.

In making these points I have largely assumed the consumer's point of view and expressed their concerns. However, and apparently as a surprise to most consumers, Internet fraud and insecure payment systems are a huge concern to the retailers themselves.

So how are these crimes committed?

Skimming

One of the most prevalent ways in which credit card fraud is undertaken in both the real and cyber worlds is known as 'skimming'.

The perpetrator of this crime carries a small technical device which incorporates a card reader and quickly, when in possession of a credit card, swipes the card, allowing the machine to read the magnetic strip and download the data. This takes seconds to do. The data which is included in the magnetic strip may then be used to make counterfeit cards which can be wrongfully used to pay for goods and services.

Identity theft

This is where a third party obtains an individual's personal details and uses these to apply for credit or goods. In many cases this will involve online purchases. A number of people have asked me how this is possible as online goods are generally delivered to a card holder's address. However, some sites allow gift sales and in many other instances the perpetrator of the crime knows the card holder and may be able to intercept the delivery.

Auctions

There have been a number of reported instances of so-called 'hackers' breaking into the accounts of individuals who sell goods through Internet auctions. If they are able to obtain the password then it has been possible for them to offer non-existent or unavailable goods for sale through the account. The fraudster then receives payment for these from the successful bidder but does not supply the goods and the fraudster cannot generally be traced.

These three examples are not exhaustive and a consumer may have legitimate concerns regarding the use to be made of their card details once these have been passed to a third party; equally, legitimate businesses are concerned to ensure that they are paid for the goods and services they provide as they are entitled to be. Not only do they need to reassure consumers that the card details provided online are secure but also they need to know that the details provided to them are correct and are provided by an individual who has a genuine right to use the payment token being offered.

7.4.3   Refunds for fraud/chargebacks

Most consumers will now be aware that as a result of the Consumer Protection (Distance Selling) Regulations 2000, card issuers are required to refund any money which has been charged for a fraudulent transaction. Historically consumers were liable for the first £50 of any fraudulent transactions on their card, but this is no longer the case.

The card issuer will then withdraw the disputed amount from its payment to the retailer. 'Chargebacks', as these repayments are called, may generally be disputed by the retailer within ten days. The retailer can dispute these by providing proof of the purchase. Chargebacks for fraudulent transactions will be borne inevitably by the retailer and may also be coupled with a charge from the card issuer for administration. As well as this, if the retailer has supplied the fraudster with the goods then it is possible that these will also be lost to the retailer. Where does this leave the innocent retailer or supplier? Unless he is lucky enough to have this risk insured the simple answer is out of pocket and looking at systems to better protect its business. Perhaps if more consumers were aware of this process they would have more confidence in shopping online as it is clearly in the vendor's interest to provide a secure environment in which to transact.

In the case of credit cards it is also worth noting that credit card issuers are jointly and severally liable with a retailer for any purchase of £100 or more. If the goods are not delivered then the credit card company would be liable to the purchaser in the same way as the retailer and should provide a refund. This adds a protection for the consumer in the event of a fraudulent 'retailer'. However, it is possible that the card company will place time restrictions on notifications for this within its card scheme rules. It may actually be safer for a purchaser to buy using a credit card rather than a debit card as the same is not true of debit card issuers.

7.4.4   *Technical solutions/the future*

Over the last few years the worlds of business and banking have thought long and hard and technical staff have spent countless hours racking their brains for the most appropriate user-friendly methods of ensuring secure payment. All sorts of processes and technology have been considered, from PIN numbers (such as are used by French credit card holders), to mobile card readers attached to key boards, from encryption to credit card chips, and so on. I have set out a short discussion of some of these below.

Chip

This involves the use of a smart card with a computer chip embedded in the card. A certain amount of money may be pre-paid onto the card and like a debit card the card holder can only spend what is available. Chip protected cards are more difficult to skim

Authentication/verification

This looks at ways of identifying individuals as the rightful card holder. It may be undertaken through digital signatures (see above).

Another method of authentication is the use of an AVS number. AVS numbers have, since 1996, been found on Visa and MasterCard credit cards. The AVS number allows the retailer to check the customer's billing address against the one held by the card issuer. However, this does not tend to be used in the online world, but in businesses where the card details are manually keyed. Failure to use this system generally subjects retailers to an additional commission charge.

CVZ numbers are perhaps the most natural progression from the AVS number and can be found on the back of a credit card by the signature strip. They are not part of the information on the magnetic strip nor embossed onto the card but are printed and so are not susceptible to skimming or to identity theft based on credit card receipts. A retailer will ask the customer to provide certain figures from this number. If a customer is able to provide a CVZ number then it is clear that you are in possession of the card at the time. I recently shopped on BA's website and was required to enter this security number as part of the payment process.

PIN – Personal Identification Numbers – are another alternative. Here the card holder has to type their personal number into the PC to verify who they are. Card holders are required to keep their PIN secret. One of the attractions of this is that generally the card does not leave its owner's sight. This system is widely used already in other countries such as France. Use of this online would probably involve providing Internet users with card holders to attach to their PCs and this is a real possibility.

Perhaps the most high tech of the proposed solutions is AADS – Account Authority Digital Signatures – which uses a combination of smart cards and PIN codes to generate a digital signature for each transaction. This then removes the need for third-party authorisation and also reduces the risk of interception of the card or payment details.

As this book goes to press the relevant bodies representing retailers, card issuers and security providers are working to find the most appropriate solution for the UK's e-businesses and are providing an increasingly wide-ranging offering. However, for any solution to become the preferred option and to be effectively implemented by e-business its cost will also have to be considered. It would be wise for all involved in e-business to follow progress and to support the most practical of these offerings.

7.4.5   *Where are we now?*

SSL

As you can no doubt imagine, at the present time a certain amount of Internet crime is perpetrated by fraudsters who have skimmed or appropriated another's identity, without the legitimate card holder having ever transacted online. The possible solutions look to stop that. Assuming that the card is being used by its rightful owner, the Internet does use existing technology to protect card holders from having their details appropriated while they are undertaking a purchase. When a customer enters a secure part of a site using SSL – Secure Sockets Layer – they will generally see an unbroken key on the bottom left-hand corner of their browser and will be made aware that they are entering a secure environment. This environment is a secure 'pipeline' for data which runs between the web browser and the web server. You may well have seen this on sites like Amazon. The URL will change to show 'https' as opposed to 'http' when the user is in this environment. To create this the site will have to have access to a server supporting the SSL application and be the holder of a digital signature.

Obviously both parties must have the appropriate technology to understand SSL. However, SSL is built into both Microsoft Internet Explorer and Netscape browsers and so most consumers' Internet use is pre-equipped with the relevant technology.

Although this technology may not provide protection from all forms of Internet crime it would certainly be advisable for all sites to use it or an equivalent.

VPN

As I have pointed out above a virtual private network may also be used to ensure that all sensitive transactional data is passed to the card authorisation provider through a secure system.

Internal housekeeping/storage of details after the transaction

From a retailer's point of view it is worth bearing in mind that it is not just the front-end system which needs to be secure. If customer card details are held securely during the sale but are then left in a human readable form internally, i.e. not encrypted, it will be possible for both corrupt employees and 'hackers' to obtain this information. On the other hand, if the data is encrypted then who is to have access to any relevant key?

It is therefore important to consider both who should have access to any such sensitive data and what form it should be stored in/what protection will be given to it. This should form part of an internal policy which should also allow for changes in personnel, passwords, etc.

The British Standard for Information Security Management BS7799 allows a business to apply for a c:cure certificate. Businesses compare their own security systems to best practices laid down by this standard.

7.5 Terrorism and cybercrimes

Terrorism is not the subject of this book but it is worth simply adding a reminder that the means to commit terrorism may be provided online and crimes which would or could otherwise have been committed may be made easier by the use of online facilities. This, in the light of 9/11, has influenced the need for anti-terrorism and in particular e-terror legislation. The Anti-terrorism, Crime and Security Act 2001 created a Code of Conduct which suggests that communications data should be kept by communications networks.

This would be applicable to ISPs and mobile phone operators, and would require the storage of names, addresses, identifiers such as telephone numbers and IP addresses from which communications were sent and to which they were sent, and details of the sites visited. It does not require any content to be retained. ISPs have unsurprisingly reacted against this and have complained of the potential cost to business. It has also been reported that they have also suggested that this may be in breach of the Human Rights Act and again the Data Protection Act's provisions may need to be complied with.

A number of crimes may be made easier by the technology and speed of e-business. A number of crimes have developed in a new format. One of these which the DTI has recently warned against is the use of e-mail and text (in some cases in breach of the requirements of the E-Commerce Regulations) to mislead individuals into believing that they have won a prize and should call a particular (premium rate number) to receive it. However, the cost of the call is more than the value of the prize, if in fact any prize exists. A number of other crimes such as obtaining goods by deception and pyramid selling schemes which are simply new technological means of committing old crimes also exist and will be covered as in the real world by existing laws. There may, however, be new laws to contend with and it is important to follow the progress of the Cybercrime Directive and the legislation it or its discussion may spawn. While this may provide protection for businesses it will also provide a compliance requirement from a technical and legal point of view which may have a cost impact on your business.

7.6   Conclusion

Like the man at the end of the *CrimeWatch* TV series I hope that you will sleep well and not be too concerned by the potential security risks highlighted here. This is and will for the forseeable future at least continue to be an area of intense development – particularly from a technical and, to an extent, legal point of view. I ask myself whether we will ever have an e-business environment which is completely safe and guess that the answer is no, but remind myself that in this as with the other areas of e-business it is unwise to expect more than one could reasonably hope to have in the 'real world' which is not and probably never will be completely secure.

What, I hope, is clear from this chapter is that the risks associated with Internet fraud, although apparently wide, are less for the consumer than they might think. Importantly, consumers and businesses are offered some commercial and legal protection and those with the ability to increase that protection – whether legally or commercially – are working constantly to do so.

CHECKLIST 7.1 SECURITY

- Undertake a security audit. ☐

- Keep virus and security software up to date. ☐

- Maintain internal housekeeping – devise a policy and process for who should have access to secure information, for how secure information is to be stored and for changes in personnel. ☐

- Policy and information for employees. ☐

- Confidentiality notices and agreements. ☐

- Use of encryption and digital signatures. ☐

- Use of technology to ensure secure transactions. ☐

- E-mail disclaimers. ☐

- Ensure employee codes apply to consultants too. ☐

ADDITIONAL INFORMATION

The Association of Chief Police Officers' Internet Crime Forum can be found at www.internetcrime.org

The Cybercrime Directive – www.oft.gov.uk

CHAPTER 8

Customer data and communications

8.1   Data collection

One of the most important aspects of a customer-facing web business is its database. The financial value attributed to each customer on a database may no longer be the outrageous sums used to value Internet companies in the run up to an IPO (initial public share offering) in the early part of 2000; however, it remains extremely important. The reason for that importance is that such a database offers access to a potential marketplace for an e-business.

Customers who have genuinely consented to be marketed can and may be a good source of ongoing income. The value in a customer is the amount that the customer can potentially bring to the business whether through direct sales or other revenue streams such as advertising. An accurate and legitimate database can therefore create a very valuable asset to an e-business, and so requires care, attention and funding to ensure that it is set up correctly.

In a recent report by the Information Commissioner the majority of e-businesses were found not to comply with data protection laws and a large proportion were found not to have data security and privacy policies. Complying is not hugely difficult but does take some time and requires appropriate systems to be in place. It is also worth noting that there are an increasing number of complaints relating to the misuse of data and also an increasing volume of adverse press coverage relating to this area, not to mention the significant negative PR implications if it is necessary to contact your customer base to rectify data protection law breaches.

Also do not underestimate the disruptive nature of being investigated by the Commissioner's office. This can be an extremely time-consuming and resource-heavy exercise.

8.2   Data Protection Act and notification

The law of data protection in the UK is governed by the Data Protection Act 1998 and various associated regulations. The Act is based on an EC Directive, and so the general principles ought to be similar throughout Europe. However, when a directive is put in place by the EU, each country must then implement that directive to give it force of law in that country. In the UK this is generally done by passing an Act of Parliament or regulations. In many directives part of the law which is to be implemented, or the way in which that law is to be implemented, is discretionary and so each country may not implement the same directive in exactly the same terms, and there may be discrepancies between local laws. This is true of the directive governing data protection and so it is not possible to rely on the rules which apply in the UK being identical in every country.

8.2.1 Notification

Any company which collects information from individuals which is personal data is required under this Act to notify the Information Commissioner (this title has recently been changed and the post was previously known as the Data Protection Commissioner). This is the case if data is collected from UK citizens or stored in the UK. Registration/notification is not particularly difficult and can be completed online at www.dataprotection.gov.uk. Completing the form is straightforward and involves inputting company details and choosing the purposes for which the data will be used and the data to be covered by clicking on the boxes which relate to the appropriate data being collected, purposes for which the data is to be held and the uses made of that data.

The notification is valid for one year and must be renewed annually. The registry sends out reminders about a month in advance. Websites or other e-businesses which hold customer data must register. The current cost is £35 per registration. Each individual company or business is required to register and it is not possible to complete a single registration for a group of companies.

8.2.2 Data controller

An individual within the business must be identified as the data controller and named on the notification form. This controller is the person who will receive any data requests from any individual who believes that their data is stored by the business whether or not they are a customer of that business. It is possible to check on the Information Commissioner's website whether any particular company or business is registered.

There is a brief guide for data controllers on the Information Commissioner's website.

8.2.3 Collection principles

The Act sets out eight collection principles which are that data must be:

- fairly and lawfully processed;

- processed for limited purposes;

- adequate, relevant and not excessive;

- accurate;

- not kept longer than necessary;

- processed in accordance with the data subject's rights;

- secure;

- not transferred to countries without adequate protection.

Traditionally the Act and UK data protection law has applied only to 'living persons'. However, it is worth noting that the Commissioner's recent guidance on e-mails states that e-mail addresses are not only personal information and that storage of them is enough to require a data protection licence but also that the Act applies to e-mail addresses of dead individuals. This may not have a great deal of significance to anyone other than ISPs, but it is certainly worth bearing in mind. The recent Naomi Campbell court case has also established that the Act applies to photos.

8.2.4   Processing data

Data processing occurs where any operation is carried out on an individual's data. Where processing is undertaken this must be done fairly and lawfully. A business may only process an individual's data where one of the following conditions has been met:

- the individual has given his or her consent to the processing; or

- the processing is necessary for the performance of a contract with the individual; or

- the processing is required under a legal obligation; or

- the processing is necessary to protect the vital interests of the individual; or

- the processing is necessary to carry out public functions; or

- the processing is necessary in order to pursue the legitimate interests of the data controller or third parties (unless it could prejudice the interests of the individual).

8.2.5 Sensitive data

The Act also creates a category of information called 'sensitive data'. This includes data on the following:

- racial or ethnic origin;

- political opinions;

- religious or other beliefs;

- trade union membership;

- health;

- sex life;

- criminal proceedings or convictions.

Where sensitive data is held, the rules applied are stricter and greater restrictions exist. As a result of this it is simpler for a business not to collect or hold sensitive data unless it is absolutely necessary for its function. If it does hold sensitive data then it would be wise to consider the advice on security in Chapter 7.

Sensitive data may only be processed if certain conditions are met. The business must:

- have the explicit consent of the individual; or

- be required by law to process the data for employment purposes; or

- need to process the information in order to protect the vital interests of the data subject or another; or

- deal with the administration of justice or legal proceedings.

8.2.6   Data subjects' rights

Data access

The Act gives individuals a right to know what data is being held about them and by whom. I am sure that you have heard of people applying to credit reference agencies to see what information is held about them. The individual is entitled to know what data is held in electronic format and also, since the Directive, in paper format where this is part of a relevant filing system. A relevant filing system is a set of information in which the records are structured, either by reference to individuals or by reference to criteria relating to individuals, in a way that makes 'specific information relating to a particular individual readily accessible'. There is an exemption scheme in place until 2007 for relevant filing systems which existed prior to October 1998. It is worth bearing in mind that the rules may not apply only to electronic data.

A business can charge up to £10 to provide that data. The individual is also entitled to have this data corrected, altered or removed. This means that it is necessary for a business which holds data of this nature to put in place a process for receipt of these requests for information and also for dealing with changes etc.

I have requested my data from at least one company and found it has included data for other people living at the same address in its response. This is in breach of the Act. I had no right to see their data and the information held on them was actually confidential.

It is important to put in place a system for responding to data requests and to then ensure that any changes or requests for removal are acted upon.

Rectification

Individuals may apply to a court to order a data controller to rectify, block, erase or destroy personal details if they are inaccurate or contain expressions of opinion which are based on inaccurate data. It is therefore wise to have a process in place to allow an individual to request rectification and to ensure that this happens.

Preventing processing

An individual can request that a business does not begin processing information relating to them where it is causing, or is likely to cause, substantial unwarranted damage or substantial distress to themselves or anyone else. This request need not always be complied with.

Where data processing has already occurred, an individual can ask a data controller to stop or not to begin processing data relating to him or her for direct marketing purposes. Where such a request is made it must be complied with. Again, it is absolutely necessary to make sure that the database which is built for direct marketing can flag where an individual has made such a request and not send any further marketing information.

Compensation

Importantly, individuals may now claim compensation from a data controller for damage or damage and distress caused by breach of the Data Protection Act.

Some uses of the data for purposes such as credit scoring (where undertaken by automatic means) and customer black or grey lists are very sensitive, and if your business is to consider this you should have particular legal advice first.

Also you may have noticed that where the electoral register has historically been used by businesses for data verification this may well not be allowed in the future.

8.2.7   Offences

In addition to the risk of being sued, there is the risk of criminal prosecution for committing a number of offences under the Act:

1. Notification offences can be committed when processing is being undertaken by a data controller who has not notified the Commissioner either of the processing being undertaken or of any changes to it. Failure to notify is a strict liability offence.

2. It is an offence to obtain, disclose, sell or advertise for sale or bring about the disclosure of personal data without the consent of the data subject. Subject to certain exceptions it is also an offence to access personal data or to disclose it without proper authorisation.

3. Subject to certain exceptions it is also an offence for a person to ask another person to make a subject access request in order to obtain personal data about that person for a specific purpose.

8.3 Collection notices

8.3.1 What is personal data?

Personal data is any data from which the customer can be identified. This can be name, address, car registration, etc. The Information Commissioner has recently issued guidelines on data protection and the Internet.

In these guidelines it is made clear that an e-mail address is personal data.

8.3.2 What action must be taken?

Every time data is collected it is possible to use the data for the purpose for which it has clearly been collected without obtaining any additional consent. In the case of an Internet sale it is possible to use the data for the purpose of the sale transaction – processing the payment and sending out the goods – without any particular or additional consent.

However, if you wish to use the data for any other purpose then you should obtain the customer's consent. This must be done each time a customer provides you with personal data that you wish to use for any purpose other than the purpose for which you collected it. For example, when a customer provides an e-mail address to allow them to participate in a prize draw, if you wish to do anything other than put the name into the draw and inform them that they have won you must first obtain their consent.

It is necessary to inform the customer or individual of the purposes for which you wish to collect their data and ask for their consent to use it. In the 'real world' this is normally done by way of a collection notice with a tick box. I am sure that you have seen these many times at the end of credit applications, competitions and surveys.

8.4   Click boxes

On the Internet or any other e-business channel the same must occur and this is normally done by way of a click box, the virtual equivalent of a tick box. Each time data is collected, if you wish to use it in a way which is not necessary for the purpose for which you have collected it, e.g. for ongoing marketing, then you should use a data collection notice and a click box. The wording of these collection notices is important. In the most basic terms a notice should at least say 'please click in the box if you do not wish us to use the data collected for the purposes listed'.

TOP TIP

An important practical consideration is to ensure that the legal wording is drafted in an attractive commercial way (or, as most marketers would view it, in the least unattractive way), for example not 'we will sell your data to others …' but rather 'we would like to share your details with carefully selected partners who may well be of interest to you …' This is, after all, a marketing tool and should as far as possible encourage people to want to be communicated with or, conversely, to reduce the fear/reluctance factor.

8.5   Opt-in and opt-out

So, you have added a collection notice to your registration page and any other page where you collect data, or perhaps you have added several notices to allow the data to be given to various third parties or to obtain the customer's consent to it being used for a number of purposes.

> *Example opt-in:*
> If you agree to your data being collected for the purpose of …
> click here [ ]
> *Example opt-out:*
> If you do not agree to your data being collected for the purpose of … click here [ ]

It is believed by many that the use of opt-out is adequate as this gives the customer the opportunity to express their opinion and stop their data being used while at the same time gives business a better chance of customers allowing their data to be used. Certainly this appears to be adequate under current UK legislation.

However, with spam as the driving force behind it, the EU has introduced the Communications Data Protection Directive (CDPD) which will be implemented in the UK in 2003. As it stands this will require an opt-in consent to e-mail marketing but there will be an exception to this where there is an existing legitimate relationship. This form of opt-in is known as a soft opt-in. The UK, at the behest of industry, argued against the introduction of opt-in requirements while other Member States were adamant that opt-out was not adequate. The soft opt-in was developed as a compromise.

What this actually means is not yet clear and probably won't be until the legislation implementing the Directive goes to consultation in 2003. However, it seems that where there is an existing customer relationship, e.g. where Dixons has sold a PC to a consumer, it is acceptable to contact that consumer without obtaining opt-in consent. Where there is no such pre-existing relationship, then communication can only be as a result of opt-in consent from the consumer. This must make anyone looking at building a new database or site consider whether it would be wise to choose to go straight to opt-in consent and so avoid the risk that they build a database or site only to find that this needs to be re-structured in 2003.

8.6   Solicited and unsolicited commercial communications

The E-Commerce (EC Directive) Regulations 2002 require that commercial communications are identified as such. This means that it is necessary to make it clear that a marketing communication *is* a marketing communication. This means that it must be clear on whose behalf the mail is sent, clearly identify the nature of any promotional offer, competition or game, and any relevant conditions relating to this must be accessible in a clear and unambiguous form. This information need not be in the same medium as the mail, i.e. it could be available in paper copy on request. There is an exclusion where a communication contains only information which allows direct access to the activity of that person such as an e-mail or geographic address.

The Regulations state that unsolicited e-mail (see section 8.8 on spam below) must be clearly identifiable as such when received. One of the principal aims of this is to ensure that there is no need for the recipient who is not interested in this communication to pay for the online time associated with opening it. However, the Regulations do not make clear how this is to be done and whether it is enough to make clear that the mail is from a business or whether it should actually state that the mail is unsolicited.

In its guidance notes the UK government makes clear that while unsolicited e-mail must make this fact clear on receipt, the same is not true for a solicited e-mail. Assuming a site collects its user data properly and uses this only where it should, then there should not be unsolicited e-mail and this should not be an issue.

8.7 Cookies

Cookies are a technology tool which allows a website to track a user on that site. This may show the site owner where the user has come from, e.g. if they have arrived at the site through a link, what pages the user views, etc. They are often viewed as a very valuable tool for sites but an intrusion of user privacy.

The information from cookies can be used in two main ways. It can either be used to provide customer-specific tracking and data analysis or it can be used to provide generic data about the site and how it is used. This second method of use involves data which is neutral and generic, and from which the customer cannot be identified.

The Communications Data Protection Directive 2002 sets out provisions which will be made law in the UK in 2003 in relation to cookies and similar devices. The possibility of active consent to cookies has been rejected and instead sites are required to provide information to consumers and allow them an effective opt-out from their use. This is in line with current good practice on sites. The requirement is one of transparency and the site should make clear to the user what devices are being used and how they are being used, what data is collected and what it will be used for.

All sites will be required to notify users of their use of these devices and to explain to a customer how they can disconnect these devices and use the site (or that if they wish to use the site that they must accept the use of the device). In this latter case they have the opportunity not to use the site and this is the effective opt-out. The Directive does not go as far as to set out the way in which an opt-out should be used and so there is room for either of these unless the UK legislation is more specific than the Directive.

Some sites require a customer to have cookies activated or the customer will not be able to access the site. I would suggest that from a commercial point of view this may turn customers away from the site, and in making such a decision there must be a balance with the commercial value of the information obtained from the cookies.

In terms of cookie use information, it will be necessary to ensure that such use is drawn to the attention of the customer at a stage in their use of the site which is early enough to stop a user who has an objection to being unwittingly 'cookied'.

8.8   Spam

Spam is unsolicited bulk e-mail. Just how much of this exists on the Internet is a matter for debate, but there are certainly many unscrupulous or careless companies who have not correctly collected customer data for the purpose that they use it for and who are viewed as spammers. In some cases this means that they have not asked the customer if they can send them communication by e-mail, or have asked but ignored customers that have said no. In other cases the data has not been collected for the purpose it is being used for. An example of this would be marketing information about car accessories being sent to someone who has just purchased a car without asking for their consent to do this, and doing the marketing by using their e-mail address which was provided to assist in the car purchase. If the customer has not specifically agreed to this type of marketing then the e-mail will be unsolicited. A third type of spam is where the data is passed to third parties with whom the individual has had no previous contact and which is then used to contact them. If they have not agreed to use of their data by third parties in general or that third party in particular then this will be unsolicited also.

There has been little case law to give us guidance in the UK, but there is a black list/register which ISPs who allow spam are added to.

8.9   Databases

On a practical note, when the wording is put onto a site (whether it is opt in or opt out) functionality which allows the data to be collected and stored on a database will need to be built. If the data is to be used for any purpose other than the one for which it was collected, e.g. marketing, then it is necessary to make sure that the database has the necessary technology to respect the wishes of any customer who has said no to their data being used. This can be done by a flag on the database for each customer who has declined to have their data used.

It is important to remember to check on each occasion that the data is used for one of the purposes set out in the collection notice only.

8.10   Preference service/opt-out registers

The Direct Marketing Association holds a number of registers of individuals who have registered their wish not to receive various types of marketing material. There are different registers for the different types of junk mail which may be received. Each of these registers is known as a 'preference service'. Since April 2001 there has been an e-mail preference service. Although the introduction of this was mooted as part of the Distance Selling Directive this was removed from the final draft. The E-Commerce Directive then resurrected it but the government has decided not to include these provisions in the Regulations. The preference service does not therefore have the force of law. Good practice would, however, dictate that the service is consulted from time to time.

8.11   Viral marketing

Viral marketing is a relatively new method of Internet marketing. It involves a method of customer referral, by which I mean 'introduce a friend' or the like. Like a virus, the information or introductions then spread.

When I first shopped at Amazon.co.uk, I made my purchase and was sent the opportunity to receive future discounts by introducing a friend. I was given a code to forward to my friends and family. If they shopped with Amazon and inserted the code in the appropriate place in the order form they would receive a discount on that order. The code was recognised by Amazon's system and as a result of this it knew that this new customer had been introduced by me. I was then rewarded with a voucher for a discount off my next purchase. I had a very lucrative few weeks introducing anyone I could think of and Amazon I know benefited from some new customers. This is a classic example of viral marketing. By incentivising me with a discount and giving me a code to pass to friends the reputation of Amazon was spread like a virus.

The structure of the system used by Amazon is also good from a data collection point of view. I did not provide them with anyone else's data and yet their name was spread and they obtained new customers. When the new customers purchased from Amazon they collected the customer's data and had an opportunity to use collection notices and click boxes so that the new customers' data was correctly collected.

Some less scrupulous or poorly advised companies have used similar viral marketing schemes in a manner which is less likely to be legal. These companies run 'introduce a friend' schemes in a way which requires the person who introduces the friend to provide third-party data directly to the e-business. That data is not correctly collected as the data's owner does not have the opportunity to consent to its use. This collection problem can be easily avoided by using a structure like Amazon's where the data is only provided by the data subject who can then consent or not.

8.12   Data from third parties

It is ideal only to use data which has been collected by you and so you yourself know what the integrity of the collection has been. You know whether you are entitled to use that data or not. Some businesses receive data from third parties through perfectly legitimate routes, such as a co-branded competition where one party collects the entries and provides the data to its partner in the promotion. The party who did not actually collect the data needs to be sure that any data passed to them has been correctly collected for their use and that the correct collection notices and click boxes have been used.

Although it is not possible to avoid liability where one uses data which one does not have a right to use, it is wise to include in an agreement with the other party certain provisions. These would include a requirement that when the data is collected a collection box is used with (opt-in or opt-out) click boxes and that one of those is specific to obtaining consent for the data being passed to you. You might even provide the wording from your own click box and ask that this be used. A method of determining which customers have declined also needs to be used.

As you are not the person actually dealing with the collection but could be responsible for the use, it would be wise to ask the provider to warrant or promise that the data has been collected in accordance with UK data protection laws and then to ask them to indemnify or reimburse you for any costs, fines, penalties, etc. incurred by you if it turns out that they have breached the warranty (broken the promise) by having failed to comply with these laws. This will help to stop any out of pocket expenses, but cannot take away any liability you would face legally.

Also one must bear in mind that where this data is to be used in the world of e-commerce, the new CDPD will require opt-in consent in such cases as no pre-existing relationship exists between the recipient of the list purchased and those on the list.

8.13   Unsubscribe

You may have received an e-mail which says something along the lines of, 'if you wish not to receive any further communication from us then please send an e-mail to this address … with the heading unsubscribe'.

This allows a customer who has received mail which has not been consented to or where they have provided consent but have now changed their mind to stop receiving mails.

As well as including a method for the customer to unsubscribe in the mail it is necessary again to put an appropriate system in place at the back end. This should ensure that there is someone who receives the mails at the particular address and who is then able to amend the database on which the personal data is stored to show that the individual has removed their consent to being contacted in this way or for this purpose.

It should also be remembered that if you are collecting further personal data in the e-mail an unsubscribe alone will not be enough as, if new data is being collected, a collection notice and click box will be necessary.

8.14   Data cleansing

Even where a customer has consented to your holding their data and using it for particular purposes, this does not allow you to hold the data for ever. The data can only be held for a reasonable time and what a reasonable time is depends on the circumstances involved. It is a question of fact. It is necessary to cleanse your database and to remove data which has passed that timescale.

It is also good practice to cleanse the database to check misspells and other circumstances which cause any individual to appear twice or more on your database. Multiple inclusions potentially cause an individual to receive particular data twice.

At least one company who I am happy to receive 'junk mail' from has me on their database twice and each time I receive mail from them I do not open the second copy but tear it up. Not only are they irritating me, they are risking losing part of their ability to market me if I destroy a communication from them which turns out not to have been identical and which I might have responded to. Many people are less patient with junk mail than I am and would destroy both copies out of irritation!

8.15   Third-party data requests

Where a third party requests data on an individual other than themselves, I would suggest that this data should not simply be handed over. This is the case even if the individual is an official body.

Ideally a policy governing release of individual data to anyone other than the data subject should be put in place within your business. I would suggest that data is only released if the person or body requesting this has a court order or a Data Protection Act notice. Such a notice is a form of notice approved under the Data Protection Act 1998 and must be signed by a senior police officer. A form of this notice has been agreed by various bodies for use by ISPs.

The legislation does allow for certain circumstances in which data can be provided without such a notice or a court order, but there are some risks attached to this and it may be safer and simpler to stick to the above policy.

This may allow you some peace of mind that what you are doing is legal, but it will not relieve the frustration of not knowing who the third parties are.

8.16   Privacy policies

Many websites favour privacy policies which may give individuals more information about what they do with data they have collected. This will set out more information than the collection notice and in effect may add commitments to the customer.

I have attached a sample policy from Freeserve at Appendix 1.

8.17   Cross-border transfers

Personal data must not be transferred to a country outside the European Economic Area (EEA) unless that country has 'adequate' levels of data protection in place. This means that there is no problem in transferring data cross border within the 18 EEA countries (the 15 EU countries plus Iceland, Norway and Liechtenstein). The European Commission has also put together a list of other countries which in its view have an adequate level of protection and to which data can be transferred. Before data is transferred to any country outside of the EEA the data controller should check that it has a 'Community Finding' allowing for this transfer. (The Community Findings can be accessed at http://europa.eu.int/eur-lex/en/oj/2001/1_21520000825en.html.)

As the US does not have an adequate level of protection, the European Commission has worked with the US to provide a means for data transfer. This has resulted in the 'safe harbor' arrangements. A set of data protection principles have been agreed and where data is transferred to a business in the US, if that business commits to comply with these and the associated guidance, then it is viewed that an adequate level of protection will exist for the transfer of data to that entity in the US. If not then there are particular contract terms which can be used and have the equivalent effect as they require that company to honour similar principles. Information on this can be found at http://europa.eu.int/comm/intenral_market/en/media/dataport/news/safeharor.htm.

Alternatively, it is possible to avoid the problems of transferring data to a country which does not have an adequate level of protection by first obtaining the individual data subject's consent to this. Consent is a generally useful 'fix' to most data protection restrictions.

The ideal solution to this will be a commercial question for any business and in reaching a decision the business should look at the commercial implications of each of the above issues.

8.18 Padlock system

The Information Commissioner has introduced a logo in the form of a padlock to give reassurance to site users. The logo appears on sites which claim to comply with the Commissioner's recommendations.

8.19 Data security

This topic has been dealt with in Chapter 7 on security.

TOP TIP

Often you will receive e-mails where there is a list of names and e-mail addresses in the address box. As the Information Commissioner has said that e-mail addresses are personal information and subject to the Data Protection Act, allowing one person, whether they are a contact or a customer, to see a list of other people's e-mail addresses is equivalent to giving their home addresses to a third party. Also for some time it has not really been considered good etiquette to do this.

There is an easy solution which is to (blind copy) or bcc the addresses, and this way each recipient will only see their own e-mail address.

CHECKLIST 8.1 DATA PROTECTION

- Processing of personal data needs consent. ☐

- Apply for a licence from the Information Commissioner. ☐

- Add a collection notice whenever you collect customer data. ☐

- Use opt-in or opt-out, but be consistent – with an eye to the future opt-in may be best. ☐

- Add a click box. ☐

- Make sure that your system notes who has said 'no' or 'yes' consistently. ☐

- Check your database when marketing. ☐

- Check with the preference services opt-out registers before e-mailing targets. ☐

- If using e-mail add an unsubscribe function. ☐

- Put in place a system for data requests and necessary amendments. ☐

ADDITIONAL INFORMATION

www.dataprotection.gov.uk

CHAPTER 9

Contracts

9.1   Background

I must begin with the usual caveat – that it is always advisable to seek legal advice on any contract before agreeing to be bound by it. However, I have set out below a general guidance on contracts and follow this with a specific review of some of the types of contract which are particular to e-commerce and which will be of interest to the readers of this text. In this chapter I cross refer to a number of standard clauses and sample contracts which are set out in Appendix 2. These were kindly provided by Ashley Winton, Partner with the law firm Pillsbury Winthrop, whose contact details can be found at the end of Appendix 5.

Contracts generally include a suite of standard form clauses called 'boiler plate' provisions. These may look the same from contract to contract, but subtle changes to the wording may allow one party or the other a greater benefit than one would normally expect. Boiler plate clauses are often overlooked or not properly considered – one does this at one's peril!

9.2   Boiler plates

Boiler plates normally include the following.

9.2.1   *Waiver*

This ensures that where a party does not enforce a breach or breaches of the contract by the other party (waives its rights) that party does not lose its right to enforce the contract for future similar breaches through its course of dealing.

9.2.2   *Severance*

This deals with the situation where a provision of a contract is unenforceable. In such circumstances that provision is 'severed' from the remainder of the contract and provision is made either to ignore it, interpreting the contract as near as legally possible had it been enforceable, or to replace it.

9.2.3   *Entire agreement and amendment*

This clause will state that the agreement between the parties is contained in its entirety in the document in question and exclude any previous discussions, documents etc. Be aware that due to recent case law it is not possible to exclude any fraudulent misrepresentation as, should that have induced the other party to enter into a contract, they may always rely on this as a get-out. Such a clause may also generally state that the contract may only be amended in writing and by signature of certain individuals.

9.2.4   'Force majeure'

This clause is used to exclude the duty to meet an obligation where a party's inability to meet the obligation is a direct result of something beyond their reasonable control, e.g. act of god, war, etc. The term 'force majeure' must always be defined. This may be a non-exhaustive list of circumstances or an agreed list. Some items such as strikes which traditionally appear in these clauses are a little out of date in the UK today. One must pay close attention as this will directly affect one's ability to terminate for non-performance or seek damages for breach. Tailor the clause appropriately as there is no such thing as a 'standard' force majeure clause.

9.2.5   Notices

This is a critically important clause, often overlooked. Any requirements as to the format they should take, where notices should be sent and for whose attention are included here. Such a clause will also generally state when a notice is deemed to be received and this will create certainty for the running of any notice period.

One should identify, for example, a post/position to which notices should be sent rather than simply a name as people move on and one needs to ensure, for instance, that a notice of termination/ breach is not overlooked and is dealt with urgently and appropriately.

9.2.6   Term and termination

It is important that a contract is certain and for a definable period of time. In some instances this will be until terminated and so it is important to state when termination may occur and what events, if any, are required to trigger this. Be careful of clauses which allow termination on or around an anniversary date only – if you miss the date you will be stuck with the contract for another year. Further, contracts can often be poor in setting out the mechanics of how any 'options' to extend, or cut short, a term are to operate.

9.2.7   Governing law and jurisdiction

The contract should state which country's laws are to apply, e.g. England and Wales, or Scotland. Note that there is no such thing as UK law for these purposes. As well as which law is to apply this clause should say which country's courts will have jurisdiction or enforce that law. This need not be the same country as the one whose laws apply.

9.2.8   Arbitration/dispute resolution

A decision as to whether or not to include this provision must be made. It may provide an inexpensive resolution to a dispute. If it is to be included it should state what the process will be, who the arbiter will be, whether its decisions are binding and who will pay the costs.

9.2.9 IT/e-commerce boiler plate

I have generally assumed that the reader will include the above clauses as appropriate and this brings their discussion to an end. However, there is also a second set of clauses which appear so often in IT and e-commerce contracts that they have almost become boiler plates. In the descriptions of the agreements which follow I have referred to them where they are appropriate (although the fact that they are not referred to should not automatically exclude them).

9.2.10 Intellectual property licence or assignment

Where any intellectual property – trade mark, copyright, design right or patent – is to be used and is not owned there should be a licence in favour of the user, allowing them to use the IP. The licence should be present and should specify who may use the IP, what for and where. Any restrictions should also be clear. If the ownership is to pass then there should be an assignment – this must be in writing and signed by both parties. This should also be in the present tense and can cover future property (i.e. property which does not yet exist). Care must be taken regarding the wording of any assignment, for example, of future copyright with reference to the appropriate section of the Copyright, Designs and Patents Act 1988 (s.91). Also there is a concept of 'full title guarantee' meaning passing the rights without any encumbrances etc., introduced under the Law of

Property (Miscellaneous Provisions) Act 1925. Reference to this will normally be included to ensure the 'purity' of what is passed.

9.2.11 Software licence

Intellectual property (IP) rights often subsist in software and, therefore, if there is to be use but not ownership then the user must have a licence to use the software. The wording should grant the licence now and not commit to do this in the future. It should make it clear who the licence is granted to, how and where the software may be used and any particular restrictions on the use.

9.2.12 Intellectual property warranties and indemnities

Where intellectual property is provided the recipient will want to be certain that the person granting the IP has the rights to do this and is not in breach of third-party rights. If they were, at a later date, to find that they are in breach then there may be the risk of secondary infringement liability and the requirement to immediately stop using the IP. This would obviously have negative PR and cost implications. One would ordinarily seek a warranty or promise that the intellectual property does not breach any third party's rights. Breach of a warranty will allow the beneficiary to claim damages for this breach but not terminate the agreement (unless stipulated otherwise as a condition of termination). An indemnity generally reimburses such out-of-pocket costs (arising out of a third party's claims) as are specified, but does not allow for damages (unless stipulated otherwise). In relation to intellectual property (and source code) the two are generally included together. A warranty/indemnity provision should allow the contract to continue but ensure that the user is not out of pocket and is compensated for breach.

This should also cover who is to conduct litigation and bear the costs and what the other party's obligations, if any, surrounding this will be. Such clauses also often provide for the grantor obtaining rights from a third party or securing alternative IP when a breach comes to the attention of the grantor of the IP.

9.2.13   Cap on liability and insurance

Liabilities under the contract should be capped (and these should make clear whether they apply to any indemnity). Where potential liabilities exist it is also wise to require insurance and to make adequate provisions for this to be taken (and any necessary proof to be provided).

This book is not intended to be an exhaustive guide to drafting contracts nor is it an exhaustive guide to negotiating contracts. However, the intention is to provide a basic commercial under-standing of the legal issues involved, so that the specific explana-tions for specific contracts make sense. Under each heading I have flagged issues in respect of that particular type of contract and highlighted relevant issues to be considered. At the end of each you are provided with a checklist to assist in negotiations.

9.3   Software licences

A software licence will grant a right from the owner of software or the legitimate licence holder to the user of the software, allowing the latter to use the software. There may, in reality, be a cascade of software licences from the original owner through a number of licensees, resulting in a licence with an end user. The standard clauses set out in Appendix 2 include a very short licence which does no more than grant the user the right to use the software in certain ways/places. This form is appropriate as part of a bigger agreement. However, in some cases there will be a whole document which is labelled software licence and which includes many more terms.

Such a document would be used where the goal of the document is to grant the right to use software and where this is not a sundry part of the agreement. In its simplest form this could be the grant of a standard form licence to use off-the-peg (standard form) software such as Microsoft Windows © XP. The document includes the basic licence, any restrictions and requirements made by the provider and also any appropriate boilerplate clauses. This type of licence may be provided in a number of forms and is binding when accepted by the user. As the user does not normally come face to face with the licensee or sign the document, it has generally become accepted that the licence is accepted by the user when the software is opened. This format has become known as a 'shrink wrap' licence (the licence being included behind the cellophane 'shrink wrapped' onto the software).

This type of licence has existed in this form for a number of years. As technology has developed to allow the downloading of software from the Internet direct, the use of this licence has been adapted. The acceptance cannot occur when the shrink wrap is opened as this never occurs and instead it is generally accepted that the acceptance occurs when the user clicks on an 'I accept' at the end of the licence terms. This is generally known as a 'click wrap' licence.

It is unlikely (although not impossible) that you will ever be in a position to negotiate these types of licence as they tend to be on a standard form basis, and the vendors generally insist that all users sign up to the same terms. This allows them certainty in the terms, and the fact that the same terms have been accepted by all also eases their enforcement.

Another type of licence you may come across is the bespoke software licence. Such a licence would be used where software is designed specifically for the user. This may also occur where part of the software is bespoke and part off the peg. This type of licence will generally be negotiated, although the software developer may well want to keep the licence as close to its standard terms as possible. As well as the right to use the software there will be the bigger issue of ownership of the source code. Software is generally licensed in machine-readable form – object code. The owner of the software will not normally want to part with the source code – human readable form (although still technical).

Ownership of the source code is an important issue as the owner has the right to do as they will with it and has the access to the human readable format of the software. The alternative to owning this is to be a licensee. The disadvantages of this are that where the owner can do as they choose with the software, what licensees can do is restricted by the terms of the licence provided by the owner and also, unless agreed otherwise, the licensee cannot restrict the owner's actions. This is particularly relevant where the commissioner of software pays a premium for the development of new software but receives only a licence of it. In these circumstances the developer can then sell the same software to third parties and possibly at a reduced price, but the commissioner who paid a premium for the development would have no say in this.

In protecting the commissioner's interests where software is commissioned from a third party, ownership should ideally be passed to the commissioner. This like copyright can only pass by a written assignment signed by both parties. Whether ownership passes (or is assigned) will generally depend on finance and the power (the bargaining position) of each party. If the creator is an employee then this is not the case and ownership (assuming this is created in the course of employment) will vest in the employer.

If it is not possible to have the ownership assigned then it may be possible to build some restrictions into the contract, so that as well as granting the licence the developer agrees not to do certain things with the software for a period of time. Clauses of this nature often also include provisions with regard to the ownership of modifications undertaken by the purchaser or licensee. Whether such clauses will be enforceable is very much dependent on what they say and in some cases these can be anti-competitive and potentially illegal.

If an assignment is not obtained then it is particularly important to think of the worst-case scenario. (I know, I'm a lawyer – I would say that.) However, without access to the source code it may not be possible to maintain and modify the software. If the supplier should go bust then how can this be done? In such agreements provision for an escrow agreement is common. This will state that the source code (all updates, modifications and documentation) is to be deposited by the developer with a trusted third party. The code will be held by that party until one of a number of circumstances occur (e.g. insolvency of the developer) and when such a circumstance occurs the source code etc. will be released to the commissioner or licensee. This service is offered by a number of third parties including the National Computer Centre (NCC). They have a number of forms for this. The provisions of the software licence should also make clear who is to pay the related costs.

There are a number of specific provisions which will also be included in a software licence:

1. The basis on which the licence is granted – for a purpose, a number of machines, a number of users etc.

2. The process for any fixes – bugs are not uncommon.

3. Upgrades – whether these are to be provided and possibly whether included in the cost of the software or at a fixed cost.

4. The right to decompile the software may well be restricted, but this exists as a statutory right under the Copyright, Designs and Patents Act 1988.

5. Provisions regarding rights to modify the software and perhaps that modification will invalidate warranties and possibly remove rights to service.

6. Circumstances which are considered abuse and grounds for termination, and provisions on termination such as return of the software and documentation if the software licence is breached.

7. If the software is bespoke then there will also be provisions regarding acceptance testing.

CHECKLIST 9.1 SOFTWARE LICENCES

- Is it off the peg or bespoke? ☐

- Is the software assigned or a licence? ☐

- How is the licence calculated – are there restrictions on where it may be used, how long it may be used for, who may use it and how it may be used? ☐

- Is there any restriction on modifications? ☐

- Are there any provisions regarding or restrictions on maintenance and support? ☐

- How do fixes work? ☐

- What provisions are there with regard to upgrades? ☐

- Are there audit rights? ☐

- If it is bespoke what is the acceptance testing? ☐

- Are there warranties? ☐

- May it be terminated? ☐

- Is there a right to an escrow agreement? ☐

Where software is purchased whether by licence or assignment it is also important to ensure that the provider has the right to provide the software and a warranty and indemnity along the lines of an IP warranty provision should be included.

9.4   Web design and build contracts

There is some overlap between content agreements and website design and build agreements. This is hopefully obvious as you read, but I will also try to cross refer.

It is necessary to split the site structure into its architecture and look and feel to understand what the site is made up of, i.e. the architecture and what the public views. There will also need to be an integration between the front-end transactional part of the site and the back-end systems which manage the order and stock. Not infrequently (depending on the scale of the project) the look and feel of a site ends up being dealt with by a different party from the overall structure design and build of a site. Where this is the case the two must be carefully integrated. Also the site will be built on a software platform which may be provided by a third party or the site architect, and a software licence for this may need to be taken as either a separate contract or part of the design and build agreement. Again the contracts for each must work together, both practically and legally.

The completed site will be hosted on a server either by a third party or by the site owner. I have seen at least one agreement which attempts to deal with the overall build of a website, content and hosting as a single agreement and should this be the case then you must ensure that the relevant issues which would be included in each of the contracts are covered.

It may seem that design and build is old hat. However, many front runners in technology have been working on or using second-generation websites, and there are still some cautious souls who are only now looking at building their first sites. With the best will in the world, although commercially it would be nice to reuse or modify existing technology for a second generation site, this can simply cause more problems than it solves. This means that even established web businesses may need to look at new or amended design and build agreements and lawyers, like the technical people involved, must build on previous experience to develop better agreements. There will be ongoing development with these as technology improves.

9.4.1   Two-phase contract?

It is always difficult for commercial or even technical people to understand what exactly they want their site to do and therefore what they are buying. Even where there is a good commercial and technical understanding of what they would like, there is also the added restriction of knowing what is achievable at the cost allowed and, further, what functionality will easily work together and what will not. A dilemma exists between having the most state-of-the-art functionality and having a site which is usable to a customer and which works quickly. The customer is often not in the best position to assess what functionality is important and what is not, although it should have an initial wish list as a starting point. This may and frequently does mean that the customer is very dependent on the site architect providing recommendations as to what is the best it can have for its money.

Having a contract where the architect may call the shots will generally not be in the customer's best interests, and the architect may not want to take on the level of responsibility which would accompany this. As a result of this it has become increasingly common for the customer to structure the relationship with the site architect so that there are either two contracts or a single contract with two phases to it. The first phase of the services or contract will involve creating the design or specification of what is to be done in the second phase, and following on from this the second phase or contract would cover how this is to be implemented.

It is important to ensure that the customer is adequately involved in this first site definition phase and that the final deliverable to be provided under this phase is subject to agreement by the customer. A process for obtaining this agreement should ideally be built into the contract. The likelihood is that the customer will be involved all the way through the discussions and that this will be a collaborative effort, but it must be remembered also that the customer is dependent on the skill and expertise of the architect and that the architect must take responsibility for the output of this phase.

It may also be worth noting that following the collapse of many e-commerce businesses the concept of 'usability' currently appears to be de rigueur and there is an acceptance in the industry that the site must be usable by customers whether they are Internet savvy or not. There is no point in bells and whistles if they slow the loading of the page to an extent that it turns consumers away or becomes overly complicated.

9.4.2 Specification and site structure

Whether the contract is effectively in two phases and the first phase is the creation of a site specification, whether the parties agree to use the ITT/ITQ (invitation to tender/invitation to quote) and response or otherwise, there will be a need for a site specification. The services to be provided will be tied to the deliverable which is the site, and the description of what this is will, in turn, be tied to a specification. The architect may choose to over-deliver on the specification but obviously will be obliged only to provide what is in that specification.

This specification must therefore not only set out what the site will do, but to an extent how it will do it, i.e. if the site is to be fully transactional then it must state not only that the site will be capable of processing transactions by particular payment methods but also the timescale for it to do so and the number of these that can be transacted at any one time.

It is also important to consider what systems the site will need to integrate with, whether these are also being built in conjunction with the service provider or are existing legacy systems with which it will need to integrate. If there are other pieces of software involved then again it is important to check that the licences for these are wide enough to allow the specified parties to undertake the work in hand. It is also important to make sure that appropriate rights are obtained in any interfaces built.

The more detail that can be provided at this stage the better.

9.4.3   Look and feel

The customer may have a particular look and feel for the site. This goes beyond the architecture and back end of the site to what the customer sees. If the customer has particular requirements for this, such as colour, fonts, space for advertising, menu layout, etc., then these should also be included in the specification. It may be that the customer wants the first phase to include the provision of mock-ups of the look and feel to provide reassurance that both parties are singing from the same hymn sheet and for the customer to have a clearer version of what it is buying. Therefore mock-ups as well as a specification may form the deliverables from the first phase. If these are very individual then it may also be worth considering restricting the use of this look and feel by the service provider for other clients or for a particular sector of those for a certain period (subject to the usual checks on unreasonable restrictions on trade).

It is also possible that the customer will consider splitting the provision of the services for architecture of the site and the site look and feel depending on the skills of the service provider. If this is the case then it is essential to ensure that the agreement between each party ties in with the other and that warranties and responsibilities in these agreements are back to back.

9.4.4   Timing and milestones

It is fairly common for the services undertaken to be done on a time-boxed basis and split into stages. This may create a commitment from the service provider to supply services in a certain timescale. The level of commitment to be provided by the service provider is always a matter of contention and the position taken very much depends on whether you are the client or the provider.

However, when reducing the level from an absolute obligation to provide the services contracted for within a timescale, it is also worth considering what level of damages will, in any event, be applicable if delivery does not occur in this timescale. Most agencies' standard terms will exclude liability for consequential loss. This is a legal term which many people believe that they understand, but which is not 100 per cent defined and it may or may not include loss of profits. Therefore, if loss of profits is to be included or excluded, then this should be specifically stated. There may also be an impact of force majeure. If the liability is only for direct loss then this too should be spelt out.

Most suppliers of services of this nature take the approach that they are working 'in partnership' with the customer. This may or may not be what the customer is looking for, but in the light of this it may instead be worth incentivising the supplier so that payments increase if a timescale or milestone is achieved – a carrot rather than a stick approach. This may also involve commitments to timescales from both parties and not just the supplier. Even without such commitments to timescales it is likely that there will be an obligation on the customer to provide reasonable assistance and co-operation.

9.4.5   *Change control*

The detail required for this very much depends on the size of the project being undertaken, but where a specification and price have been agreed, there needs to be an agreed process for any proposed changes to be made by either party, to either that specification or the associated price. This will not only allow the customer to come back and ask for more or different functionality, but will also allow the agency or architect to point out authorisation problems. This obviously also requires a process for authorising the agreement to the change (if this is given) and in turn for making any necessary amendments to the contract.

9.4.6   Key personnel

Again depending on the volume of work undertaken and the skills required of the individuals involved it may be felt that it is necessary to specify that certain key personnel will undertake the work. If the agency has been chosen to do the work on the basis of the skills of certain people, and these same skills are not shared by all employees who work for it, then it is essential that these are the people who undertake the work. The use of subcontractors may also be something which should be considered and where appropriate restricted.

9.4.7   Payment terms

The basis for charging needs to be clear in the contract – is it charged on a fixed fee or a time and materials basis? If it is time and materials, are there any restrictions or caps on the amount to be charged? Beware that for some suppliers time and materials can be a licence to print money! The contract should of course state when payment is due and on what terms. As well as the standard payment terms one should note in particular with the smaller agencies that there is a statutory requirement to pay interest if no interest amount is specified. (The Late Payment of Commercial Debts (Interest) Act 1998 was fully implemented on 7 August 2002.) This means that if no amount of interest is specified a statutory amount of the 'official dealing rate' plus 8 per cent will be charged where there is late payment for goods or services and the supplier and the provider are dealing in the course of their business. Take care when contracting out of this by setting your own interest rate in a contract, as this will only be enforceable rather than the statutory rate if it is viewed as being a substantial remedy which must be fair and reasonable and of a sufficient amount.

Also be careful to ensure that if you believe expenses are included in the fees there are no additional provisions allowing these to be charged. If they can be charged check whether there are any restrictions on this and if there are not whether there should be.

9.4.8 Intellectual property and code

The intellectual property in the site should be assigned in full to the customer. Importantly, as the agency may have contractors in its team, there should be appropriate commitments from the agency ensuring that all third-party rights have also been assigned and moral rights waived. Remember that the assignment must be in writing and signed to be valid – so do not leave the unsigned contract in the bottom of a cupboard.

There is a natural but conflicting reaction from each of the parties to the ownership of code. The agency will of course wish to retain ownership of all code which it brings to the table and will only provide the customer with a licence to use the object code for the purpose it is provided. It is worth considering whether any other third parties, other consultants or group companies might need to use the code on behalf of the customer and extending the grant of licence to them or obtaining the right to sub-licence to them.

The problems usually begin where new code is being developed for the project and, as he is paying for its development, the customer believes it should belong to him. The agency on the other hand is likely to consider this new software as a development which has benefited from its previously existing experiences and code and which should, like that previously existing code, form part of its stock in trade. As a result it will not wish to assign any of the code to the customer.

If the customer does accept this it will again require a full licence to use it and one must consider the parties to whom it may be licensed, the duration of the licence, the purpose of the licence and its geographical scope. This is also discussed as an issue in section 9.3 on software licences and more detail can be found there.

9.4.9   *Upgrades, modifications and enhancements*

As time passes it is likely that the customer will want to change the site or add pages or functionality to it. It is necessary at this early design phase to make sure that the future is considered and, if making such changes will require access to code not provided, how this should be dealt with in the future must be clearly set out.

Part of the agreement on look and feel may involve agreeing what content is coded into the site as a constant and what content will be open to the customer to change without recoding. It is also important to establish who will own the changes and whether there is any commitment to go back to the original service provider to make them.

9.4.10 Maintenance and training

Once it has been built the site will need to be maintained and, as this is frequently undertaken by the site architects, the provisions relating to this frequently manage to find their way into the design and build agreement. If these are included then it is key to ensure that these cover proactive and reactive maintenance and that the detail of the types or levels of maintenance to be provided and response times are clearly defined in the form of SLAs (service level agreements). If there is to be any service credits for failing to achieve these then this would also need to be considered here.

If maintenance is to be brought in-house or to be provided by a third party the agreement needs to deal both with the use of the site and its code by someone other than the site owner and should include a provision allowing this. It may also be sensible to have provisions for a training requirement which might allow knowledge transfer from the designer. There will also be a need for other related provisions such as documentation transfer and generally handover between the site architect and the maintenance provider. If maintenance comes from a third party from the point of acceptance this will also have to tie into a fault analysis in order to be clear as to whether this is a maintenance or a warranty issue and cost. The handover may be staggered and involve a run-down period where the knowledge transfer occurs.

It would also be wise, if the agreement is particularly restrictive in relation to either of these, to have this type of provision for handover and knowledge transfer should the provider be in breach of the agreement.

9.4.11   *Warranty and indemnity*

As well as setting out what is warranted, the period during which this is effective must be stated. It should be clear when this commences, how long it is for and what the level of obligation during the warranty period will be.

There ought to be warranties from the supplier that the service will be provided possibly in accordance with industry standards, but certainly by appropriately skilled individuals using reasonable skill and care. Although such terms are covered to some extent, one should not overly rely on implied terms that may apply by law. These can sometimes assist in the event of a dispute and the absence of clear express terms; however, it is much better to expressly tie down anything of importance. Also note that where express warranties are given the party giving these may want to exclude implied terms.

The site should further be warranted to comply with the specification and to be free from viruses or be virus checked. A standard intellectual property warranty should also be included, and this must also cover IP provided by third parties and in turn the code. Indemnities for breach and for breach of intellectual property should also be added and the cap on these and/or the general liabilities should be included. If content is being provided by either party then there may also need to be warranties relating to this.

9.4.12 Testing and acceptance

The contract must set out the tests which will apply when the supplier has completed the deliverable(s). It may be possible to state what these tests are or if not what they should demonstrate, who will undertake them and in what timescale. If one party is to undertake them (and it may need assistance from the other) this should also be made clear and they should each be obliged to provide this assistance. It may be that the tests cannot actually be defined until a later date, but the general provisions around these can be added with a commitment to agree the tests in certain timescales. This is of course not desirable.

When acceptance is achieved then a process for notification of the fact ought to be set out as well as a process for the situation where testing draws out problems. Assuming it is agreed that there will be further work and retesting, who will pay for this and how many times will it be undertaken before there is a decision that acceptance has not occurred? What if acceptance is not achieved after two or three sets of testing? What will be the consequences of not achieving this?

9.4.13 Additional services

Many agencies will offer various additional services. It is not uncommon for them to offer hosting or content preparation. They may also offer domain name registration.

Some agencies offer an additional and related name registration service. If this is to be opted for then how this process will work going forward must be considered. If the agency registers the name,

CHECKLIST 9.2 SITE DESIGN AND BUILD

- Specification of site structure – architecture and look and feel. ☐

- Will contract be phased to allow creation of specification by third party? ☐

- Timing for delivery and possible milestones. ☐

- Change control – process for suggesting and agreeing. ☐

- Key personnel – is this why you have chosen a third party? ☐

- Payment terms – how payment is structured. ☐

- IP ownership – if not with you what protection do you have? Ensure that you can maintain, upgrade and modify. ☐

- Maintenance and training – is this required from the designer? ☐

- Warranties – IP and also that it will do what you want it to do. ☐

- Testing and acceptance – process and what if not achieved? ☐

do they commit to hand it over to the customer at a later date should the customer request it? If not, the customer may be vulnerable to the agency. Will the name be registered to the customer or the agency's IP address? Also, what is to happen to renewal notices, which one can assume will be sent to the agency – what if they fail to renew? This is a potentially risky area, but one most companies have to face.

9.5   Web content contracts

The recognition that quality of content is key to attracting and retaining customers on the Internet has led to a growth in businesses specialising in content provision. But website owners are still legally responsible for the content provided and a watertight website content agreement is becoming increasingly important.

Content forms the heart of a website. In the same way as an attractive shop window may bring a customer through the shop door, an attractive home page may interest a browser. But once through the door, dull or sparse content will not encourage the browser to stay, and will certainly not encourage the browser to buy the website's services or goods. The nature of the content will depend on what the goals of the website are. Whether the economic model of a web business is based on visitor clicks, staying time or sales, site 'stickiness' (retention of users for a long period or repeat visits) is essential to website success.

This need to interest and retain users has led to a rise in businesses specialising in the provision of site content which can facilitate the regular update of the materials on a site. Content providers offer their services in many different ways. In much the same way as a traditional magazine would receive and include features to fill its pages, it is not uncommon for the content to be passed to a site owner for inclusion in his site in this way. Another popular content provision method is by way of a link from the content provider's website to the content purchaser's site. Site users may not even be aware that they have passed across a link when moving from one page of a site to what appears to be no more than another page of content.

A website owner is responsible to the public at large, and in particular to users of its site, for the content of its site. The legal obligations faced will apply equally to the content provided by website owners or third parties. An agreement which seeks to cover the legal issues raised by the provisions of the content must therefore cover not only the issues which would have arisen under a traditional magazine, but also those issues which arise as a result of the Internet 's structure. The principle issues of a website content agreement are set out below.

9.5.1 Specification of what is purchased

The content agreement must first make clear what is being purchased or provided and should include a clear and fairly detailed description. The description should cover the following basics:

- subject matter of the content – for example daily international news, London theatre reviews;

- length of each piece of content – in terms of either copy or pre-agreed web space;

- up-to-dateness of content – particularly relevant for news, for example the story should have broken in the preceding 24 hours;

- frequency, timing and method by which the content is to be updated – particularly important, as this must not only tie in with the availability of the content but also the needs of the site;

- particular look, feel and format required for the content – both the fact that this should happen and what it is to be must be made clear;

- degree of customisation required – for example, the content may be provided free from all links or from e-commerce placements or may need additional local information.

It may often be simpler, from a lawyer's point of view, to base this content description on the pitch for the contract. Such a document will normally be completed by the content provider before the contract is awarded. Other issues to be addressed in the content agreement are looked at in more detail below.

9.5.2   Exclusivity of content

If there is to be exclusivity of use of the content, this must be carefully reviewed by each side and included in the agreement.

The grant of exclusivity of use of the content by a content provider will mean that the value of the content needs to be recouped in this single, exclusive provision. This may well mean that the cost makes this a prohibitively expensive and unattractive option for the purchaser.

From a content purchaser's point of view, the purpose of the content must be considered against the cost of exclusivity of the use or display.

Would a customised version of general content, for example, fulfil the purpose at a cheaper price? If the content is intended to make the website unique or distinct from competitors, then there may well be a sound commercial reason for exclusivity.

9.5.3   Delivery of content

The timing of content delivery may be of particular importance, depending on the nature of the content and the frequency with which it is updated. If your site is updated through the night then there is little point in purchasing same-day news stories that are not delivered until 9 a.m.

The method by which the content is to be provided/delivered should also be stated. For example, is this to be a CD-ROM delivered daily or a link to a website? Many content providers supply content through links direct to their website where the content is then framed or otherwise customised for the purchaser. The purchaser must be clear what method is to be used, as the obligations that surround each will be different.

If the content is accessed through a link, then the content agreement should have the same provisions as a standard linking agreement. These would include the need for the link to be built and maintained by one or other of the parties and to comply with a particular specification. The specification should include where the link is from and to – is it to and from a home page, or to and from a particular part of the site? There may also be a need for the link to be secure and provision will have to be made to this effect, along with service levels for its uptime and a right to remove the link. In each case it may be necessary to ensure that the content is backed up. It may also be sensible to ask that the content is provided free from viruses or time bombs. If providers cannot stipulate this, then they should at least provide that the content will have been virus-checked by a state-of-the-art anti-virus software before it is passed to the purchaser.

9.5.4   *Service levels*

There should ideally also be some measure of the content provision. In the case of provision by link this ought to cover both uptime and provision for maintenance of the website, particularly where this creates downtime. For a site which is heavily reliant on content via links, obvious dangers attach to content downtime and site mainten-ance being performed by the provider during peak times. Any such service level will need to be monitored and measured and should be backed by either service credits or a right to terminate (preferably both) if the content provided fails to meet these measures.

9.5.5   *Content use*

It is important to bear in mind that if the content is to be used on anything other than a straightforward website, then other issues may apply. An ITC public consultation looked at issues regarding content used in interactive television, where the compliance issues may differ, due to the regulators struggling to come to terms with the 'convergent' media. Differences may also apply where content is to be used in m-commerce or any other new type of technology. If the content supplied for a website might be used through such alternative media, then the agreement will need to include a right to use the content on such media and also, where necessary, to repurpose the content for that media.

It is also important to specify not only what media the content can be used in, but also how long the content may be used for. In some agreements the licence to use the content will be perpetual, but in other agreements there may be a right to use the content only for a limited period of time. The licence may not last for the term of the agreement and may effectively mean that the content is frequently updated but back copies cannot be used. In such agreements it may well be necessary to procure a right to keep copies of the content as part of the site's audit trail.

9.5.6   Legality of the content

Content purchasers will generally find that their right to edit the content is restricted by the content provider. Content providers justify this on the basis that they will aim to provide the content in a form which is legal, and they will be required to warrant the legality of this. The content provider may also wish to be identified as the provider of the content, and for its own reputation will not want to be identified with misleading or otherwise illegal content.

A provision restricting the purchaser's ability to edit the content obviously protects the provider from the eventuality that changes could make the content illegal and from any liability that the provider might face for the amended content.

The normal form of a content legality warranty will be to list a number of offensive or illegal types of content, such as that which is defamatory, pornographic or discriminatory, and to state that the content will not include such types of materials. It ought also to state that the content will not in any way breach UK laws or regulations and may then specify codes with which one must also comply. Often the British Codes of Advertising and Sales Promotion (BCASP) policed by the Advertising Standards Authority (or, in the case of interactive television, the ITC code) will be mentioned. In some areas there will be other specific regulators. In these cases the particular regulators, such as the Financial Services Authority (FSA), should be specified.

One problem which may arise is the fact that the content will be accessible all over the world where many different laws may apply. However, it is unlikely that a local content provider will be willing to warrant the legality of the content anywhere in the world, and will be likely to restrict the warranty to the UK or, exceptionally, Europe. Whether this is acceptable is a question which must be looked at in all the commercial and legal circumstances of each individual case.

In recent times there have been a number of reported cases in other European countries where a foreign site has been prosecuted, and in certain cases found guilty, of providing a promotion or advertisement which does not meet that country's legal requirements but which can be accessed and utilised by its nationals. Against the background of such real risks, purchasers would obviously prefer wider protection from their providers. However, the price paid by the purchaser will be a very relevant factor in the risk that the provider may be willing to bear. Taking on the liability may be possible for the provider but prohibitively expensive for the purchaser.

9.5.7   Intellectual property rights

The second area of legal responsibility for content relates to the relevant intellectual property rights attached to the content. The content itself may be made up of many forms of media and each of these will have particular rights attached. The provider should grant a licence (or possibly a written assignment if there is exclusivity) for the use of the content provided.

Depending on the number of contributors to the content and the media provided, such as music and film, there may also be additional licences and consents required and it is necessary to ensure that the relevant acknowledgements are included.

The content purchaser should have a general clause confirming that the provider has all necessary consents, licences and permissions for the use of the content, and the provision of this to the purchaser for the purchaser's particular use.

The licence will need to cover the use, transmission and display of the content and may also, in certain technical structures, need to allow the use of the provider's software.

If the content is to include particular trade marks or logos, the permission to use these may be separately noted. This would be likely to tie into a provision which grants a right for each contractual party to use the other's trade marks and which may also cover the right to make a press release or other announcement about the parties' relationship. This may also include restrictions or consents which are necessary to make such a licence and frequently you may see trade mark schedules and specifications setting out exactly how a mark should be reproduced and/or used. If a contract refers to such a document, make sure that it is attached and that there is a process for changes to be agreed or at worst notified.

There should be an undertaking from the provider that the content provided does not breach any third party's intellectual property rights and a warranty and indemnity should back this.

If a restriction on the right to edit is accepted, then this should be qualified by the right to edit illegal or potentially illegal content. It may also be wise to tie this obligation to another obligation on the content provider, requiring it to provide replacement content within a certain time period where illegal content is discovered. There may be additional obligations on each party to cover the removal and replacement of illegal content.

9.5.8 *Advertising and sponsorship*

Content may contain advertising or sponsorship for third parties. It may be possible for a purchaser to specify that the content should be provided free from all e-commerce placements and third-party advertising. Where there is a risk that this will be adverse to the purchaser if included, then it is necessary to do so. However, the willingness of the provider to remove such materials will be dependent on the economic basis for the provision of the content. Whether the provider requires the sponsorship or advertising to make the content provision economically viable will be a major consideration.

This highlights beyond any other issue the need for a clear understanding of what is being bought at what price. The relationship will only work if the provider makes the level of profit it needs and the purchaser buys content that is usable and boosts site stickiness.

9.5.9   Warranties and indemnity

The warranty of the legality of the content should extend to all relevant rules and regulations. There should be a standard intellectual property warranty, warranting that all necessary consents have been maintained and that the content provided is not in breach of any third party's rights.

The amount of the indemnities is normally hotly debated. Although the purchaser will want the general indemnity to be for a large amount, this may be limited by the provider's view of risk.

9.5.10   Cost and payment terms

Of course content is not always provided free of charge. The cost structure of a straightforward content agreement will often be based on a volume of content over a period of time. Many content agreements are actually much more than content agreements and are in fact true e-commerce agreements, with complex cost structures.

CHECKLIST 9.3 CONTENT AGREEMENT

- Definition of the subject matter: length, frequency, timing, method of updating, format. ☐

- Exclusivity of content: exclusive or customised? If the latter, specify the degree. ☐

- Time of delivery: when is the site to be updated? How often? ☐

- How is the content to be accessed? If via a link, then how is this to be maintained? Think about service levels and uptime. Where is the link to and from? ☐

- Is the content intended for use on other media? If so, there may be other compliance issues and the content may have to be re-purposed. ☐

- Service levels: consider the quality of the content. If via a link, then uptime and maintenance provision need to be factored in. Have you a rebate provision for delays or failures? ☐

- Legal warranties: the content should not be in breach of UK laws, codes or regulations (whether statutory or otherwise) or include offensive material. ☐

- Intellectual property rights: all necessary consents, licences and permissions for use of the content must be in place. A warranty and indemnity should be considered. ☐

- If vouching for the legality of the content, to what extent should the content purchaser be allowed to edit the content? Advertising: is the content to be free of placements? ☐

- Cost structure. ☐

The more complex agreements may actually amount to distribution agreements and the payment may link to the volume of sales or the number of visitors to a site through the content. Such economic structures may also raise issues of customer ownership and data protection.

9.6   Web hosting contracts

The hosting agreement will be needed where there is a third party whose server is used as your site's physical location and the point from which the site is to be transmitted. The agreement may be on a standard form from the hosting ISP or on a bespoke or negotiated contract. As is often the case, the facility to make demands and alter the agreement will depend to a large extent to the power of the parties and in this case the size of the site, the volume of traffic and the revenue from hosting the site.

Maintenance of the site itself may be part of the hosting agreement or it may form part of the agreement with the site developer. If it is with a party other than the host or is to be done internally, there need to be arrangements in place with the host to allow secure access of these parties to the site at convenient times. The party who provides the maintenance should be subject to service levels covering the response and fix time of any problems. Maintenance will be split into ongoing or preventative maintenance and also to reactive maintenance responding to a problem. The provisions relating to each of these may be different and there may also be a requirement for ongoing maintenance not to be done during trading hours or at worst at peak hours. The site will need to be maintained, but there should also be a provision to allow for future developments such as upgrades and fixes and ongoing modifications. There may even be a need for it to adapt to new technology. This will be relevant to the site designer but also to anyone who maintains the site. Ideally the host and maintenance provider will cooperate without being required to but it is again wise to require this in the agreement.

As well as the maintenance of the site itself there will be a need for maintenance of the equipment on which the site is hosted and this will always fall to the host. The standards for this and details for reactive maintenance as described above will need to be included. Again it may be essential for the site maintainer and host, if the two are different, to work together.

Like so many other areas of e-commerce the details of the hosting service will be set out in the agreement and generally through a specification. The specification should set out certain details including the server the site is located on and the site address location. There is a decision to be made as to whether the deal is based on the hosting of the site on certain equipment or whether it is results based. Where the site owner does not have the same expertise as the host it may be wise for this to be results based. In the case of an equipment-based service then there should be a list of the equipment to be used. This should also then say what is to happen if there is any problem with that specific kit and whether there is another or mirror server to which the site would transfer.

Where the service is provided on the basis of what the host will deliver the results to be achieved should be clearly set out. Sadly it is difficult to achieve this without using technical measures such as the site capacity and connectivity. This may also set out the security of the site and require a customer data security log. In particular, where the specification is based on equipment it is important to include a procedure to deal with change control.

In considering the initial environment it is worth bearing in mind that there may be initial glitches and it would be advisable to create a staging environment to trial the site as first launched and then the various modified versions of it through time. Having this may allow you to avoid a number of embarrassing situations where glitches occur just as a new development goes live.

In either case there is a need to ensure that the service as specified is provided and the host must report on its ability to achieve these requirements and also any faults, problems and outages. These will normally be measured against a set of service levels which will relate back directly to the specification of the service where it is results based, or on a similar basis where this is based on equipment. In order to report the service levels there must be a level of monitoring in place and details of this should be agreed in advance. The results of the monitoring should be included in any reporting.

Service levels of themselves may not be adequate as there is nothing other than walking away from the contract to support them. It is therefore sensible to agree service credits/rebates to back these with the host.

It is essential that a site is backed up at regular intervals and particularly where changes are made to it. The frequency of these is a cost issue but it would be wise to do this at least daily. Back-ups may be stored at the host or off-site and this ties neatly into the concept of disaster recovery and whether the site is so valuable to your business that the additional costs of disaster recovery should there be a problem at the host's premises or server farm is worth paying for. If it is then these provisions ought to include the time for recovery and the location of the recovered site.

The host should agree to host the content and display this as provided and not to make any changes to it. In return, it is normal for the host to require the site owner to ensure that the content is legal and to warrant to the host that this will be maintained on this basis and that all illegal content will be removed. Some hosts will also reserve the right to withdraw hosting if they are notified that the content is illegal. You might well stipulate that you should be notified first and have an opportunity to look into the problem and correct it before such action is considered.

The site owner is not the only provider of warranties and the host should also warrant that the service will be provided in accordance with the specifications and the service levels. There should also be a mutual intellectual property warranty and indemnity.

When the hosting comes to an end there will be a period of handover between the current and new host. As this end may not be on the best of terms, a wise site owner will always add provisions surrounding this to the contract. This will cover the rundown of the service and cooperation between the parties, and may cover knowledge transfer.

CHECKLIST 9.4 WEB HOSTING

- Basis of service provision – list of equipment or delivery of a service/result? ☐

- Specification of services – does it include site maintenance and what this is – access for maintainers? ☐

- Duty to maintain equipment. ☐

- Service levels and service credits to enforce these. ☐

- Back-up and disaster recovery. ☐

- Content/editing – display as provided. ☐

- Change control and handover. ☐

- Possibility of staging environment. ☐

9.7 Advertising contracts

At a time when advertising revenues appear to be contracting in the online world, it may appear strange to be suggesting that it is important to have a basic understanding of online advertising agreements. However, there have been movements in technology and the structure of these agreements that make the issue worth considering or at least updating. This section aims to give an overview of issues which should be considered where adverts are commissioned for use on a website or where space is purchased on a site for these to be displayed.

9.7.1 Form of advert

Internet advertising has traditionally consisted of click-through advertising, the revenue stream or royalty for the advert often being based on the number of click-throughs. Banner ads appear to have been a disappointment to many advertisers as they have not resulted in large numbers of click-throughs.

Pop-ups have existed since the Internet was in black and white! Due to the fact that you have to click on them whether you are interested or not, they need to be carefully targeted as they can be a cost (time online) and an annoyance to the user. A recent trend has been for pop ups to appear on sites in a competing or 'piggy back' fashion. So, for example, when opening the site of a car retailer, there might be a pop up for a car listings magazine. The legality of this type of guerrilla advertising is debatable.

9.7.2   Advert placement

Consider the following:

- What form of advertising space is being bought and where will it be located? If this is on a site page, what page is it?

- Exactly what size and form will the advert take? The content of that page and the prominence of the ad should all be specified.

- Will the advert be static or will it be in a swap situation where it is replaced by another advert every so often. If the space is shared, how is this to work?

- What is the length of time it is displayed each time it is shown and how often is it shown in a period of time? Bear in mind that where there are swaps, the time the advert is displayed should allow the user to notice the ad and click on the link. The frequency of its display in a given period of time should also be stated.

- If the advert is one of many on a page it is worth considering what the other adverts will be, both in terms of their form and their content. Is a competitor advertising on the same page?

9.7.3   IP and code

If a third party is being paid to design an advert, all IP rights arising now or in the future should be assigned in full to the party who has commissioned the ad. In the UK, this should include a waiver of moral rights. The contract should obligate the producer to obtain assignments on the same, or similar, terms from any third party who may have worked on the ad. These should be backed up with appropriate warranties and indemnities.

The advert may involve the building of code by a third party. If the code is their stock in trade, it is important to obtain a wide licence that covers the purpose for which it is being used and also the right to modify or adapt this in the future. If the code commissioned is unique to the client, then this should be assigned in full.

9.7.4   Revenue

- If the revenue stream is to be measured on the number of click-throughs, there must be certainty in the accuracy of the method by which these are monitored. Does the advertiser have a way of checking this? If not, then some form of audit should be considered.

- If another method of pricing, such as a straight cost for space, is used, then this should be noted. Whether payment is in a single lump sum or parts should be specified and the payment process, timing and terms should also be set out. Interest should be specified or a statutory amount may apply.

9.7.5   Legal and regulatory considerations

The ASA has backed away from its regulation of Internet content and narrowed this to advertising for websites and true Internet advertising. This includes banners and pop-ups as well as adverts in commercial e-mails and sales promotions. Ensure that the content of any advert complies with the BCASP Code, the main principles of which are that the advert is legal, decent, honest and true.

Is the advert to be used in another form of media? In the case of television, this would be subject to the ITC Code. Given the blurring of the lines of distinction between different media there is potentially an interrelationship between the ASA and ITC and this must all be considered in checking whether content is legal.

The advert content must also comply with a number of consumer laws. If a click-through takes a consumer to a location on your site from which you intend to sell to a consumer, consider the impact of the Distance Selling and E-Commerce Regulations.

The site on which the advert is to be displayed will undoubtedly request a contractual commitment to the legality of the content of the advert. As many Internet advertisers wish to push back barriers there may be more risk of this in the Internet arena. Provisions such as immediate notification of the removal and reason, coupled with an ability to rectify or replace, should therefore be built in.

If one moves away from the basic click-through to include moving images or music, obtain the relevant usage rights or consents. Like all IP, this should also be subject to relevant warranties and indemnities. A more detailed explanation of this process and the rights surrounding this can be found in http://www.marketinglaw. co.uk.

9.7.6   Spec/site commitment

If a contract is for advertising space on a site, state the commencement date of the contract; the date the advert will be started; the length of time (or other measure, e.g. number of clicks) during which it will be displayed, whether this can be extended and when it terminates. If the advertiser has not sold the space to a third party at the end of the advert, then will the advert remain for free or at a discounted price?

The site should commit to display the advert on a 24 by 7 basis (or such other basis as is agreed) and offer some sort of rebate if the site is not working during that time. If the management of the technology of the link or the swapping of adverts is down to the site, then the site must commit to achieving this and resolving problems within an agreed timescale. It must also commit to display the advert as provided and to respect the look and feel of the advert in doing so.

Note that although some pre-clearance advice is available through different bodies such as the CAP (Committee of Advertising Practice) such advice is not binding (i.e. even if your copy is 'approved' the ASA can still find you in breach subsequently); therefore you must consider legal advice. This is particularly important the more novel or cutting-edge the campaign.

CHECKLIST 9.5 ADVERTISING

- How does the revenue stream work? If it needs monitoring how is this done? ☐

- What kind of ads are covered – banners, buttons, links, pop-ups? ☐

- What kind of placing on the site has been agreed? ☐

- When and how long will ad be on the site? ☐

- Who is building and maintaining any links? ☐

- If any IP arises whose is it? ☐

- Provisions regarding legality of site and advert and liability. ☐

- Right to remove advert for each party and to reinstate. ☐

9.8   Linking contracts

Linking agreements have progressed a great deal over the last couple of years. Originally they were little more than a method of regulating the links between sites which creates the giant network of links forming the World Wide Web. However, the commercial thinking behind links has developed substantially and links these days will often represent a commercially beneficial arrangement between the linking parties. Obviously the purpose of the link will affect the considerations for the contract which governs the relationship, but there are also certain general issues which must be considered irrespective of the commercials.

As the economic model of linking has developed, links have moved from being clicks through a banner advert to being sophisticated and often integrated links allowing seamless e-commerce in relationships such as click to buy.

It cannot have escaped the notice of anyone who has been following the development of the Internet and related legal matters, that there have been a number of hotly debated issues surrounding links. There has been no statute law but a large number of cases in many jurisdictions. From the early Shetland Times case to the more recent Playboy cases, the law has struggled with the legalities of the link. A formal agreement between parties who wish to link is advisable.

9.8.1   Link itself

The first consideration once it is agreed that there will be a link will always be how it is to work and the need for a technical specification or agreement in this regard. If it is possible, as well as specifying who will set up and maintain the link, the agreement should specify what this will be. In some instances a specification of the technology will be attached as a schedule and this will provide both parties with the information they need to make sure that this link works with their site and technology.

9.8.2   Look and feel

The link will be made from a word or graphic on one website to a page of the other. It is important, as the clip, word or mark which the customer clicks through to use the link will be a form of brand representation, that the parties commit to displaying the link in the agreed format. This ought to specify not only the size of any link icon, but also the look and feel of the icon and any content provided with this. For example, it may state that the link will be in the text describing a product, it may be a button in blue which says click to buy in green, etc. It is also normal to see not only a commercial description of the link but a detailed technical requirement covering the form and size of the icon, often using technology such as GIFs or pixels.

It is also worth bearing in mind that some links will be from promotions or adverts and if this is the case it may also be worth specifying how often that link is to be upgraded.

9.8.3   Intellectual property licence

If the link involves a trade mark it will be necessary for the holder of the trade mark to grant a licence to use the trade mark to the other party. This may restrict what the trade mark is used for and may also tie into a publicity clause. The licence may also need to extend to other forms of intellectual property depending on the commercial reality of what is being done, e.g. whether product images or other content is provided, and whether technically a copy of the site or part of it is made when the link is used.

9.8.4   Location of link on page

It is essential that, as well as agreeing what the link will look like to consumers, the agreement considers where the link icon is to be located. Is this to be somewhere on the home page or on another particular page of the site? If the link is from a book review on a magazine site to a bookseller's sales of that book, then it will be essential that the agreement specifies that the link is placed on the relevant product page.

It may be important to consider not only what page the link is on but where on the page the link is. In particular, if a site provides indexes or menus of third parties to whom the site links, one may want to specify details of menu placement such as which category the link is stored under, where in the menu the listing will be or how prominent the icon will be.

It may be necessary to specify not only where the link goes from but also where it goes to.

9.8.5   Home page or deep links

It is possible that due to a commercial relationship such as the book review magazine linking to the bookseller there will be a need to link directly to a page on the site. This is known as a deep link. This is distinct from a link to the home page.

There may be policy, security or technical (not to mention legal) issues surrounding deep links and it is not uncommon for sites to prohibit deep links while allowing home page links. Again, if any such policy or prohibition exists it is important to spell this out in the agreement.

9.8.6   One-way or two-way link

Many links are placed from site A to site B to drive users or consumers from one site to the other. Whether this is with the intention of increasing sales or site traffic, this one-way flow of users is essential to the linking relationship. However, a question often arises as to whether the link should flow in one or two directions. Should a user who has linked from A to B have a reverse link back to A? Also, should users of site B who may not have arrived via the link from site A, or who in fact may not even know site A, be offered the opportunity to link to site A?

Again, there are a number of factors involved in this decision. If the link is part of a commercial or commission relationship, the direction in which the commission flows may dictate the direction of the link. If the link flows in two directions should the commission flow in two directions?

If a site allows links in to drive traffic to that site, will it allow that traffic to move to another site directly from it? This may lead a customer to be confused as to the relationship between the site or may be viewed as diluting the brand. Marketing concerns such as these are a factor in the decision by many major e-commerce sites to prohibit links out.

Another influential factor is the fairly unresolved issue of liability for links to third-party content. Where a user links from the book review site to the bookseller it may not always be clear that they are moving sites. Initially some sites tried to avoid the risks of liability through links with the use of pop-up boxes explaining that the user was leaving the site and moving to a third-party site, the content of which was not associated with the site it linked from. However, this extra click and delay has proven unattractive to users and marketers and is relatively uncommon. Although the legal aspects may not be a major factor in the decision as to linking out, a decision to prohibit this certainly removes some of the legal concerns.

The commercial importance of this highlights the need for any prohibitions to be clear in the contract.

9.8.7   *Warranty and indemnity*

The warranties are as always largely a question of circumstance and what is agreed commercially. It is likely that as a minimum there should be a mutual IP warranty with indemnity. There ought also to be a warranty of the legality of the content of the website to which the link takes the customer. Whether this needs to be mutual is obviously dependent on whether the links flow in one or two directions. This particular warranty should extend to relevant codes and regulations to encompass the BCASP code and the like. If a link transcends countries of site ownership then there may also be issues around the extent of this warranty and what countries it should cover.

9.8.8   Competitors

If a link to a site takes a customer from company A to company B then A may well want to make sure that the page on B's site does not include advertising for its arch competitor C. Even worse might be linking from A to B to find that the user arrives at the site and is immediately faced with a link to arch rival C!

It may be necessary to take specific competition advice where it is intended to include prohibitions or exclusions in a linking agreement. However, it is important to consider whether there may be any room for prohibiting such practices within the terms of the agreement. It could also be necessary to consider a most favoured nation clause as a form of protection where it is not possible to have a straight prohibition of a particular activity.

9.8.9   Customer data collection and customer ownership

If it is not the most contentious issue in e-commerce then it is certainly one of them: who owns the customer? The fact that the user in a linking arrangement moves between sites in at least one direction creates questions as to who 'owns the user' – is it the original site the user linked from, the site they link to, or both? It is generally accepted that both sites may have 'rights' to the customer and what these are will depend on what data is collected from the customer on that site. Data collected will generally be owned by the recipient site (i.e. the site where the customer provided his/her data) and be provided to the site from which the user linked only to the extent necessary to monitor the financial relationship between the sites. Unless the data has been collected by one site on behalf of the other, then the data will often (and should, in light of data protection law restrictions) be provided on a generic or neutered basis and will not contain any personal information relating to the customer.

If either site requires the other to provide it with more information then it is essential that the contract makes this clear and contains an obligation to comply with the data protection legislation in force at the time. Also it is wise to include a clear list of what that data is and, if relevant, confidentiality provisions and details of the uses or restrictions which attach to it.

9.8.10 *Financial model*

The financial models which accompany the link have developed almost as quickly as the technology behind it. The trend for links to e-commerce sites has gradually moved from a pay per click to payment of a commission or bounty where a customer registers or purchases on a site having accessed the site by way of the link. It is obviously essential that the payment model and how it is to work are clear in the contract. In particular, if the model is a commission one then it is important to consider exactly what the commission is payable on and what action the user must take before they become worthy of a bounty – i.e. is it only on sales by new customers and is it net of the delivery charge and VAT? If the user has to register and purchase do they still attract a bounty even if they are already a customer? If they do then will a bounty be payable for each link they come to the site through? As links often take customers to a special promotion it is more than possible that a customer will follow several promotional links to a site.

Where the link is to another form of site which is traffic dependent, then the financial model is likely to be based on a reward to the traffic provider being related to or a proportion of advertising revenues. Where this is the case it is important to ensure that the definition of advertising revenues is correct in relation to the commercial reality of how this is dealt with on the site.

As the financial models for this type of relationship are constantly evolving it is important not only to rely on past experience but to obtain a full commercial understanding. Only once this has been garnered will it be possible to describe the terms of the finances and to make the appropriate definitions.

9.8.11   Payment terms

The agreement should state when and how payment is to be made and also how much interest is due on late payments. Obviously the payment will be dependent on the reporting of the number of users who have followed the link or who have completed the necessary prerequisites to qualify.

9.8.12   Monitoring and measuring

The measure of whether a user attracts a bounty is largely dependent on the financial model. However, it is wise to state not only what this measure is but also how that will then be monitored, what technology will be used to monitor a customer to whom a bounty attaches and how this will work. If the customers who link through to the site need to be measured then this may require different technology from the case where it is only customers who register or buy. A further point to consider is whether it will be dependent on any technology such as cookies which the user can remove.

Once agreement has been reached on the form of monitoring it is then necessary to specify how often this will be reported and how that reporting will tie into the payment process. Will that reporting be something which can be challenged by the other party to the agreement or is it accepted as being accurate? Depending on the size of the potential relationship and the amounts of money involved it may also be necessary to consider whether there is a need to audit the reporting and monitoring systems or whether it would at least be wise to have a right to do this.

9.8.13   Right to cut links

It is essential to have a right to cut a link to or from your site if the link is to a site which appears to have become illegal due to its actions or its content. The grounds on which you may wish to cut the link are often wider than this to the extent that the parties may want a right to cut the link without reason. The grounds which are acceptable and any consequences of this should be set out in the agreement.

As linking has developed it has become more common to find it as part of a separate agreement which covers not only linking but content. Other forms of agreement which are essentially linking agreements have also become common, in particular affiliate or partnership agreements.

9.8.14　Term and termination

The link being cut may be a ground for termination, but depending on the terms and the reason that the link was cut it may simply mean that some work needs to be done on the link or the site before the link is reconnected.

The agreement should set out not only the terms and grounds for termination, but also post-termination provisions dealing with any reporting and financial commitments and how these are to be dealt with and within what timescales post-termination.

9.8.15　Affiliate/partnership/loyalty agreements

Affiliate agreements may involve a relationship which is largely linking but is part of a larger scheme of linking to or from a particular site. A site may almost be an index or hub of links to other sites with other sites paying to be part of that index. Alternatively, a site may have hundreds or thousands of links driving customers to it. Where such a large financial structure is put in place the parties who provide the links may well do so on similar if not identical terms.

This type of affiliate programme creates some additional considerations such as vetting of the site which provides the link. This will allow the affiliate programme owner to avoid the embarrassment of finding that the site they are linked to/from conducts immoral or illegal activities. Almost as important as the legal consequences of this are the brand protection issues which arise where the brand is associated with another as a result of a link which has been paid for.

It is not uncommon for schemes of this nature to be similar to a franchise agreement to the extent that the owner of the programme will want all sites to which it links to sign a similar agreement with similar obligations in order to be sure that certain brand and legal compliance issues are met.

9.8.16 *Click to buy*

A more complicated model arises where the links are from a click to buy type of site. This may be a fairly simple exclusive relationship or be part of a more complicated shopping mall type solution. In the case of a shopping mall, issues of whether the content is provided by way of a link or repurposed content, who collects the customer details and who conducts the sale transaction and on what terms also arise.

CHECKLIST 9.6 LINKING

- Specification of the link itself – who is to build and maintain it? ☐

- Look and feel of the link on the third-party site. ☐

- TM licence if used? ☐

- Location of the link on the third-party site. ☐

- Home page or deep links or both? ☐

- One-way or two-way? ☐

- Legality of each site and mutual warranties. ☐

- Warranty and indmenity – IP and legality. ☐

- Competitors? ☐

- Data collection and provision of data to each other? ☐

- Financial model and any necessary monitoring to measure this. ☐

- Right to cut links. ☐

9.9 Download contracts

9.9.1 Overview

The Internet is not only an alternative channel through which one is able to sell in the traditional method to a customer, but by the very nature of its technology it also offers novel opportunities for sales and marketing. One of the novel sales methods is electronic download. This allows the consumer to purchase a product, whether it is music, a movie or software, and to download that product directly to a PC etc. There is of course no need for delivery and the product should arrive at the customer's PC etc. almost instantly (although the larger (content/memory wise) the product obviously the longer that takes).

It is easy to imagine that through time this form of interactive relationship will develop and become commonplace for many varying goods and services, such as books, training, etc. Issues raised by the download site Napster have of course highlighted some of the problems of electronic download of music from the Internet. However, it is not intended to comment here on the legitimacy or otherwise of this form of download, but rather to look at the legal relationships which may apply to a legitimate business which includes software download sales as a service to its customers. It is likely that many of the same issues and considerations would exist for the download of other goods and services, but when dealing with downloading these it would also be necessary to consider what specific issues might arise in relation to them and to ensure that the contract is tailored to cover them.

It is possible that a site owner will own or have appropriate licences to software allowing it to provide its customers with the software directly. However, it is common for a third party which owns or has the rights to a substantial software library to provide the benefit of that software library to the site and its customers, and for this the site owner to provide customers with software, via download, as part of an outsourced arrangement. It is therefore necessary to consider the contractual implications of the outsourcing arrangement where this is the case.

Considerations would include: who contracts with the consumer? will the third party contract with the consumer direct? if they do then how is this achieved? how does the buying process work? These and the various other considerations are set out below.

9.9.2 Services

The outsourcer will typically provide services which can be split into two:

- the provision of content via which the customer will contract, either through the initial build/alteration of the site to allow for this form of transaction or a link to the outsourcer's site; and

- an ongoing supply of software, probably direct to the consumer.

9.9.3 Site structure, amendment and linking

The first decision which needs to be made is how the software is to be sold and by whom. Having decided this it is then necessary to decide whether the sale will be through the site or by way of a link to a part of the outsourcer's site. As providers of this type of outsourced service tend to have a structure for the sales of the software provided by them, this will generally come from their established sale structure.

The contract should set out how the technical structure which supports the sale of the software, to be delivered electronically, will work. This will include not only whether the third party or the site owner contracts with the consumer, but the detail of how this happens and whether this is done by a link, or whether the third party provides content to the site owner. If the website structure is to be amended or any links etc. are to be built then it is necessary to consider what these will be, who is responsible for the work on them and what the timescales for putting them in place are to be. Any amendments by the outsourcer or links will raise issues of liability.

Any amendment to the structure will have to be tested when it is built and although there may not need to be formal acceptance testing by the site owner, there will need to be adequate checks to ensure not only that the software download works in itself, but also that it does not in any way affect the working of the remainder of the site before it is launched.

The infrastructure of this needs to be maintained on an ongoing basis and it is important that this maintenance is also provided for. There may also be a need to ensure that where any problems of a serious nature occur, e.g. discovering that software is being sold illegally, there is the possibility of closing down the part of the site or the link which allows for the electronic download.

It is possible that where a link is provided to the outsourcer's site this will be to the same content as other site owners use. It is therefore necessary to consider whether this content is unique, tailored to the site owner or generic content which customers from many sites see. Naturally, the site owner will probably want to ensure the framing and 'get up' of the relevant section of the outsourcer's site is suitably tailored to provide the customer with a seamless and appropriately branded experience (and, of course, this should be addressed in the contract).

At this point it is also worth considering the possibility of service levels. As a third party is providing a service to customers on behalf of the site it may be natural to expect a service level. This would obviously be dependent on any restrictions or delays caused by a site itself. However, the site owner will need to have reassurance that the outsourcer will meet a reasonable uptime and transactional capacity and may also look for service levels relating to the ease of download and time that this takes. If service levels are to be included then provisions for reporting and monitoring and what the consequence of these not being met will be also need to be incorporated into the agreement. Credits may not be enough given the potential damage to the site owner's brand and possible loss of customers. Other remedies, the ability to switch providers and the provision of handover assistance in such a case should all be considered for the contract.

If the site is to include content provided by the outsourcer or a link to the outsourcer's site then it will be necessary to consider whether there is any link to third-party sites from this. It may well be that there are other site owners who are provided with the same service and the site owner will generally not be happy to see its customers being provided with links to its competitors. A similar principle applies to advertising for third parties within the outsourcer's content or site. A blanket prohibition on advertising on the content which the site owner's customers see as a result of their purchasing software may also be included.

If the software is sold direct by the outsourcer then it is important to have a commitment that the sale will comply with the laws of the country in which the software is sold. Depending on the site owner they may also want to have some participation in signing off the content their customer will see or perhaps, as mentioned above, to have co-branding of the content.

9.9.4 Software itself

As the third party is selling software through the site it is important for the site owner to have reassurance, probably in the form of warranties and indemnities, that the site is legal and that the outsourcer has all of the necessary rights to advertise, sell and license the software in the way he proposes. This must cover not only the country of origin of the software supplier but also the rights to do this in the countries in which the consumers are able to purchase the software. Many providers of software are US based and where the software is to be sold in Europe it is particularly important to ensure that the provider has the rights to sell/license the software in these particular countries.

It is also worth considering asking for a warranty/indemnity from the outsourcer confirming that the software is not in breach of any third party's IP in the countries in which it is to be sold and is otherwise not illegal in those countries. However, as many of the providers of this type of service are reliant on a number of third parties' catalogues of software and those various third parties' commitments and confirmations, the outsourcer may not be willing to provide this strength of commitment to the site owner and this in turn may create a risk to the site owner.

9.9.5   *Taxation*

The issue of taxation may arise where the outsourcer is not based in the EU. Is the outsourcer liable to pay VAT or equivalent sales tax if the server from which he sells is not based in the UK or even the EU? This is a hotly debated topic and one which has for some time been discussed by the EU and the OECD. It is wise to add a provision to the contract to make clear that any liability or potential liability for this is to be borne by the outsourcer and to ensure that the payment structure will not be affected by any such liability.

9.9.6   *Customer data collection and data transfer*

If the customer is to transact direct with the outsourcer then the outsourcer may well collect data from that customer and it is necessary to consider issues of customer ownership and potential data sharing. This will involve not only the relationship between the site owner and the outsourcer but also the outsourcer and the third parties who have provided software. Not only is it appropriate to set out what data should be collected on behalf of the site owner (if any), that the data should be legally collected and any proposed restrictions on its use, but also it is important to consider whether data will be passed outside of the EU. If it is then it may be necessary to incorporate safe harbour wording and this may need to be on the basis of the new standard contract terms for this.

Further, do not assume consents obtained when the data is captured (by the outsourcer) will extend to the data being passed back to and used by the site owner. In addition to covering this in the contract with the outsourcer, appropriate notices and privacy policy should be agreed and used.

9.9.7 Distance selling and returns

Where software is obtained via download and is not provided on a disk format then issues arise as to the customer's rights as consumers purchasing at a distance and any ability to change their mind or return the software if it is faulty or otherwise unsatisfactory. It is necessary to give due consideration to the Distance Selling Regulations which apply to consumer transactions, in particular their provisions for software.

It is also wise to consider the risk of software piracy where a customer is able to download the software, possibly use, save or copy it, and then require a refund. The relationship has a potential risk and this is one which may be countered to some extent by use of a digital seal or other digital rights management system. It is important to raise this with the outsourcer and to try to find a satisfactory solution within the realms of the legal requirements.

9.9.8 After-sales

If the customer is purchasing from the outsourcer direct then does the outsourcer provide customer after-care, a helpline and the like, and if it does then where does the customer obtain these details? If the outsourcer does not provide them then who will? If the site owner itself is to provide them then where does it obtain the information it needs to do so? Also, with either of these relationships, what hours are any helplines to be open? This is of particular relevance where the outsourcer is based outside of the UK where time differences can apply.

A general point may be made here. Consider carefully whether you want a third party handling your customer enquiries and complaints and if so impose tight performance criteria in the contract with that party. Tremendous damage to a brand can result from poor handling of these aspects.

If an e-mail after-care system is provided then it is also worth considering the need for service levels relating to response times. Also, if the outsourcer is to provide the after-sales service it will be wise for the site owner to require some form of reporting and to consider what this should entail. Again, without this the site owner may have no clarity of the level of customer satisfaction relating to these aspects.

9.9.9   Exclusivity

The outsourcer may simply provide access to generic content, but on the other hand it may provide tailored or bespoke content. It is important to consider whether this or the relationship in general is subject to any exclusivity in either direction. Can the site owner provide ESD (electronic software delivery) from its site via a number of outsourcers, and if not then is there an exclusivity commitment from the outsourcer? All of this should be viewed within the restrictions which may exist under relevant competition legislation.

9.9.10   Warranty and indemnity

As has already been mentioned, the site owner may be wise to ask for various warranties. In particular, he may wish to have a warranty that the content provided by the outsourcer is legal, that any link or structure for sales provided by that party will not affect the working of the site detrimentally and that neither of these are in breach of a third party's IP. The site owner should also seek this form of confirmation of the outsourcer's rights to sell/license the software, that the software is not in breach of third-party IP rights and that the process of sale is legal.

9.9.11   Payment

The commercial relationship between the site owner and the outsourcer is obviously central to the relationship and the contract. If the outsourcer sells direct, then on what basis is the site owner recompensed for passing the customer to him? If this is a commission, is it on all sales to that customer or only on sales where the customer accesses the outsourcer through the original site? How are these sales to be monitored and is there a method of this being audited by the site owner? If the sale is a commission then is this on a net sale and if it is then what charges (such as sales tax) are to be deducted? It is also important to clarify what is to happen where software is returned or a fraudulent transaction occurs on the site.

Also, how often is the commission accounting payment made and on what terms?

9.9.12   Terms of sale and software licences

Having established that the third party has the rights to sell the software one must also ensure that the way it is sold is legal. The process of sale involves two legal relationships with the consumer: first the actual terms of sale and secondly the software licence. Whether the sale is undertaken by an outsourcer or the site owner, the customer contract of sale and software licence need to be considered.

It is of course necessary to ensure that the provisions of all local consumer legislation are complied with, but in particular it is worth highlighting the Distance Selling Regulations which require that the consumer is made aware of who they are dealing with and of certain rights such as any right to return, prior to their transaction taking place. If there could be any confusion in the structure of the sale then it is particularly important to make clear who the vendor is. The circumstances in which a return may be made and how this is to be dealt with should also be made clear to the consumer. The consumer contract should also not exclude any of the consumer's statutory rights. It may also be worth considering how these are to be brought to the customer's attention, particularly where these are different from the other terms of sale used on the site.

The second element of the sale is the software licence and ideally this should made available to the consumer in advance of the software being provided. It may well be that the sale process will include a 'click wrap' rather than a 'shrink wrap' licence where the consumer clicks to accept the terms of the licence.

CHECKLIST 9.7 DOWNLOAD

- What is being downloaded and how does the process for this work? ☐

- Who has the right to license the software and how will this work – i.e. who contracts with the consumer? ☐

- Who provides customer-facing content and how is this approved or agreed with any third-party provider? ☐

- How will the site structure or any links work and who will own/take responsibility for it? If there is any amendment to the structure who does it, how is it maintained and are there any SLAs? ☐

- Consumer rights in software, e.g. quality, distance selling, etc. – who has responsibility? ☐

- Where is the provider located – tax issues? ☐

- Customer data collection and ownership. ☐

- Payment structure. ☐

9.10 Interactive TV contracts

9.10.1 Overview

The future of the Internet has been seen by many for some time to be likely to follow a path of convergence. However, for convergence to be achieved the technologies which will provide access to the converged medium need to develop, and the players in these markets need to consider a multi-channel policy. One of the principal technologies where there will be convergence is TV. Although PC penetration is high in the UK it is not at the same level of penetration as TVs. Almost every home in the country has at least one TV and this high level of access is one of the many reasons that this may be viewed by retailers as an attractive medium though which to conduct sales. Not only is the penetration high, but the medium of TV lends itself very well to marketing activities such as product placement and links from those programmes. It is not difficult to imagine a high level of interactivity between customer, broadcast programmes and sales. Certainly there is the possibility of entertainment TV, such as gaming, direct selling through a TV/virtual shop and direct marketing where there is a direct response by the customer to advertising.

Over the last couple of years it has become apparent that many parents are concerned about Internet security and the risks to which they may be exposing their children. These same parents may well be more comfortable with the older and more familiar medium of TV, with its watershed programming. Some of the concerns raised by the Internet may seem to be alleviated by traditional TV and by the existence of private networks used by many iTV providers. The security of a private network may be one of the attractions of access through TV rather than PC.

9.10.2 *Walled garden*

Many iTV providers have created private networks or 'walled gardens' in which the stores on their platform can be accessed. These private networks stand alone and may not be accessed from the Internet, or if they are then this will be through a link out of the private network. This may remove many consumer concerns relating to the perceived dangers of the Web and may also make this medium appear more secure from a transactional point of view, as well as safe for users and in particular their children who may be barred from or unable to step outside the walled garden. However, if the user steps outside of the walled garden environment, then the World Wide Web accessed through the TV will be just the same as that accessed through the PC.

The fact that the providers have in some cases selected a walled garden environment has other consequences. A series of such secure networks may mean that retailers who want to maximise their exposure via this medium are forced to enter into agreements with several service providers. If the technology in each is different there are also cost implications to this situation, as sites are amended to be used on each or several of these.

At least one company has launched a product which delivers an aggregation of content to a number of platforms as a response to this and there may also be a need to consider the use of these services and an agreement for this type of service where multiple platforms are used.

9.10.3   Specification

As always with a contract for a site it is necessary to be clear as to what is being paid for and what technology is being provided by each party. It is therefore important to have a clear service description including the technology and requirements of each party in the form of the specification. The pitch provided by the service provider may well be a good starting point in drafting this.

Any restrictions on content, such as a restriction on the sale of advertising by the site owner, should also be included in this.

9.10.4   Repurposing of an existing site/content

Where a site owner wishes to sell through an interactive portal then there is a need to 'repurpose' or modify its existing content to make it suitable for access through multimedia or TV, or to create entirely new content for that site. In the case of TV the user who accesses this is going to be in a very different position from the user of a website. They will be not be sitting close to the TV in the way they would be for a PC. The screen is likely to be larger (although this is not guaranteed) and TVs offer a greater number of pixels and quality of picture. Bearing in mind these and many other factors, the content needs to look good in this particular medium and must be clear from a greater distance than a traditional website. It is also possible that the service provider will be able to offer varying types of interactivity which need to be considered in the content design.

If existing content is used then this may prove difficult and it is necessary to consider the nature of the content which will be accessed and whether this will be unique and developed for this purpose or a modification of existing content. If the latter is to happen, then consider how the repurposing of the existing content is done. This will depend in large part on which of the providers is being used, but will also depend to an extent upon whether the content is going to be accessed through TV and other media or simply through TV. If new content is to be developed then what this looks like may be dependent on the service provider's platform.

If there is to be repurposing, this may be done by the site owner or host, depending on the structure of the business. If the site host is undertaking this work then it is necessary to ensure that warranties as to the quality and look and feel of the repurposed content are obtained, as well as ensuring that the content will not be edited. If the host is not undertaking this but supplying a software tool for the site owner to undertake this work themselves then it is necessary for there to be a software licence for this tool.

All of this is relevant not only to the initial content provided but on an ongoing basis to amendments or additions to the content. This content maintenance should be covered not only by the same provisions but requires additional provisions to clarify when and how this is to be done and to make clear what if any restrictions on changes exist. If there is a problem with content, e.g. illegality, how this is to be resolved and how quickly should also be addressed.

9.10.5 Licences

The licence from the service provider must cover the use which the software tool provided is being put to, and it is likely that the host will either want to have confirmation of its destruction at the end of any agreement or its return. This licence may also restrict any other use of the software tool and limit copies, as this is a very valuable commodity for the service provider. If a third party is being used to manage or provide the content then it may be necessary for the grant of licence to extend to them also.

The site owner will normally be required to provide the service provider with a standard licence to allow for the content's use, display, etc. by it.

9.10.6 Customer experience

It is essential to understand whether any customer sale transaction will be undertaken by the service provider on behalf of the site or whether this is handled by the site itself. If the service provider is responsible for the customer transaction in terms of authentication and authorisation (i.e. ensuring that the customer is who they say they are and has the appropriate funds to pay) then appropriate obligations must be placed upon them. A consideration must also be given to how fraud is to be dealt with and who will bear any associated risk.

Customer relationships and management may also vary between providers of iTV services and it is essential to establish how the customer relationship will be managed. If the customer is in contact only with the service provider and not the site owner then it is necessary to consider what obligations will lie with that service provider. Will they collect customer data only on their own behalf or on behalf of both parties? Also in such a relationship it will be necessary to have clear reporting requirements and warranties. These are particularly important if the service provider is also responsible for the sales transaction.

9.10.7 Customer data collection

There are two elements to customer data collection which must be borne in mind. Data may be collected in any registration process and also in the transaction (whether this is a sale or part of a promotion or competition), as well as through any marketing initiative. How this data is captured and what the customer is to be told needs to be clarified at this stage in order that the service provider involvement, if any, can be documented. If all data is collected by the service provider then is it correctly collected for use by the site owner or is its use restricted to the service provider?

9.10.8 Fulfilment, delivery and after-sales

Any transactions which take place through the iTV service will need to have these and it is essential to ensure that the site on the iTV platform has the ability to communicate with these back-office systems or that there is a process for this to be conducted efficiently in place. Customer communication with these services will need to be captured and interfaced with the appropriate systems and the responsibility for this should be clarified. A process for customer returns through the iTV service needs to be put in place and this may involve the service provider if they have been responsible for the transaction as well as the site owner.

9.10.9 Framing of the site

It is possible and likely that the iTV site will be framed with a frame from the service provider. If this is the case then there may need to

---

be provisions to ensure that this will not affect the look and feel of the site. Also it may be wise to have an opportunity to see the frame and to agree what will be included in it. If it is to include adverts then it is essential to make sure that these are appropriately restricted.

9.10.10 Linking

It may be possible that there will be links to a shop from other parts of the iTV platform or even from broadcasts. In the main these are likely to be from menus but it is also important to understand where else links may come from if they are used at all.

9.10.11 Menu placement

iTV platforms generally provide site indexes or menus which give their customers information on the sites available. These may list the sites by name or by product sold. It is important to consider if there are any requirements as to which menus the site is included in and where it is placed or how it is described, e.g. by the use of a logo.

There may also be space on such a page for the advertising of particular promotions and any rights to be included in this advertising should be set out.

9.10.12 Legal compliance

There is likely to be a warranty in the contract requiring that the site content is legal and possibly offering some form of indemnity to the host if the content breaches any law or relevant code. The various

ITC Codes (e.g. programme sponsorship, advertising, programme content and so on) may well apply to sales made through interactive TV. This means that a site which sells through this method will have to comply with the codes. It is important to check not only the appropriate terms of the codes but also to remember that the media is quite different and something which may be clear on a PC where one sits immediately in front of the screen may not be clear from the other side of a room where one shops via a remote control.

It would be advisable for one's legal adviser to review the TV site fairly early in its production stage to check how this will appear on a TV.

There is still some confusion in relation to the boundaries of the ITC's remit. For example, the ITC Codes will not apply to the part of an interactive TV experience where the customer goes online. After some confusion over the appropriate regulator, the ASA stepped forward to claim a remit over the Internet. However, this has now changed with the clarification that the ASA's role does not include the regulation of Internet content per se, rather it regulates pure advertising on sites, e.g. banners. This in turn has confirmed that general consumer and trading laws apply as always to product descriptions, price indications and so on and will continue to fall under the remit of Trading Standards and the OFT. It is understood that Trading Standards are now working towards a team with skills allowing them to be Internet 'experts'.

The DTI has issued its White Paper, *A New Future for Communications*, with proposals for a single regulator (OFCOM) to regulate all interactive services, combining the roles of the existing regulators. Various bodies have responded (including the ASA) and progress needs to be followed by anyone interested in or advising on these services. In the meantime, from the point of view of interactive or Internet TV, it is important to remember who the existing regulators are and what content they cover and to be clear on what regulations need to be complied with.

The rough and ready position for the moment is still that the ITC is for 'broadcast' and the ASA for 'non-broadcast' advertising and commercial promotions. Where interactive activity falls currently is very much something to be grappled with depending on your particular circumstances and how you fit into the current definitions/interpretation.

In a recent separate survey, the Chamber of Commerce has concluded that only 5 per cent of websites are compliant with the Distance Selling Regulations. iTV like any other means of distance selling is regulated by this and the site content must include the necessary information and otherwise comply. The customer, of course, has the same rights as any other distance purchaser. Where relevant, both parties need to take specialist advice and comply accordingly.

9.10.13 *Warranty and indemnity*

In terms of content legality it is necessary to ensure that this covers not only all laws but also codes of conduct. The service provider will also expect the site owner to provide fairly expansive IP warranties of the content provided.

9.10.14 Testing and acceptance

Before the site goes live and where any major changes are made to either its architecture or content there should be an opportunity for testing. How this is to be undertaken should be clear.

9.10.15 Payment

The customer will pay the service provider for use of its service. This may be by way of a percentage of transactions or a flat 'rental' for the site. The structure for calculation of the payment and how and when this is to be paid should be set out in the agreement.

What the payment is for should be clearly set out and if this is to include additional services, such as inclusion in any advertising campaigns for the platform, then this must be stated.

9.10.16 Term and termination

As always there should be a term for the agreement and provisions for termination. There may also be a process for renewal of the agreement, or even for developing the relationship between the parties as the service expands and technology develops. This may also deal with suspension of the services by either party and when this amounts to termination.

No sample contract has been provided as these tend to be very specific to the service provider.

CHECKLIST 9.8 INTERACTIVE TV

- Is it a walled garden or not? ☐
- Specification of what is being purchased and the technology requirements. ☐
- Will existing content be repurposed and if it is does it have to be unique? ☐
- How will it be amended and upgraded? ☐
- Software licence for repurposing tool if appropriate. ☐
- Who does customer deal with and provisions regarding customer experience? ☐
- Service levels and credits if appropriate? ☐
- Customer ownership and data collection and ownership. ☐
- Customer consumer relationship – delivery etc. ☐
- Framing of the site. ☐
- Linking. ☐
- Legal compliance of the site content, terms and conditions etc. – may be different from the Internet. ☐
- Testing and acceptance – and failure to achieve this. ☐
- Payment. ☐

APPENDIX 1

Sample terms

A1.1 Freeserve.com – Acceptable Use Policy

IMPORTANT NOTICE: This policy (the "Acceptable Use Policy" or "this Policy") sets out the terms between you and us under which we will provide you with access to the information and services we offer from time to time via the Freeserve website located at www.freeserve.com (the "Freeserve Service"). It is, therefore, very much in your interests to read them carefully.

If there is anything in this Policy that you do not understand then please contact our Customer Care Department as soon as possible by calling 0870 872 0099 (the "Customer Number"). Please note that calls to the Customer Number are charged at national rate and may be monitored for training, security and quality assurance purposes. If you do not understand any of the terminology used in this Policy then please refer to our internet glossary at **www.freeserve.com/help.jargon.htm**.

Unless otherwise stated, the Freeserve Service is provided to you by Freeserve.com plc, a company registered in England and Wales (company number 3014367) whose registered office is located at Maylands Avenue, Hemel Hempstead, HP2 7TG ("Freeserve"). References to Freeserve in this Policy are to "we", "our" and "us".

1   Your use of the Freeserve Service

1.1   The Freeserve Service is intended to appeal to a wide range of audiences and as such not all of the Freeserve Service is suitable for use by children. Parents and guardians are reminded of the importance of supervising young children's use of the Freeserve Service. Parents or guardians of children shall be responsible for the actions of any children using the Freeserve Service.

1.2 You may use the Freeserve Service only for lawful purposes. You may not use, and shall take all reasonable steps to ensure that no other person uses, the Freeserve Service:

1.2.1 in a way that does not comply with the terms of any laws applicable to you or that is in any way unlawful or fraudulent or has any unlawful or fraudulent purpose or effect;

1.2.2 to send, knowingly receive, upload, download, use or re-use any material which is abusive, indecent, defamatory, obscene or menacing, or in breach of any copyright, confidence, privacy or any other rights;

1.2.3 to spam or send or procure the sending of any unsolicited advertising or promotional material;

1.2.4 to cause annoyance, inconvenience or needless anxiety;

1.2.5 to send or upload any material that contains viruses, trojan horses, worms, time bombs or any other harmful programs.

1.3 If you do not follow the guidelines set out under paragraph 1, you agree to indemnify us against all claims, demands, actions, costs, expenses (including but not limited to reasonable legal costs and disbursements), losses and damages arising from or incurred as a result of your actions.

2   Intellectual property rights

2.1 You agree that the material and content contained in, or provided by Freeserve as part of, the Freeserve Service is for your use only and may not be distributed to anyone and you are prohibited from using such content commercially without our permission.

2.2 Your use of the Freeserve Service carries with it no rights in relation to copyright, trademarks or other intellectual property rights that belong to us or third parties that have granted us licences to use their intellectual property. The Freeserve.com logo and Freeserve.com name are trademarks of Freeserve.com plc.

2.3 You may not display the contents of the Freeserve Service or any part of them in a frame surrounded by other material not originated by us.

3   Limitations on the Freeserve Service

3.1 You should note that various elements of the Freeserve Service are not provided by us but instead by other companies. We are therefore unable to guarantee that such products and services or any websites accessible via the Freeserve Service are virus or error free. You should check all emails, attachments and files before downloading them.

3.2 Your dealings with, and interest in, promotions, services, or merchants found via the Freeserve Service are solely between you and the person with whom you are dealing unless we expressly state otherwise.

3.3 We, or merchants and content providers found via the Freeserve Service, may provide links to other web sites or resources. We are unable to accept responsibility for these web sites or resources; neither have we endorsed their content, products or services merely because they are accessible via the Freeserve Service.

3.4 We make all reasonable efforts to ensure that all information provided by us in connection with the Freeserve Service is accurate at the time of its inclusion, however, there may be errors, inaccuracies or omissions in respect of which we exclude all liability. We make no representations or warranties about the information included on our web pages (including links to third parties' web pages). You shall be solely responsible for any decision based on the information contained on such web pages.

3.5 Information provided by Freeserve does not constitute legal or professional advice and should not be relied upon without taking independent advice.

3.6 We take reasonable steps to safeguard the security of any information you input or send to us in connection with the Freeserve Service by using secure services and encryption technology where we deem appropriate, however, we accept no responsibility for any damages that you may suffer as a result of the loss of confidentiality of such information.

3.7 You acknowledge that licensed telephone operators provide the telephone networks which are utilised by us and therefore we cannot guarantee that the Freeserve Service will be uninterrupted or error free. Similarly, we cannot guarantee that the transmission of information over the Internet will be secure or that you will be able to access the Internet at all times or at the speeds that we have indicated are available.

3.8 If you intend to use the Freeserve Service for business or commercial purposes, you agree that, unless we specifically state otherwise, we shall provide the Freeserve Service to you without any conditions, warranties or guarantees whether express or implied, including but not limited to any implied warranties or conditions as to satisfactory quality or fitness for a particular purpose, which are expressly excluded, to the extent permitted by law.

4   Our liability to you

4.1 We do not limit our liability if you die or are injured as a result of our negligence or you suffer loss as a consequence of any fraud by us.

4.2 We shall not be liable to you in contract, tort (including negligence) or otherwise for:

4.2.1 any damage or loss arising from the consequences of viruses received by you via the Freeserve Service or of our failure to provide the Freeserve Service in accordance with this Policy; or

4.2.2 any economic losses (including loss of business, contracts, profits, revenues, capital or anticipated savings), any indirect, special or consequential loss, loss of data, goodwill or reputation or for any wasted expense including but not limited to losses caused by viruses.

4.3 Except as set out in paragraph 4.1 any liability we may have to you whether in contract, tort (including negligence) or otherwise for any loss or damage suffered by you in relation to the Freeserve Service is limited to £500 in any 12 month period.

4.4 We are not liable for any failure to perform our obligations if we are prevented from doing so by an event beyond our reasonable control (which may include, without limitation, strikes, labour disputes; acts of God; war; riot; civil action; malicious acts or damage; compliance with any law, governmental or regulatory order, rule, regulation or direction; any act or omission of any government or other competent authority; accident; equipment or services failure, including the unavailability of third party telecommunications services, lines or other equipment; fire; flood or storm).

4.5 Each provision of this section 4 operates separately. If any part is held by a court to be unreasonable or inapplicable then the other parts shall still apply.

5   Suspension and termination of the Freeserve Service

5.1 We may suspend or terminate the Freeserve Service without giving notice to you.

6   Changes to the Freeserve Service

We may alter and/or amend the Freeserve Service at any time without giving notice to you.

7   Other things you need to know

7.1 We will only use any personal data you provide in accordance with our Privacy Policy located at **www.freeserve.com/privacy**.

7.2 If any part of this Policy is found to be illegal or unenforceable, this will not affect the validity and enforceability of the remainder of the Policy.

7.3 The provision of the Freeserve Service and the application of this Policy are governed by English law and the parties hereby agree to submit to the exclusive jurisdiction of the English Courts in respect of any dispute or matter arising out of or in connection with this Policy.

A1.2   Freeserve.com – Data Collection Notice

Personal Information

Please complete the following information:

First Name [_____]   Last Name [_____]

House No./Name [_____]   Street [_____]

Town [_____]   Post Code [_____]

Gender   ○ Male ○ Female

Date of Birth (e.g. 12/12/1968) [___|___|___] (Enter complete 4 digit year)

Daytime Telephone [_____]

Evening Telephone [_____]

How we use your data (Data Protection)

Freeserve.com plc ("Freeserve") is an online service provider. As part of the Freeserve service, you will have access to information, online services and Internet access. Freeserve and other companies who provide goods and services as part of the Freeserve service ("Commercial Partners") will hold and process your personal information for the purposes of administration, satisfying orders, information mailings, running competitions, business development, customer service, trend and profile analysis and data matching.

Some of our Commercial Partners are based outside the European Economic Area (where the law may not protect your details to the same extent). You may from time to time decide to use some of their products and services and your personal details will therefore be passed to them.

Apart from the uses outlined above, we may also wish to use your details for other purposes such as contacting you for marketing purposes and to inform you of special offers. Please tick the appropriate box if you **do not want** the parties listed below to make use of your details in this way:

☐ Freeserve.com plc

☐ Wanadoo and other members of the France Telecom Group

☐ Commercial Partners and selected third parties

Freeserve may wish to share your personal information with Commercial Partners and selected third parties who are resident outside the EEA for promotional purposes.

☐ Please tick the box if **you do consent** to us sharing your information in this way.

Your internet use

How many people use this computer? [Select] (optional)

What do you intend to use Freeserve for? ☐ Personal use ☐ Work (optional)

How did you hear about Freeserve? [Select] (optional)

Current internet connection: [Select] (optional)

A1.3   Freeserve.com – Privacy Policy

The following provides detail about our Privacy Policy. Freeserve.com Plc ("Freeserve.com"), treats your privacy seriously. In general, we use the personal information that we collect from you to identify personal preferences and match your needs with relevant products, and process any orders that you may make through our web site.

NOTICE: This policy only applies to web sites hosted at and comprising part of the Freeserve.com service and not to the companies, individuals, organisations or other websites to which there are links.

1.   **Consent**

Your use of this web site signifies your consent to us collecting and using personal information about you as specified below in accordance with this Policy. Should we choose to change our Policy for any reason, the changes will be posted here, so that you are always kept informed of how we collect and use your personal information, and when we may disclose it. If you are a Freeserve.com member this policy will be applied subject to any particular limitations or choices you made as part of the membership application procedure.

2.   **How Do We Collect Information About You and How Is It Used?**

2.1   You may provide personal information when communicating with us.

2.2   You may order a product or a service and give your name, e-mail address, delivery address, credit or debit card number and expiry date so that the order can be processed and your products (or services where appropriate) delivered to you. Sometimes you may be asked for your telephone number.

2.3   If you enter a competition or promotion we will ask for your name, address and e-mail address.

2.4   We will collect information about your tastes and preferences both when you tell us what these are and by analysis of customer traffic, including by using cookies (see below).

2.5   It may be that some of the personal information you give us (for instance about your lifestyle or health) is sensitive personal data within the meaning of the Data Protection Act 1998. Any such information ("sensitive information") will only be disclosed with your express consent.

2.6   It may be that you provide to us details of credit or debit cards or bank accounts in order to make payments to us. Any such information ("confidential financial information") will be dealt with as described below.

2.7   We may use personal information collected about you to personalise your visits to our web site and recommend goods or services to you. We also use the information to help us develop the design and layout of our web site to ensure that our sites are as useful and enjoyable as possible.

2.8   We may use personal information collected about you to let you know about functionality changes to our web site or changes to our terms and conditions of use.

2.9 Sometimes (and only in accordance with any preferences selected by you) we or our affiliated companies might use the personal information collected about you to let you know about new goods, services or offers that you might find interesting.

3.   Traffic Data

3.1 We may provide aggregate statistics about our sales, customers, traffic patterns and other site information to third parties, but these statistics will not include any information that could personally identify you.

4.   Other Disclosures

4.1 Freeserve.com reserves the right to access and disclose individually identifiable information to comply with applicable laws and lawful government requests, to operate its systems properly or to protect itself or its users.

5.   How Do We Protect Your Information?

5.1 When you review your account information or order products, Freeserve.com offers the use of a secure server. The secure server software encrypts the information that you input before it is transmitted to us. In addition, we have strict security procedures covering the storage and disclosure of your information in order to prevent unauthorised access and to comply with the Data Protection Act 1998. This means that sometimes we may ask you for proof of identity before disclosing any personal information to you.

6.   Cookies

6.1 A cookie is a piece of information that is stored on your computer's hard drive by your web browser. On revisiting this site our computer server will recognise the cookie, giving us information about your last visit. Most browsers accept cookies automatically, but usually you can alter the settings of your browser to prevent automatic acceptance. If you choose not to receive cookies, you may still use most of the features of our web site, including purchasing items.

Updated – September 2000

A1.4   Freeserve.com – Registration Terms (October 2002)

Please read the following information. To proceed, click 'Accept' at the bottom of this page to indicate your acceptance of the Terms of Use.

Please click on any of the following sections to take you directly to your area of interest

BECOMING A FREESERVE MEMBER
WHAT YOU WILL GET AS A FREESERVE MEMBER
OR ANYTIME SUBSCRIBER
CHARGES FOR NO TIES OR ANYTIME
YOUR USE OF THE SERVICES
LIMITATIONS ON THE SERVICES
SUSPENSION AND TERMINATION OF THE SERVICES
OUR RIGHTS AND OBLIGATIONS
TERMS AND TERMINATION OF THIS AGREEMENT
OUR LIABILITY TO YOU
COMPLAINTS PROCEDURE
GIVING NOTICE
CHANGES TO THE SERVICES OR THE TERMS OF USE

OTHER THINGS YOU NEED TO KNOW

TERMS OF USE

IMPORTANT NOTICE: These terms and conditions (the "Terms of Use" or this "Agreement") set out the agreement between you and us under which we will provide you with access to the Internet using our No Ties or AnyTime services and related services and applications, for example, email facilities and personal web space. It is, therefore, very much in your interests to read them carefully.

If there is anything in the Terms of Use that you do not understand then please contact our Customer Care Department as soon as possible by calling 0870 872 0099 (the "Customer Number"). Please note that calls to the Customer Number are charged at national rate and may be monitored for training, security and quality assurance purposes. If you do not understand any of the terminology used in the Terms of Use then please refer to our Internet glossary at www.freeserve.com/help/jargon.htm

Access to the Internet and our related services and applications consist of two distinct service elements, a telephone access element and Freeserve member services. The Freeserve member services comprise various Internet based services available to members of Freeserve, for example email facilities, personal web space, access to the World Wide Web and other services and applications (the "Member Services"). The telephone access element enables your equipment to be connected to and access the Member Services. The telephone access element is provided either by the No Ties service, a metered product with per minute call charges ("No Ties"), or by AnyTime, a flat-rate product with a fixed monthly fee ("AnyTime"). In this Agreement the term "Services" will mean the Member Services together with whichever of the telephone access elements you use from time to time to obtain access to the Member Services.

Unless otherwise stated, the Member Services and No Ties shall be provided to you by Freeserve.com plc, a company registered in England and Wales (company number 3014367); whose registered office is located at Maylands Avenue, Hemel Hempstead, HP27TG ("Freeserve").

AnyTime will be provided to you by Freeserve Servicos de Internet LDA, a company registered in Madeira (company number 05431/2000.09.08) whose registered office is located at Avenida do Infante, 50, 9004 – 521 Funchal, Madeira, Portugal ("Freeserve LDA"). Please note that all correspondence should be addressed as specified in Clauses 10 and 11 below and not to the above address which is Freeserve LDA's corporate headquarters. Freeserve LDA has been granted by Freeserve the right to provide the AnyTime telephone Internet access service to you.

References to both Freeserve LDA and Freeserve are to "we", "our" and "us" and where a clause refers to "we", "our" and "us" in connection with the following terms it shall be taken to mean the company or companies indicated: the Services, to both Freeserve and Freeserve LDA; Member Services and No Ties, to Freeserve only; and AnyTime, to Freeserve LDA only. For the avoidance of doubt, only Freeserve will be able to exercise any rights and will bear all obligations under this Agreement in relation to the Member Services and No Ties. Only Freeserve LDA will be able to exercise any rights and will bear all obligations under this Agreement in relation to AnyTime.

1. BECOMING A FREESERVE MEMBER

1.1 You can only become a member of Freeserve (a "Member") if:

1.1.1 You have a valid contract with BT for telephone services; and

1.1.2 You have a PC with Internet Explorer 4.0 or above.

1.2 You can sign up for No Ties using a signup CD ROM or via our website at www.freeserve.com. If you prefer, you can call the Customer Number and complete the initial registration steps by telephone. Once you have successfully registered for No Ties (which will include agreeing to the Terms of Use) then you will become a Member and you will automatically be able to use the No Ties service and the Member Services.

1.3 You can sign up for AnyTime only after you have become a Member by following one of the sign-up procedures outlined above. To subscribe to AnyTime you must complete the AnyTime registration by supplying the registration data requested. You may subscribe to AnyTime using a sign up CD ROM or via our website at www.freeserve.com or by calling the

Customer Number. Once you have successfully registered for AnyTime you will become an AnyTime subscriber and you will be able to use AnyTime to access the Member Services.

1.4 You must ensure that the information that you give to us during registration is true, correct and complete. If there are any changes to your registration details you must inform us immediately either by calling the Customer Number or by sending us an email addressed to admin@freeserve.com.

1.5 By signing up for the Services you consent to our using and/or disclosing your registration details as follows:

1.5.1 processing your application or changes to your registration details, which may involve credit checking by a credit reference agency who may record that a credit check has been made;

1.5.2 disclosing certain personal details including account details to a bank, credit card operator or other payment processor for the purposes of setting up a continuous payment authority;

1.5.3 providing registration details to any telecommunications provider who operates the telephone access network used to provide No Ties or AnyTime; and

1.5.4 providing or arranging for third parties to provide customer care facilities and bill you for the Member Services, which may involve disclosing information about you to third parties solely for this purpose.

1.6 Otherwise, we will only use any personal data you provide in accordance with our Privacy Policy located at www.freeserve.com/privacy and subject to any limitations you select or choices you make during the registration process.

1.7 During registration for any of the Services, we will issue you with a username and a password which are essential for your secure use of the Services. You will be responsible for keeping this information confidential and agree to take all necessary steps to ensure that it is kept secure and not disclosed to any unauthorised person. If you think that your username or password has been discovered or is being misused by someone else then you must tell us immediately and take all steps necessary (or requested by us) to prevent such use. If we think there is likely to be a misuse of the Services because of a breach of security we may:

1.7.1 suspend your use of the Services; and/or

1.7.2 change your password and then notify you that we have done this.

1.8 We may accept instructions in connection with the Services from someone we are satisfied has your authority and you agree that you will be responsible for all use of the Services whether or not authorised by you.

1.9 When you become a Member, we will provide you with Member Services and the No Ties service immediately. When you have registered for AnyTime we will provide you with AnyTime immediately subject to you completing the install procedure. The Member Services, No Ties and AnyTime are provided immediately when you register, therefore, you will not be able to cancel the contract under the Consumer Protection (Distance Selling) Regulations 2000.

2. WHAT YOU WILL GET AS A FREESERVE MEMBER OR ANYTIME SUBSCRIBER

2.1 By becoming a Member, you will be able, using access equipment, for example a personal computer, PDA, Internet enabled television or WAP telephone (each meeting the relevant specification described on the Freeserve website at www.freeserve.com), to access the Member Services through a No Ties dial-up telephone connection charged on a per minute basis. By becoming an AnyTime subscriber, you will be able, using a PC, to access the Member Services through an AnyTime dial-up telephone connection on payment of a monthly charge. AnyTime dial-up connection is only available from the telephone number that you gave during registration or subsequently notified to us. Our Internet call packages are described on the Freeserve website at www.freeserve.com/time.

2.2 You will be responsible for any access equipment that you use in connection with the Services and you must use such equipment in accordance with any instructions and safety and security procedures applicable to it. Failure to do so may mean that you are unable to access the Internet and the Member Services.

2.3 You will be able to use certain web pages owned and operated by Freeserve (including their content, search facilities, directory services, personal web space, email, newsgroups and other Internet services as amended and updated from time to time) that are not available to non-Members. We also offer a number of services that are available to both Members and non-Members through our portal site at www.freeserve.com, in respect of which specific terms and conditions, available on our website at www.freeserve.com, will apply.

2.4 Calls made to access the Member Services must be made either by the No Ties service or AnyTime using dial-up numbers and any dial-up application software (the "Dialler") that we will provide you with at the time you register for No Ties or AnyTime. Any calls made without using the correct dial-up numbers provided to you by us will remain your sole responsibility. We may make changes to your dial-up numbers at any time. Freeserve LDA will provide AnyTime telephone access to you, if you have registered for this service, and Freeserve will provide all other Member Services and No Ties telephone access to you with reasonable skill and care and in accordance with the provisions of this Agreement.

3. CHARGES FOR NO TIES OR ANYTIME

3.1 The charges we will make will depend on the Internet call package that you selected during registration or subsequently. All charges will be made in pounds sterling and a price list for the standard Internet call packages that we offer is available at www.freeserve.com/time. Other charging packages may be separately notified to you from time to time.

3.2 In respect of AnyTime we will collect payment from you for all charges in advance using the payment method you selected when you registered or subsequently notified to us. Your first payment will be debited from your selected payment method within 28 days of you completing the registration process and subsequent payments shall be made by means of a continuous payment authorisation using the credit or debit card or through your bank account using the details that you provided to us during registration or which you subsequently notify to us.

3.3 If we are unable to collect the payments from you as they fall due, we may suspend or cancel No Ties or AnyTime and may forward the debt to an external agency for collection. You will pay our reasonable costs and expenses for collecting any late payments.

3.4 We reserve the right to vary the charges for No Ties or AnyTime and to introduce new payment methods at any time by writing or sending an email to you notifying you of the changes.

4. YOUR USE OF THE SERVICES

4.1 In order to access the Services you must make your telephone number or Caller Line Identification available when connecting to the Services. If you choose to restrict presentation of your telephone number or CLI, we may take such steps as we consider necessary to override that restriction on a per call basis. You consent to any steps we take to override the restriction on the telephone number or CLI presentation in order for us to provide you with the Services.

4.2 You may not use the Services for business or commercial purposes, unless you have obtained our express prior written consent.

4.3 You shall comply with any policies or guidelines we publish governing how you are allowed to make use of the Services ("Acceptable Use Policy").

4.4 You shall not use, and shall take all reasonable steps to ensure that no other person uses, the Services:

4.4.1 in a way that does not comply with the terms of any laws or any licence applicable to you or that is in any way unlawful or fraudulent or has any unlawful or fraudulent purpose or effect;

4.4.2 to send, knowingly receive, upload, download, use or re-use any material which is abusive, indecent, defamatory, obscene or menacing, or in breach of any copyright, confidence, privacy or any other rights;

4.4.3   to spam or send or procure the sending of any unsolicited advertising or promotional material;

4.4.4   to cause annoyance, inconvenience or needless anxiety;

4.4.5   to send or upload any material that contains viruses, trojan horses, worms, time bombs or any other harmful programs;

4.4.6   in a way that does not comply with any instructions that we or our agents have given to you (including instructions that we or our agents believe are necessary for health or safety reasons or to maintain the quality of the Services);

4.4.7   to store more than 100Mb of emails or 1,000 emails in your email account with us;

4.4.8   to send emails with attachments greater than 10Mb in size;

4.5   If you have not followed the above guidelines or Acceptable Use Policy, you agree to indemnify us and/or our agents against any costs or losses we and/or our agents may incur as a result of any claims or legal proceedings that are brought or threatened against us and/or our agents by anyone else.

5.   LIMITATIONS ON THE SERVICES

5.1   You should note that various elements of the Services are not provided by us but instead by other companies. We are therefore unable to guarantee that such products and services or any websites accessible via the Services are virus or error free. You should check all emails, attachments or files before downloading them.

5.2   We take reasonable steps to safeguard the security of any information you input or send to us in connection with the Services by using secure servers and encryption technology, however, we accept no responsibility for any damage that you may suffer as a result of the loss of confidentiality of such information.

5.3   You acknowledge that licensed telephone operators provide the telephone networks which are utilised by us and therefore we cannot guarantee that the Services will be uninterrupted or error free. Similarly, we cannot guarantee that the transmission of information over the Internet will be secure or that you will be able to access the Internet at all times or at the speeds that we have indicated are available.

5.4   As part of the Member Services we may provide you with email facilities, web hosting and other services that involve us providing storage space on our computers. In order to manage our computers and services we may restrict the amount of storage space provided. Limits may be by reference to the physical amount of web space made available to you, the number of email messages held, the size of any attachments sent or any other method we may specify. We reserve the right to vary these limits from time to time and we will keep you informed by email of any changes. We also reserve the right to refuse to accept material and/or to delete material, which exceeds the relevant limit. The current limit is as set out in Clause 4.4.7 above.

5.5   Internet access is subject to our network traffic management controls. We reserve the right to disconnect you from the Internet after 2 hours continuous use and/or 10 minutes of inactivity during connection. As a consequence, our No Ties or AnyTime dial-up Internet access packages may not be suitable for downloading files, which require continuous connection in excess of these times.

5.6   We may provide you with software that enables you to use the Services. You must not copy or modify this software (unless allowed by law) or use it for any purpose other than to access the Services in accordance with these Terms of Use. If specified by us, you must only access the Services using this software or in an alternative way that we have authorised.

5.7   The Services and associated software are provided to you for your use only and you must not resell, transfer, assign or sub-license them or any part of them to any other person.

6.   SUSPENSION AND TERMINATION OF THE SERVICES

6.1   If you do not follow the guidelines set out under Clause 4 then we may suspend or terminate the Services. We may also suspend or terminate the Services or any part of them if you fail or have failed to pay any charges for any other service that we or our affiliates may supply or you have used such services in breach of the applicable terms and conditions.

6.2   We reserve the right to terminate your use of the Services without notice if you do not connect to the Internet using the Member Services at least once in each period of 90 days.

6.3   We reserve the right to suspend, restrict, or terminate your access to the Services or any part of them if we believe your use of the Services causes or is likely to cause the whole or part of the Services to be interrupted, damaged, rendered less efficient or in any way impaired.

6.4   You understand that as a flat rate Internet user, AnyTime is not intended to be available on an "always on" basis and we may suspend your access if we think that you are using AnyTime in a manner which, in our opinion, makes abnormal demands on the network from a single connection and/or amounts to unreasonably excessive use of AnyTime.

6.5   We may need to temporarily suspend any or all of the Services without notice in order to repair, maintain or improve the Services or our network, or in an emergency. If we need to do this we will try to keep you informed and to keep interruptions to a minimum, although we cannot always guarantee to do so.

7.   OUR RIGHTS AND OBLIGATIONS

7.1   We reserve the right to forward your contact details to the police, or other regulatory or government authorities where properly requested to do so; we may also forward contact details where a complaint arises concerning your use of the Services and where that use is deemed by us to be inconsistent with these Terms of Use.

7.2   If subject to the approval required pursuant to Clause 4.2, you intend to use the Services for business or commercial purposes, you agree that, unless we specifically state otherwise, we shall provide the Services to you without any conditions, warranties or guarantees, whether express or implied, including but not limited to any implied warranties or conditions as to satisfactory quality or fitness for a particular purpose, which are expressly excluded, to the extent permitted by law.

7.3   Your dealings with, and interest in, promotions, services, or merchants found via the Member Services are solely between you and the person with whom you are dealing unless we expressly state otherwise.

7.4   We, or our merchants and content providers found via the Services, may provide links to other web sites or resources. We are unable to accept responsibility for these web sites or resources; neither have we endorsed their content, products or services merely because they are accessible via the Services.

7.5   We make all reasonable efforts to ensure that all information provided by us in connection with the Member Services is accurate at the time of its inclusion, however, there may be errors, inaccuracies or omissions in respect of which we exclude all liability. We make no representations or warranties about the information included on our web pages (including links to third parties' web pages). You shall be solely responsible for any decisions based on the information contained on such web pages.

7.6   Some modifications may need to be made to your PC to use the Services and it is your responsibility to ensure that such modifications do not invalidate the terms of any warranty or contracts you may have in relation to the PC. We shall have no liability for any claim that your warranty has been invalidated or a contract breached as a result of work carried out by you, us or our agents in order to make your PC operate with the Services.

8.   TERMS AND TERMINATION OF THIS AGREEMENT

8.1   This Agreement will operate from the time we accept all your registration details during the registration process and will continue unless and until terminated by either of us as set out under Clause 6 and this Clause 8.

8.2   You may terminate either:

8.2.1   your use of AnyTime and continue to use No Ties and the Member Services (with the use of No Ties or the Member Services being in accordance with this Agreement); or

8.2.2   your use of all the Services and this entire Agreement;

at any time and without reason, on the same day as you give notice to us by telephone.

8.3   We may terminate this Agreement or any part of it, at any time for any reason on 30 days notice to you, unless we terminate pursuant to Clause 6 without notice.

8.4   We may also terminate the Agreement or any part of it or suspend the supply of any of the Services to you, immediately and without notice if:

8.4.1   you breach these Terms of Use;

8.4.2   you or any person using your account misuses the Services in any way, including, without limitation, misuse in the manner set out under Clause 4.4;

8.4.3   bankruptcy or other insolvency proceedings are brought against you, or if you are unable to pay your debts as they become due, fail to make payments as they fall due, or you cancel your continuous payment authorisation preventing us from collecting payment as it becomes due;

8.4.4   you are no longer able lawfully to receive the Services;

8.4.5   you no longer have an appropriate residential telephone account from which the Internet is accessed or satisfy the conditions for becoming a Member as set out in Clause 1.1; or

8.4.6   we can no longer provide the Services or provide the Services in a way that we deem appropriate.

8.5   If the Services are suspended or restricted by us, as described under Clause 6, you must continue paying charges (if applicable) unless and until this Agreement is terminated.

8.6   In the event that this Agreement is terminated for any reason other than under Clause 8.3, you will remain responsible for all charges due under this Agreement until the end of the month in which this Agreement is terminated but you will not be entitled to a refund of any charges already paid in advance. Where we terminate this Agreement under Clause 8.3 and do not offer comparable services to replace the Services you shall be reimbursed for amounts you have paid in advance on a pro-rata basis from the date of expiry of the notice given under Clause 8.3.

8.7 In the event of termination, all the information we are storing on your behalf on our servers may be deleted and in particular we may delete all the emails in your email account.

9. OUR LIABILITY TO YOU

9.1 We do not limit our liability if you die or are injured as a result of our negligence or you suffer loss as a consequence of any fraud by us.

9.2 We shall not be liable to you in contract, tort (including negligence) or otherwise for:

   9.2.1 any damage or loss arising from the consequences of viruses received by you via the Services or of our failure to provide the Services in accordance with these Terms of Use; or

   9.2.2 any economic losses (including loss of business, contracts, profits, revenues, capital or anticipated savings), any indirect, special or consequential loss, loss of data, goodwill or reputation or for any wasted expense including but not limited to the cost of using any other service or losses caused by viruses.

9.3 Except as set out in Clause 9.1 any liability we may have to you whether in contract, tort (including negligence) or otherwise for any loss or damage suffered by you in relation to the provision of the Services is limited to £500 in any 12 month period.

9.4 We are not liable for any failure to perform our obligations if we are prevented from doing so by an event beyond our reasonable control (which may include, without limitation, strikes; labour disputes; acts of God; war; riot; civil action; malicious acts or damage; compliance with any law, governmental or regulatory order, rule, regulation or direction; any act or omission of any government or other competent authority; accident; equipment or services failure, including the unavailability of third party telecommunications services, lines, or other equipment; fire; flood or storm).

9.5 Each provision of this Clause operates separately as between you and Freeserve and between you and Freeserve LDA. If any part is held by a court to be unreasonable, inapplicable or unenforceable then the other parts shall still apply. If any part is held by a court to be unreasonable, inapplicable or unenforceable against either one of Freeserve or Freeserve LDA, that part shall, for the avoidance of doubt, still apply for the benefit of the other company.

10. COMPLAINTS PROCEDURE

10.1 If you have a complaint about any aspect of the Services, please let us know by calling the Customer Number and we will endeavour to resolve any complaints as soon as is reasonably possible.

10.2 If you are not satisfied that your complaint has been resolved, you can escalate your issue, in writing, to the Customer Action Team, PO Box 452, Leeds, LS2 7SW. Once your complaint has been fully investigated we shall reply back to you.

11. GIVING NOTICE

11.1 Unless otherwise provided in these Terms of Use, any notices must be sent by email, post or delivered by hand as follows:

11.1.1 to you, at the address you have given us or the email address given to us in your registration details or to any other address you provide to us subsequently in accordance with Clause 11.1.2; and

11.1.2 to us by telephone by calling the Customer Number or by post addressed to Customer Action Team, PO Box 452, Leeds, LS2 7SW.

11.2 In the case of notices sent by email, such notices shall be deemed to be received when capable of being accessed by you. In the case of notices sent by post, such notices shall be deemed to be received on the second business day after posting.

12. CHANGES TO THE SERVICES OR THE TERMS OF USE

12.1 We may alter and/or amend at any time:

12.1.1 any aspect of the Services upon giving you 21 days notice in advance, of such alteration taking effect, provided such alteration or amendment does not require any material change to this Agreement; and

12.1.2 this Agreement upon giving you 21 days notice in advance of any such amendment taking effect. If, upon receiving any such notice, you do not wish to continue with the Services, you may terminate the Agreement upon giving us written notice. Your notice shall take effect upon the earlier of 7 days from our receipt of your notice or the date upon which the amended Agreement would otherwise have taken effect.

12.2 You will be deemed to have accepted any alteration and/or amendment to the Agreement and/or the Services if you continue to use the Services after the relevant period of notice has expired.

13. OTHER THINGS YOU NEED TO KNOW

13.1 You may not transfer this Agreement or any part of it to anyone else.

13.2 We may transfer the benefit and burden of this Agreement to any person taking over the supply of the Services or any part of the Services without your prior consent by giving you notice. We may also sub-contract or assign the provision of the Services or any part of the Services to any other person.

13.3 If any part of this Agreement is found to be illegal or unenforceable, this will not affect the validity and enforceability of the remainder of the Agreement.

13.4 If either of us delay or fail to enforce any right under this Agreement that will not be deemed to be a waiver of that right and will not prevent that right or any other right or remedy from being exercised or enforced.

13.5 This Agreement constitutes the entire agreement between us relating to the provision of the Services and supersedes any previous agreements and understandings between us relating to the Services (except that we do not limit or exclude our liability to you in respect of any fraudulent misrepresentations).

13.6 Nothing in this Agreement is intended to create any rights under the Contracts (Rights of Third Parties) Act 1999, which is enforceable, by any person who is not a party to this Agreement. Nothing in this Agreement shall affect any right or remedy of a third party which exists or is available other than as a result of the aforementioned Act.

13.7 The provision of the Services and the application of this Agreement are governed by English Law and the parties hereby agree to submit to the exclusive jurisdiction of the English Courts in respect of any dispute or matter arising out of or in connection with this Agreement.

A1.5 McDermott, Will & Emery – Employee Policy

A1.5.1 *Use of e-mail and the Internet*

The use of both e-mail and the Internet in order to correspond with customers/clients is a fast and reliable method of communication with significant advantages for [*insert name of Company*] (the '**Company**'). Staff should also be aware, however, that its use involves them exposing both themselves and the Company to certain risks and offences and that the misuse of this facility can cause problems for both a member of staff and the Company.

The purpose of this policy in relation to e-mail and Internet use is to highlight some of the main areas where problems could potentially be encountered and to provide a number of guidelines which, if followed, will assist staff in avoiding such difficulties arising.

A1.5.2 *Use of external e-mail*

- Staff should always be careful of what is said in e-mail messages as the content could give rise to both personal liability or create liability for the Company by virtue of their acts. Staff should take care to avoid entering into either personal commitments or commitments on behalf of the Company over the Internet without having received prior and express permission to do so or unless this forms part of their normal day-to-day activities and has been so authorised by the Company.

- Staff are reminded that all e-mails will identify both themselves personally and the Company as the sender and that, as such, the content will have a reflection on both their and the Company's image and reputation with its clients/suppliers/customers. Staff are reminded that they should word all e-mails appropriately in the same professional manner as were they composing a letter for that particular client/customer/supplier.

- Staff should ensure at all time the content of any e-mail message sent is neither defamatory, abusive nor illegal and accords with the Company's policies concerning harassment and equal opportunities, [*which is set out in section [...] of the Company Manual*]. Employees should note that the sending and receipt of obscene or pornographic or other offensive material may constitute an offence under the Obscene Publications Act and that they may face criminal liability for any such breach. Staff should note that the Company's IT Department has the facility to monitor the content of e-mails sent and received and that any member of staff found breaching these guidelines will be subject to disciplinary action which, in some cases and depending upon the circumstances and seriousness of the breach, may include summary dismissal.

- Staff are reminded that there is a danger that e-mails may be misdirected or intercepted by third parties. You should ensure that they have the correct e-mail address for the intended recipients. If you are unsure concerning the correct address then you should either clarify this with the recipient or avoid sending the e-mail and use an alternative means of communication.

Staff, in any event, should not send any information that the Company considers to be confidential or sensitive by way of e-mail. [*You should consult the Code of Conduct in section [...] of the Company Manual for discussion of your confidentiality obligations.*]

- Staff should ensure, in any event, that all e-mails sent contain an appropriate confidentiality notice.

- If staff inadvertently misdirect an e-mail they should contact [*member of the IT Department*] immediately on becoming aware of their mistake. Failure to do so may lead to disciplinary action being taken against them.

- Staff are reminded that the e-mail facility is provided primarily for business purposes and that this facility should not be abused. Staff are requested to limit personal usage to a minimum and to abide by the above guidelines concerning the content of e-mails. Excessive personal usage or abuse of the guidelines concerning the content of e-mails may lead to the withdrawal of e-mail and Internet access and/or disciplinary action.

- Staff should ensure that a confirmation of receipt is obtained or sent with particularly important e-mail messages. A hard copy of such confirmation should also be retained.

- Staff should at all times remember that e-mail messages could have to be disclosed as evidence at any Court proceedings or investigations by regulatory bodies and therefore may be prejudicial to both their or the Company's interests. Hard copies

of e-mails may be taken and backup disks may retain records of
e-mails even when these have been deleted from the system.

A1.5.3   Internal e-mail

- The above guidance upon the content of e-mails applies equally
  to e-mails sent internally within the Company.

- E-mails sent containing pornographic, sexist or otherwise
  offensive or abusive material may entitle affected employees to
  bring harassment claims against both the sender and the
  Company under the Sex Discrimination Act, Race Relations
  Act or Disability Discrimination Act.

- Should any employee receive an e-mail which they consider
  offensive, abusive or sexually or racially derogatory material
  they should [contact [...] or use the Anti-harassment policy
  contained in section [...] of the Company Manual].

A1.5.4   Copyright issues

Staff are reminded that the downloading, onwards transmission or
copying of works of third parties without their express permission
may constitute a breach of copyright. Staff should note that
information placed on the Internet may not have been put there
with the consent of the copyright owner and that they should
exercise extreme care and caution in the use of such information.

A1.5.4   Use of the Internet

Employees are provided with Internet access for business use. While you may access the Internet during lunch hours and before or after normal business hours, you should not access non-business-related sites during working hours.

A1.5.5   Downloading information from the Internet

Staff should be aware that information which may be downloaded from the Internet may contain a virus and therefore should not be downloaded from the Internet without first obtaining the approval of [*member of the IT Department*]. Staff should follow instructions of [*member of the IT Department*] concerning the downloading of such information without fail. Staff should only download such information that is required for a business purpose. The downloading of information of whatever nature for personal purposes is not permitted.

©McDermott, Will & Emery 2002

A1.6   McDermott, Will & Emery – E-mail Disclaimers

A1.6.1   E-mail confidentiality and monitoring disclaimer

Please note: This e-mail is confidential and may also be privileged. Please notify us immediately if you are not the intended recipient. You should not copy it, forward it or use it for any purpose or disclose the contents to any person. [*Company name*] may monitor e mail to ensure compliance with business policies and for training or quality control purposes.

A1.6.2   E-mail/web posting general disclaimer

You understand that all information, data, text, software, music, sound, photographs, graphics, video, messages or other materials ('**Content**'), whether publicly posted or privately transmitted, are the sole responsibility of the person from which such Content originated. This means that you, and not the Company, are entirely responsible for all Content that you upload, post, e-mail, transmit or otherwise make available via e-mail or other service. The Company does not control the Content posted via e-mail or other service and, as such, does not guarantee the accuracy, integrity or quality of such Content. You understand that by using e-mail or other service, you may be exposed to Content that is offensive, indecent or objectionable. Under no circumstances will the Company be liable in any way for any Content, including, but not limited to, for any errors or omissions in any Content, or for any loss or damage of any kind incurred as a result of the use of any Content posted, e-mailed, transmitted or otherwise made available via e-mail or other service.

You acknowledge that the Company does not pre-screen Content, but that the Company and its designees shall have the right (but not the obligation) in their sole discretion to refuse or move any Content that is available via e-mail or other service. Without limiting the foregoing, the Company and its designees shall have the right to remove any Content that violates the terms of service or is otherwise objectionable. You agree that you must evaluate, and bear all risks associated with, the use of any Content, including any reliance on the accuracy, completeness, or usefulness of such Content.

You acknowledge and agree that the Company may preserve Content and may also disclose Content if required to do so by law or in the good faith belief that such preservation or disclosure is reasonably necessary to: (a) comply with legal process; (b) enforce the terms of service; (c) respond to claims that any Content violates the rights of third-parties; or (d) protect the rights, property, or personal safety of the Company, its users and the public.

You understand that the technical processing and transmission of e-mail or other service, including your Content, may involve (a) transmissions over various networks; and (b) changes to conform and adapt to technical requirements of connecting networks or devices.

A1.7　Dixons.co.uk – Terms of Sale

Looking after our customers

Our terms and conditions comply with UK legislation and are designed to ensure that all of our customers can shop easily and with confidence at Dixons. Please keep and print a copy for reference.

Pricing

All prices are in £ sterling inclusive of VAT and exclusive of delivery and installation charges. Delivery charges can be found at "Delivery" accessible from the Customer Service Menu and are confirmed in the order. You may pay by any major credit card or debit card. Prices, offers and products are subject to availability and may change.

Accepting orders and security

When you place an order we will treat it as an offer to buy. We will send an e-mail (first e-mail) to confirm receipt. This does not mean your offer has been accepted. If we accept your order, we will send you a confirmation e-mail (second e-mail) with your order number, at which point your offer is accepted and we make a legal contract with you. However, we will be entitled to refuse to accept your order if we feel it necessary, in which case we will e-mail you as soon as we can to let you know.

When you order you have an opportunity to check the details and correct any input errors. In deciding whether to accept your order we may use the information you have given us, or we already hold about you, or which we receive from any enquiry we may make with Experian Limited, to confirm your identity. Experian will check any details we disclose to them against any database (public or private) to which they have access and will keep a record of that check. Experian will also retain this information and may use it in the future to assist other companies with identity verification. This assists us to protect you and us from fraudulent transactions. More details of the steps we take to offer our customers security can be found by going to our Customer Service Menu and clicking on "Security Issues".

If we decline your offer on security grounds we may contact you to seek an alternative payment method or to advise you of the location of your nearest store.

Age requirements

If you order a product where a minimum age requirement is indicated, by ordering you confirm that you are of the required age or over.

Delivery

Delivery is restricted to the United Kingdom. Delivery must be to the address at which your credit or debit card is registered. All deliveries must be signed for and you should keep your receipt. Delivery times and more details about delivery can be found in the "Delivery" section accessible from the Customer Service Menu.

Although we do everything we can to meet delivery times described in that section, delivery times may be affected by factors beyond our control and therefore cannot be guaranteed.

Cancellations and Returns

All products: You may normally cancel your purchase provided you notify us either before or within 14 days after delivery. Your product may be returned to a Dixons store or collected from the delivery address free of charge. If another method of return is used you will be responsible for the costs.

Faulty within 28 days: If there is a fault with your product (or other defect with your order), you may return the product to us within 28 days of delivery for a replacement or refund. This does not apply to faults caused by accident, neglect or misuse.

Faulty after more than 28 days: If your product develops a fault after more than 28 days, it will normally be covered by a minimum 1 year guarantee.

(To see full details of our cancellation and returns policies see the section entitled Returns Policy.)

Miscellaneous

Sales on the web site are governed by English law and you agree to submit any dispute to the non-exclusive jurisdiction of the English courts. All orders are subject to these terms and conditions and no amendments will be accepted by us. Sales may be conducted in English only.

These terms and conditions only cover the Dixons web site. Any links within this site to other web sites are not covered by this policy and we accept no responsibility or liability for the content of the web sites which are not under our control.

We may supply substitute goods.

These terms and conditions do not affect your legal rights.

Dixons is a trading name of DSG Retail Limited, Maylands Avenue, Hemel Hempstead, Hertfordshire, HP2 7TG.

This contract will not be filed.

A1.8 Dixons.co.uk – Terms of Use

We do not guarantee that this web site will be compatible with all customers' PCs.

DSG Retail Limited owns the copyright in all materials on this site, which may be used, downloaded, copied, reproduced, republished, posted, broadcast, transmitted or linked only for your own personal and non-commercial use. You agree not to adapt, alter or create any derivative work from any material on this site, or to restrict or inhibit the use or enjoyment of this site by anyone else.

It is not permitted to create any link to this web site without our prior written consent.

I ACCEPT

A1.9   Pubs247.co.uk – User Terms

Terms

Please read this carefully. By accessing the pubs247.co.uk Website at www.pubs247.co.uk (the "Site") you are agreeing to the terms (the "Terms") that appear below, whether or not you register as a user. If you have any questions, please contact help@pubs247.co.uk.

pubs247 reserves the right to alter any and all of these Terms at its own discretion. Changes to the Terms will be notified to you on the Site. You will be agreeing to these Terms and any future Terms by using the Site. If you do not wish to agree to these Terms, do not use this Site.

Site Access

Access to this site does not require you to become a registered user. If you wish to be able to post pub reviews ("Reviews") or to receive e-mail from pubs247.co.uk ("pubs247") you will need to register.

In order to become a registered user of the Site you must provide pubs247 with complete and accurate registration information. Furthermore, it is your responsibility to ensure that this information is kept up to date by informing pubs247 of any changes to your registration information (including in particular your e-mail address). This is done by emailing help@pubs247.co.uk.

Any personal information obtained by pubs247 from you in operating this Site will be treated in accordance with the Data Protection Act and pubs247 Privacy Policy. The pubs247 Privacy Policy does not apply to any other site including, without limitation, those which are co-branded.

As a part of the registration process you must choose a user name and password (your "ID"). This information should not be shared with anyone else. Each registration is for a single user only. pubs247 does not permit persons to share ID's, nor does it permit multiple users to access the Site via a network using a single ID.

You are responsible for all use of the Site by your ID, whether this is by you or anyone else using your ID. You are responsible for any unauthorised use of your ID. If you are concerned that the security of your ID has become compromised, you must notify pubs247 immediately by e-mailing security@pubs247.co.uk.

pubs247 provides a service to pubs to enable them to send Alerts to their regular customers about forthcoming events. pubs247 does not pass your details on to the pubs, you must register directly with the pub as a regular in order to receive Alerts from that pub.

All Alerts transmitted are the sole responsibility of the pub from which they are sent. pubs247 do not review, edit or modify the content of the Alerts and takes no responsibility for them but reserves the right to delete, edit and to insert advertisements into them.

You may unsubscribe from receiving the Alerts by notifying the pub from which they were sent, either directly or by going to the relevant pub homepage. Occasionally, pubs247 will send you Alerts on behalf of the pub which will remind you how to unsubscribe.

pubs247 hopes that you find the Alerts useful but if you do have any complaints about them or their content, you should speak to the pub. If you are still dissatisfied, email complaints@pubs247.co.uk or write to pubs247, Fourth Avenue, Burton-on-Trent, DE14 2WT and we can help prevent you from receiving further Alerts.

Notice

pubs247 reserves the right to suspend or, with cause, terminate your access to all or any part of the Site at any time with or without notice at our discretion. If notice is to be served, this will be deemed to have been adequately served three hours after e-mail transmission to your e-mail address as notified to pubs247.

Consumer Reviews

pubs247 offers users the facility to post Reviews to the Site on pubs they may have visited. pubs247 does not control, and takes no responsibility for, the content of Reviews. However, pubs247 reserves the right to delete, edit or move any Review. You waive any moral right you may have in regard of the Reviews.

You are solely and entirely responsible for the content of any Review you post. You agree to comply with any and all rules posted by pubs247 in relation to Reviews.

You may not post, link to or otherwise publish any Reviews which contain:

- any form of advertising or promotion for goods and services;
- unlawful, threatening, abusive, libellous, defamatory or indecent remarks or infringe copyright or other rights of third parties;
- any other form of illegal content;
- any virus or other harmful component.

You may not impersonate any person or entity (including pubs247 employees) or misrepresent any affiliation with any person or entity or otherwise disguise the origin of any Reviews.

You are not permitted to collect or store other users' personal data, or restrict or inhibit any other user from using the Reviews.

You agree to indemnify and hold harmless pubs247 from all claims, costs and reasonable expenses (including reasonable legal expenses) that arise as a result of you posting any Review that is in breach of these Terms.

pubs247 takes no responsibility for, and cannot guarantee the accuracy, quality or integrity of any review submitted. You must note that some users may submit Reviews that are misleading, inaccurate, untrue or offensive and consequently you should not place any reliance on the accuracy of any Review.

Through submitting a Review you grant pubs247 a perpetual royalty free non-exclusive licence to reproduce, modify, translate, make available, distribute and sub-licence the Review in whole or in part. This will also include personal information such as your user name or alias (if available) and your expressions of opinion.

pubs247 does not have the ability to ensure that Reviews do not infringe the copyright, or any other right, of third parties. If you feel that a Review infringes any legal rights you may have, or you wish to complain about the content of a Review you should immediately contact pubs247 by e-mailing complaints@pubs247.co.uk with full details of your complaint and accurate details of how we may contact you.

Content

All material on the Site and its selection and arrangement (the "Content") belongs to pubs247 or its licensors. pubs247 permits you to access and display Content on your computer screen, to store Content for personal, non-commercial use and to print individual pages on paper. You may not photocopy Content.

pubs247 permits specified parties to advertise and offer for sale certain goods and services. Any contract that you make for the purchase of goods or services from these parties will be with the specified third party and not pubs247. pubs247 will not be responsible for any error or inaccuracy in advertising material. Advertisers and sponsors are responsible for ensuring that any material they submit to the Site is compliant with all relevant laws.

You may not commercially exploit the Content. You may not, without the prior written authorisation of pubs247, remove the trade mark or copyright notices from copies of Content made under these Terms. You may not create an electronic or manual database of any or all of pubs247 Content.

Any competitions, prize draws or promotions on the Site are subject to terms that will be made available at the time of the competition, prize draw or promotion.

Governing Law

These Terms shall be governed by, and construed in accordance with, English Law. Your rights under these Terms may not be assigned, sub-let or otherwise transferred. Rights and remedies under these Terms will not be waived by a failure of either party to exercise any right or remedy under these Terms. If this term or any of these Terms is found to be invalid by a court with competent jurisdiction, the remaining Terms will be unaffected and remain valid.

DISCLAIMER

The Site is for public access and is not intended to cater for individual requirements. The Content does not constitute any form of advice, recommendation or other arrangement by pubs247. You should not rely on the Content in making, or refraining from making, any decision. Any arrangements made between a third party named on this Site and yourself are at your sole risk and responsibility.

PUBS247 IS PROVIDING THIS GENERAL INFORMATION SITE FREE OF CHARGE. WHILST WE ENDEAVOUR NOT TO MAKE THE SITE MISLEADING WE CANNOT REPRESENT THAT THE INFORMATION ACCESSIBLE VIA THIS WEB SITE IS ACCURATE, COMPLETE OR CURRENT. OTHER THAN SET OUT IN THESE TERMS AND CONDITIONS OF USE, PUBS247 MAKES NO (AND EXPRESSLY DISCLAIMS ALL) REPRESENTATIONS, WARRANTIES, CONDITIONS AND OTHER TERMS EXPRESS OR IMPLIED BY STATUTE, COLLATERALLY OR OTHERWISE WITH RESPECT TO THIS WEBSITE OR ITS CONTENTS.

Except as specifically stated on this Website, to the fullest extent permitted at law, neither pubs247 nor any of its affiliates, directors, employees or other representatives will be liable for damages arising out of or in connection with the use of this Website. This is a comprehensive limitation of liability that applies to any and all losses, damages or costs of any kind, including (without limitation) direct, indirect or consequential damages, loss of data, income or profit, loss of or damage to property and claims of third parties. For the avoidance of doubt, pubs247 does not limit its liability for fraudulent misrepresentation, death or personal injury to the extent only that it arises as a result of the negligence of pubs247, its affiliates, directors, employees or other representatives.

pubs247 Site contains links to other sites. Such links are clearly indicated although such sites may be co-branded with pubs247 and so may include pubs247 trademark. pubs247 is not responsible for the content or availability of such sites and will not be contractually implicated in any transaction for goods or services available from such Third Party Sites.

pubs247 is owned by barbox Limited a company registered in England & Wales under number 4256310 whose registered office is at 137 High Street, Burton-on-Trent, Staffs. "pubs247" and "pubs247.co.uk" are trade marks and may not be used without the prior written permission of pubs247.

If you wish to link to the Site, please contact us at links@pubs247.co.uk.

APPENDIX 2

Contract precedents

The following precedents were kindly provided by Ashley Winton of Pillsbury Winthrop Solicitors.

The first of these is the boiler plate or standard form which should be used in conjunction with the bespoke versions of the agreements which follow. These may be used by readers at their will; however, neither the author nor Pillsbury Winthrop accept responsibility or liability for the accuracy of the same or any loss sustained by any person acting or placing reliance on these.

A2.1 Boiler plate

This Agreement is made the [ ] day of [   ]

Between:

(1)   [Company Name] a company incorporated in England under registration number [   ], the registered office of which is at [   ] ("**Company**"); and

(2)   [Customer Name] a company incorporated in England under registration number [   ], the registered office of which is at [   ] ("**Customer**").

Definitions and interpretation

In this Agreement the following words and expressions shall have the meaning set out below:

"**Agreement**" means this Agreement and any Schedule;

"**Confidential Information**" has the meaning set out in clause 13.1;

"**Commencement Date**" means [/the date of this Agreement];

"**Force Majeure**" has the meaning set out in clause 12.1;

"**Intellectual Property Rights**" means any and all registered and unregistered copyright patents, design rights, database and compilation rights, Marks (and related goodwill), trade secrets and other intellectual property rights, howsoever arising and in whatever media, and any applications for their protection or registration and all renewals and extensions anywhere in the world;

"**Marks**" means any and all names, brands, logos, trade marks, service marks, trade names and domain names; and

"**Term**" has the meaning set out in clause 9.1.

Except where the context otherwise requires, words denoting the singular include the plural and vice versa, words denoting any gender include any other genders, and words denoting persons include firms and corporations and vice versa.

Unless otherwise stated, a reference to:

a Clause or Schedule is a reference to a clause of or schedule to this Agreement. Clause headings are for ease of reference only and do not affect the construction of this Agreement;

"include" and "including" shall be construed without limitation; and

2

any Act of Parliament shall be deemed to include any amendment, replacement or re-enactment thereof then in force and to include any bye-laws, statutory instruments, rules, regulations, orders, notices, directions, consents, licences, conditions or permissions made thereunder.

[Clauses 2 to 8 – Insert main provisions of the Agreement]

Term

The Agreement shall commence on the Commencement Date and shall continue for a period of one year unless and until terminated in accordance with clause 14 ("**Term**"). On each anniversary of the Commencement Date this Agreement shall renew for a further period of one year unless either party gives the other not less that three months' prior written notice to expire on or before such anniversary.

Indemnities

Each party shall indemnify and keep the other party fully and effectively indemnified on demand against any liability, damage, expense, claim or cost (including reasonable legal costs and expenses) suffered by the other party as a result of any breach by the first party of the warranties set out in clause [   ] of this Agreement, provided that where products are concerned the latest version of the products have been used in normal circumstances without modification.

To take benefit of an indemnity, that party shall: (i) notify the other party promptly in writing and in any event within ten (10) business days of first learning of any such claim, lawsuit, action or proceeding; (ii) consent to the other party having the sole authority to control the defence and/or settlement of any such claim, lawsuit, action or proceeding; and (iii) provide reasonable co-operation and assistance to the other party, at that party's expense, in defending any such claim, lawsuit, action or proceeding.

Limitation of Liability

Save as provided in clause 11.3, neither party shall be liable in contract, tort (including negligence), statutory duty, pre-contract or other representations (other than fraudulent or negligent misrepresentations) or otherwise arising out of or in connection with this Agreement for: (a) consequential, indirect or special loss or damage; or (b) any loss of goodwill or reputation; or (c) any economic losses (including loss of revenues, profits, contracts, business or anticipated savings). In each case whether advised of the possibility of such loss or damage and howsoever incurred.

3

Save as provided in clause 10.1 and 11.3, both parties agree that the maximum liability of either party in contract, tort (including negligence), statutory duty, pre-contract or other representations (other than fraudulent or negligent misrepresentations) or otherwise arising out of or in connection with this Agreement, and each part thereof, including its execution and performance; shall, in respect of any one or more events or series of events (whether connected or unconnected) taking place within any twelve month period, be limited to the Licence Fees paid by Licensee in such period or [£10,000], whichever is the greater.

Nothing in this Agreement shall exclude or limit liability for death or personal injury resulting from the negligence of either party or their servants, agents or employees acting in the course of their duties.

Force Majeure

Either party will not be liable for any failure or delay in performing its obligations under this Agreement to the extent that this failure or delay is the result of any cause or circumstance beyond the reasonable control of that party including acts of god, war, civil commotion or industrial dispute and that failure could not have been prevented or overcome by that party acting reasonably and prudently. If either party is prevented from performing its obligations for a period exceeding six (6) months due to Force Majeure then the other party may terminate this Agreement on one month written notice.

Confidentiality and Data

During the term of this Agreement and for two (2) years thereafter, each party will treat as confidential all information that they obtain concerning, but not limited to, the business, finances, technology and affairs of the other, ("**Confidential Information**"). Each of the parties will use at least the same degree of care (and not less than a reasonable degree of care) it uses to prevent the disclosure of its own confidential information of like importance, to prevent the disclosure of Confidential Information of the other party. Each party will promptly notify the other party of any actual or suspected misuse or unauthorised disclosure of the other party's Confidential Information.

The provisions of this clause 13 shall cease to apply to: (i) information that has come into the public domain other than by breach of this clause or any other duty of confidence; (ii) information that is obtained from a third party without breach of this clause or any other duty of confidence; and (iii) information that is required to be disclosed by a regulatory or government body or court of competent jurisdiction with power to compel the disclosure.

4

In the event of termination or expiration of this Agreement, each party shall return or on request of the other party, destroy the Confidential Information of that party.

Each party will comply with its obligations pursuant to the Data Protection Act 1998 and any subordinate legislation and official guidelines.

Termination

Each party shall have the right to terminate this Agreement on written notice in the event that the other:

commits any material breach of the terms of this Agreement which, in the case of a breach capable of remedy, is not remedied within 30 days of service of a notice specifying the breach and stating the intention to terminate the Agreement if not remedied; or

holds any meeting with or proposes to enter into or has proposed to it any arrangement or composition with its creditors (including any voluntary arrangement as described in the Insolvency Act 1986); has a receiver, administrator, or other encumbrancer take possession of or appointed over or has any distress, execution or other process levied or enforced (and not discharged within 7 days) upon the whole or substantially all of its assets; ceases or threatens to cease to carry on business or becomes unable to pay its debts within the meaning of Section 123 of the Insolvency Act 1986.

Forthwith upon the termination of this Agreement each party shall return all licensed and/or confidential materials, and all copies in whole or part, of the other or if requested by the other party, shall destroy them and certifying in writing to the Licensor that they have been destroyed.

Termination or expiry of this Agreement shall be without prejudice to any rights, liabilities or remedies of a party accrued before termination nor shall it affect any provision of this Agreement which is expressly intended to come into or continue in force after termination or expiry.

Severance

To the extent that any provision of this Agreement is found by any court or competent authority to be invalid, unlawful or unenforceable in any jurisdiction, that provision shall be deemed not to be a part of this Agreement, it shall not affect the validity, lawfulness or enforceability of the remainder of this Agreement nor shall it affect the validity, lawfulness or enforceability of that provision in any other jurisdiction.

5

Waiver

No failure or delay exercise by any party in exercising any right, power or remedy under this Agreement will operate as a waiver of that or any other right, power or remedy nor will any single or partial exercise by either party of any right, power or remedy preclude any further exercise of any other right, power or remedy.

Time of the Essence

Any times, dates or periods specified in the agreement may be extended or altered by agreement in writing between the parties. However, time shall not be of the essence except where it is expressly stated to apply.

Insurance

Each party must have in force and maintain with a reputable insurance company professional indemnity insurance exceeding [£1,000,000].

Further Assurance

Each party shall at the cost and expense of the other party use all reasonable endeavours to do all such further acts and things and execute or procure the execution of all such other documents as that party may from time to time reasonably require for the purpose of giving that party the full benefit of the assets, rights and benefits to be transferred to the other party under this agreement.

Relationship

Nothing in this Agreement shall or shall be deemed to create a partnership or joint venture or contract of employment of any kind between the parties nor shall it be deemed to grant any authority to the other not expressly set out in the Agreement or create any agency between the parties.

Assignment and Sub-contracting

Either party shall not be entitled to assign, transfer, charge or license the whole or any part of its rights and/or obligations under this Agreement to any party without consent of the other party [which shall not be unreasonably withheld or delayed].

[Neither/either] party may engage any person, firm or company as its sub-contractor to perform any of its obligations, but shall not be released from any liability therefor.

6

E-Business: The Practical Guide to the Laws

Rights of Third Parties

Nothing in this Agreement shall create or confer any rights or other benefits whether pursuant to the Contracts (Rights of Third Parties) Act 1999 or otherwise in favour of any person other than the parties to this Agreement.

Notices

Any notice given under this Agreement will be in writing and shall be deemed served if hand delivered to the other party or sent by pre-paid post, facsimile transmission or confirmed email copy to the address or transmission number of that party specified on page 1 of this Agreement or such other address or number as may be notified under this Agreement by that party from time to time for this purpose. Notices will be deemed to be effective on personal delivery, within 48 hours of posting (if the address is in the UK or within 96 hours otherwise), or upon confirmation of receipt of facsimile or email.

Entire Agreement

Each party confirms that this Agreement sets out the entire agreement and understanding between the parties and that it supersedes all previous agreements, arrangements and understandings between them relating to the subject matter of the Agreement. Each party confirms that it has not relied upon any statement, representation or understanding that is not an express term of this Agreement and shall not have any remedy in respect of any statement, representation or understanding which is not an express term unless made fraudulently.

Governing Law and Jurisdiction

This Agreement shall be governed by and construed in accordance with the law of England and each party hereby irrevocably submits to the non-exclusive jurisdiction of the courts of England.

Dispute Resolution

If any dispute arises between the parties out of this Agreement, the parties shall attempt to settle it by mediation in accordance with the Centre for Dispute Resolution (CEDR) Model Mediation Procedure.

If the parties have not settled the dispute by mediation within [42] days from the initiation of the mediation, the dispute shall be referred to arbitration under the Rules of the London Court of International Arbitration in force at the date of this Agreement. The parties hereby agree that:

The tribunal shall consist of [one/three] arbitrator[s] who [specify qualifications/nationalities etc.];

7

If the parties do not agree on the appointment of the arbitrator[s], the London Court of International Arbitration shall determine the arbitrator[s];
The place of arbitration shall be London; and
The language of the arbitration shall be English.

General

The rights and remedies of the parties under this Agreement are cumulative and in addition to any rights and remedies provided by law. Any variation to this Agreement must be in writing and agreed by the parties. This agreement may be executed in counterpart.

This Agreement has been signed on the date appearing at the head of page 1.

Signed by   )
for and on behalf of   )   Director
Company   )
)   Director/Secretary
Signed by   )
for and on behalf of   )   Director
Customer   )
)   Director/Secretary

8

A2.2 Software Licence and Maintenance Support

This Agreement is made the [   ] day of [   ]

Between:

(1) [Company Name] a company incorporated in England under registration number [   ], the registered office of which is at [   ] ("**Company**"); and

(2) [Customer Name] a company incorporated in England under registration number [   ], the registered office of which is at [   ] ("**Customer**").

Definitions and Interpretation

In this Agreement the following words and expressions shall have the meaning set out below:

"**Agreement**" means this Agreement and any Schedule;

"**Confidential Information**" has the meaning set out in clause 13.1;

"**Commencement Date**" means [/the date of this Agreement];

"**Documentation**" means the operating manuals, user instructions, technical literature and other related materials supplied to the Customer by the Company for aiding the use and application of the Software;

"**Environment**" means the network(s), file servers and computers specified in the Schedule, or as may be agreed from time to time, on which the Software is installed and/or used;

"**Fees**" has the meaning set out in the Schedule;

"**Force Majeure**" has the meaning set out in the clause 12.1;

"**Intellectual Property Rights**" means any and all registered and unregistered copyright patents, design rights, database and compilation rights, Marks (and related goodwill), trade secrets and other intellectual property rights, howsoever arising and in whatever media, and any applications for their protection or registration and all renewals and extensions anywhere in the world;

"**Maintenance Support Service**" means the provision of Updates by the Company as they become available and the provision of the maintenance support services set out in the Schedule, and "maintenance" and "maintain" shall be construed accordingly;

"**Marks**" means any and all names, brands, logos, trade marks, service marks, trade names and domain names;

"**Number of Users**" has the meaning set out in the Schedule;

9

"**Software**" means the software specified in the Schedule and any and all Updates and Upgrades, all in object code form, and Documentation which may be supplied by the Company from time to time;

"**Support Fees**" has the meaning set out in the Schedule;

"**Support Period**" has the meaning set out in the Schedule;

"**Term**" has the meaning set out in clause 9.1;

"**Update**" means a version of the Software consisting of corrections and minor functional enhancements to the prior version of the Software. Updates are registered by means of a change of the number to the right of the decimal point, e.g. 1.0 >> 1.1; and

"**Upgrade**" means a version of the Software consisting of substantial new functionality or other substantial changes to the prior version of the Software. Upgrades are registered by means of a change of the number to the left of the decimal point, e.g. 1.0 >> 2.0.

Except where the context otherwise requires, words denoting the singular include the plural and vice versa, words denoting any gender include any other genders, and words denoting persons include firms and corporations and vice versa.

Unless otherwise stated, a reference to:

a Clause or Schedule is a reference to a clause of or schedule to this Agreement. Clause headings are for ease of reference only and do not affect the construction of this Agreement;

"include" and "including" shall be construed without limitation; and

any Act of Parliament shall be deemed to include any amendment, replacement or re-enactment thereof then in force and to include any bye-laws, statutory instruments, rules, regulations, orders, notices, directions, consents, licences, conditions or permissions made thereunder.

Company Obligations

Within [30 days] of the date of this Agreement Company will provide Customer with a current version of the Software on CD-ROM.

Company will, from time to time, issue to the Customer Upgrades or Updates which the Customer should promptly apply to the Software.

Customer Obligations

The Customer must provide the Environment for the Software.

The Customer shall promptly notify Company of any actual or suspected infringement of Company Intellectual Property Rights including use of the Software in excess of the permitted Number of Users and Customer shall give

10

Company all reasonable assistance in detecting such infringement or access and preventing further infringement or access.

The Customer shall ensure that the Software is not used in any manner which reflects adversely upon the name, reputation and/or goodwill of Company and shall ensure that the Software is used in accordance with all applicable laws and regulations.

Licence Grant

Subject to clause 5, the Company grants to the Customer, and the Customer accepts, the following non-exclusive and non-transferrable rights for the duration of this Agreement:

to install the Software [in the Environment];

for the Customer's employees to use the Software; and

for the Customer to create one copy of the Software for backup or archival purposes only.

Licence Restrictions

At any time the number of people using the software must not exceed the Number of Users and the Customer must use reasonable safeguards to ensure that the Number of Users is not exceeded.

Customer and Customer's clients may not copy, modify or disassemble the Software except to the extent as permitted by applicable law and on prior written notice to Company.

The Customer shall not remove, alter, cover or obliterate any copyright or other proprietary rights notice used on or in connection with the Software without the prior written consent of Company. The Customer shall not permit any third party use of the Software whether by way of bureau, time-share, rental, sub-licence or other service to third parties.

Title and Intellectual Property Rights in the Software and any modifications and adaptations thereto shall vest in Company and its suppliers.

Support and Maintenance

Company warrants that, so long as Support Fees are not outstanding, it will during the Support Period provide the Maintenance Support Service to the Customer using reasonable skill and care.

Where the Environment has not been properly provided or maintained or where all Updates and Upgrades have not been applied Company may provide the Maintenance Support Service but only at an additional cost and only on an "as is" and "as available" basis.

11

Notwithstanding the generality of clause 6.1, Company makes no representations or warranties as to the period of time it will take to resolve any problem or query. The parties acknowledge that time is not of the essence. Company reserves the right to alter the Maintenance Support Service or any of the relevant provisions set out in this Agreement at any time by thirty (30) days prior written notice to the Customer.

Payment

Company shall invoice the Customer and the Customer shall pay the Fees and any other charges due to Company within thirty (30) days of the invoice date. All Fees and other charges are subject to VAT at the prevailing rate and are payable in Pounds Sterling. All Fees described herein are exclusive of any taxes, including any excise, sales, use, value added (VAT), withholding and similar taxes. Customer shall be liable and shall pay all applicable taxes associated with Fees. Customer shall gross up any payments to compensate for any withholding tax payable and Company shall credit Customer with any tax credit received within 6 months by Company in respect of such withholding.

If any sum due to Company remains outstanding after thirty (30) days from the invoice date then, without prejudice to any other rights and remedies of Company, such sums shall attract interest at the then current rate of [Bank] plus two percent, before and after judgement, from the invoice date until payment is made in full, compounded at monthly intervals.

In the event that Company has to resort to collection enforcement as a result of the non-payment of its charges, Company will charge any reasonable expenses it has incurred associated with such collection including, but not limited to reasonable legal costs, lawyers' fees, court costs and collection agency fees.

Warranties

Each party warrants to the other that it has the full right, power and authority to enter into and perform this Agreement and has not entered into any arrangement which in any way conflicts with this Agreement or inhibits, restricts or impairs its ability to perform its obligations under this Agreement.

Company warrants that the Software with all Updates and Upgrades applied shall operate substantially in accordance with the Documentation for a period of 90 days from the date of delivery. Company does not warrant that the Software will meet the Licensee's requirements or that the operation of the Software will be uninterrupted or error free or that defects in the Software will be corrected.

12

Company warrants that the Software shall not infringe any copyright, right of privacy, right of publicity or personality or any other like right of any person in the UK and does not incorporate any unlicensed third party source material.

Except as expressly provided in this Agreement, each party expressly disclaims any further representations, warranties, conditions or other terms, express or implied, by statute, collaterally or otherwise, including but not limited to implied warranties, conditions or other terms of satisfactory quality, fitness for a particular purpose or reasonable care and skill.

Term

The Agreement shall commence on the Commencement Date and shall continue for a period of one year unless and until terminated in accordance with clause 14 ("Term"). On each anniversary of the Commencement Date this Agreement shall renew for a further period of one year unless either party gives the other not less that three months' prior written notice to expire on or before such anniversary.

Indemnities

Each party shall indemnify and keep the other party fully and effectively indemnified on demand against any liability, damage, expense, claim or cost (including reasonable legal costs and expenses) suffered by the other party as a result of any breach by the first party of the warranties set out in clause 8 of this Agreement, provided that where products are concerned the latest version of the products have been used in normal circumstances without modification.

To take benefit of an indemnity, that party shall: (i) notify the other party promptly in writing and in any event within ten (10) business days of first learning of any such claim, lawsuit, action or proceeding; (ii) consent to the other party having the sole authority to control the defence and/or settlement of any such claim, lawsuit, action or proceeding; and (iii) provide reasonable co-operation and assistance to the other party, at that party's expense, in defending any such claim, lawsuit, action or proceeding.

Limitation of Liability

Save as provided in clause 11.3, neither party shall be liable in contract, tort (including negligence), statutory duty, pre-contract or other representations (other than fraudulent or negligent misrepresentations) or otherwise arising out of or in connection with this Agreement for: (a) consequential, indirect or special loss or damage; or (b) any loss of goodwill or reputation; or (c) any economic losses (including loss of revenues, profits, contracts, business or anticipated savings). In each case whether advised of the possibility of such loss or damage and howsoever incurred.

Save as provided in clause 10.1 and 11.3, both parties agree that the maximum liability of either party in contract, tort (including negligence), statutory duty, pre-contract or other representations (other than fraudulent or negligent misrepresentations) or otherwise arising out of or in connection with this Agreement, and each part thereof, including its execution and performance; shall, in respect of any one or more events or series of events (whether connected or unconnected) taking place within any twelve month period, be limited to the Licence Fees paid by Licensee in such period or [£10,000], whichever is the greater.

Nothing in this Agreement shall exclude or limit liability for death or personal injury resulting from the negligence of either party or their servants, agents or employees acting in the course of their duties.

Force Majeure

Either party will not be liable for any failure or delay in performing its obligations under this Agreement to the extent that this failure or delay is the result of any cause or circumstance beyond the reasonable control of that party including acts of god, war, civil commotion or industrial dispute and that failure could not have been prevented or overcome by that party acting reasonably and prudently. If either party is prevented from performing its obligations for a period exceeding six (6) months due to Force Majeure then the other party may terminate this Agreement on one month written notice.

Confidentiality and Data

During the term of this Agreement and for two (2) years thereafter, each party will treat as confidential all information that they obtain concerning, but not limited to, the business, finances, technology and affairs of the other, ("Confidential Information"). Each of the parties will use at least the same degree of care (and not less than a reasonable degree of care) it uses to prevent the disclosure of its own confidential information of like importance, to prevent the disclosure of Confidential Information of the other party. Each party will promptly notify the other party of any actual or suspected misuse or unauthorised disclosure of the other party's Confidential Information.

The provisions of this clause 13 shall cease to apply to: (i) information that has come into the public domain other than by breach of this clause or any other duty of confidence; (ii) information that is obtained from a third party without breach of this clause or any other duty of confidence; and (iii) information that

14

is required to be disclosed by a regulatory or government body or court of competent jurisdiction with power to compel the disclosure.

In the event of termination or expiration of this Agreement, each party shall return or on request of the other party, destroy the Confidential Information of that party.

Each party will comply with its obligations pursuant to the Data Protection Act 1998 and any subordinate legislation and official guidelines.

Termination

Each party shall have the right to terminate this Agreement on written notice in the event that the other:

commits any material breach of the terms of this Agreement which, in the case of a breach capable of remedy, is not remedied within 30 days of service of a notice specifying the breach and stating the intention to terminate the Agreement if not remedied; or

holds any meeting with or proposes to enter into or has proposed to it any arrangement or composition with its creditors (including any voluntary arrangement as described in the Insolvency Act 1986); has a receiver, administrator, or other encumbrancer take possession of or appointed over or has any distress, execution or other process levied or enforced (and not discharged within 7 days) upon the whole or substantially all of its assets; ceases or threatens to cease to carry on business or becomes unable to pay its debts within the meaning of Section 123 of the Insolvency Act 1986.

Forthwith upon the termination of this Agreement each party shall return all licensed and/or confidential materials, and all copies in whole or part, of the other or if requested by the other party, shall destroy them and certify in writing to the Licensor that they have been destroyed.

Termination or expiry of this Agreement shall be without prejudice to any rights, liabilities or remedies of a party accrued before termination nor shall it affect any provision of this Agreement which is expressly intended to come into or continue in force after termination or expiry.

Severance

To the extent that any provision of this Agreement is found by any court or competent authority to be invalid, unlawful or unenforceable in any jurisdiction, that provision shall be deemed not to be a part of this Agreement, it shall not affect the validity, lawfulness or enforceability of the remainder of this Agreement nor shall it affect the validity, lawfulness or enforceability of that provision in any other jurisdiction.

15

Waiver

No failure or delay by any party in exercising any right, power or remedy under this Agreement will operate as a waiver of that or any other right, power or remedy nor will any single or partial exercise by either party of any right, power or remedy preclude any further exercise of any other right, power or remedy.

Time of the Essence

Any times, dates or periods specified in the agreement may be extended or altered by agreement in writing between the parties. However, time shall not be of the essence except where it is expressly stated to apply.

Insurance

Each party must have in force and maintain with a reputable insurance company professional indemnity insurance exceeding [£1,000,000].

Further Assurance

Each party shall at the cost and expense of the other party use all reasonable endeavours to do all such further acts and things and execute or procure the execution of all such other documents as that party may from time to time reasonably require for the purpose of giving that party the full benefit of the assets, rights and benefits to be transferred to the other party under this agreement.

Relationship

Nothing in this Agreement shall or shall be deemed to create a partnership or joint venture or contract of employment of any kind between the parties nor shall it be deemed to grant any authority to the other not expressly set out in the Agreement or create any agency between the parties.

Assignment and Sub-contracting

Either party shall not be entitled to assign, transfer, charge or license the whole or any part of its rights and/or obligations under this Agreement to any party without consent of the other party [which shall not be unreasonably withheld or delayed].

[Neither/either] party may engage any person, firm or company as its sub-contractor to perform any of its obligations, but shall not be released from any liability therefor.

16

Rights of Third Parties

Nothing in this Agreement shall create or confer any rights or other benefits whether pursuant to the Contracts (Rights of Third Parties) Act 1999 or otherwise in favour of any person other than the parties to this Agreement.

Notices

Any notice given under this Agreement will be in writing and shall be deemed served if hand delivered to the other party or sent by pre-paid post, facsimile transmission or confirmed email copy to the address or transmission number of that party specified on page 1 of this Agreement or such other address or number as may be notified under this Agreement by that party from time to time for this purpose. Notices will be deemed to be effective on personal delivery, within 48 hours of posting (if the address is in the UK or within 96 hours otherwise), or upon confirmation of receipt of facsimile or email.

Entire Agreement

Each party confirms that this Agreement sets out the entire agreement and understanding between the parties and that it supersedes all previous agreements, arrangements and understandings between them relating to the subject matter of the Agreement. Each party confirms that it has not relied upon any statement, representation or understanding that is not an express term of this Agreement and shall not have any remedy in respect of any statement, representation or understanding which is not an express term unless made fraudulently.

Governing Law and Jurisdiction

This Agreement shall be governed by and construed in accordance with the law of England and each party hereby irrevocably submits to the non-exclusive jurisdiction of the courts of England.

Dispute Resolution

If any dispute arises between the parties out of this Agreement, the parties shall attempt to settle it by mediation in accordance with the Centre for Dispute Resolution (CEDR) Model Mediation Procedure.

If the parties have not settled the dispute by mediation within [42] days from the initiation of the mediation, the dispute shall be referred to arbitration under the Rules of the London Court of International Arbitration in force at the date of this Agreement. The parties hereby agree that:

17

The tribunal shall consist of [one/three] arbitrator[s] who [specify qualifications/nationalities etc.];

If the parties do not agree on the appointment of the arbitrator[s], the London Court of International Arbitration shall determine the arbitrator[s];

The place of arbitration shall be London; and

The language of the arbitration shall be English.

General

The rights and remedies of the parties under this Agreement are cumulative and in addition to any rights and remedies provided by law. Any variation to this Agreement must be in writing and agreed by the parties. This agreement may be executed in counterpart.

This Agreement has been signed on the date appearing at the head of page 1.

Signed by	)	
for and on behalf of	)	Director
Company	)	
	)	Director/Secretary
Signed by	)	
for and on behalf of	)	Director
Customer	)	
	)	Director/Secretary

18

Schedule to contain details of:

- Environment
- Fees
- Maintenance Support Services
- Number of Users
- Software
- Support Fees
- Support Period

19

A2.3 Web Services Development and Provision

This Agreement is made the [   ] day of [   ]
Between:
(1) [Company Name] a company incorporated in England under registration number [   ], the registered office of which is at [   ] ("**Company**"); and
(2) [Customer Name] a company incorporated in England under registration number [   ], the registered office of which is at [   ] ("**Customer**").

Definitions and Interpretation

In this Agreement the following words and expressions shall have the meaning set out below:

"**Acceptance**" means the passing of the acceptance tests pursuant to clause 2, and "**Accepted**" shall be construed accordingly;

"**Agreement**" means this Agreement and any Schedule 2;

"**Brand Features**" means trade marks, service marks, logos, insignias, devices and other distinctive brand features (whether registered or unregistered) including those set out in the Schedule 2;

"**Confidential Information**" has the meaning set out in clause 13.1;

"**Commencement Date**" means [/the date of this Agreement];

"**Content**" the information, data and software provided to Company by the Customer for incorporation into the Web Services as specified in the Schedule 2;

"**Error**" any reproducible and material failure to comply with the Specification;

"**Force Majeure**" has the meaning set out in the clause 12.1;

"**Fees**" has the meaning set out in the Schedule 2;

"**Intellectual Property Rights**" means any and all registered and unregistered copyright patents, design rights, database and compilation rights, Marks (and related goodwill), trade secrets and other intellectual property rights, howsoever arising and in whatever media, and any applications for their protection or registration and all renewals and extensions anywhere in the world;

"**Marks**" means any and all names, brands, logos, trade marks, service marks, trade names and domain names;

20

"**Password**" means the codes which facilitate access to the Web Services and their configuration;

"**Project Plan**" the plan set out in the Schedule 2;

"**Representative**" a person or persons nominated by each party in writing from time to time;

"**Response**" has the meaning set out in clause 3.2;

"**Specification**" the description of Web Services as set out in the Schedule 2, as amended pursuant to clause 3;

"**Term**" has the meaning set out in clause 9.1; and

"**Web Services**" the web services provided from [www.Company.com] or such other address notified to Customer by Company.

Except where the context otherwise requires, words denoting the singular include the plural and vice versa, words denoting any gender include any other genders, and words denoting persons include firms and corporations and vice versa.

Unless otherwise stated, a reference to:

a Clause or Schedule is a reference to a clause of or schedule to this Agreement. Clause headings are for ease of reference only and do not affect the construction of this Agreement;

"include" and "including" shall be construed without limitation; and

any Act of Parliament shall be deemed to include any amendment, replacement or re-enactment thereof then in force and to include any bye-laws, statutory instruments, rules, regulations, orders, notices, directions, consents, licences, conditions or permissions made thereunder.

Development and Acceptance

Subject to the payment of the Fees and the provision of Content by Customer in an agreed format and on a timely basis, Company agrees to customise and implement the Web Services using reasonable endeavours and in accordance with the Specification, the Project Plan and the other provisions of this Agreement.

Company shall notify the Customer when the Web Services are available for testing. As soon as reasonably practicable (and in any event within 5 working days) after such date, the Customer shall notify Company of any Errors in that version of the Web Services.

If the Customer notifies Company of any Errors, Company shall endeavour to correct such Errors and make the Web Services available to the Customer pursuant to clause 2.2 above.

21

If the Customer does not notify Company of any Errors within five (5) working days of Company making that version of the Web Services available, or if the Customer notifies Company that there are no Errors in that version, then the Web Services shall be Accepted.

Amendments to Specification

The parties agree that amendments to the Specification and/or Project Plan can only be made in writing. If at any time the Customer wishes to amend the Specification or any aspect of the implementation of the Web Services the Customer shall provide Company with full written details together with such further information as Company may require in order to assess the proposed amendments.

Company shall within a reasonable time of receipt of all of the information specified in clause 3.1 submit to the Customer a revised Specification, Project Plan and quotation for any additional Fees required in order to implement the amendments proposed by the Customer ("Response").

If the Customer wishes to accept the Response then it shall do so within 5 working days of its receipt, in which case this Agreement (including the Specification, Project Plan and the Fees) shall be amended in accordance with the Response otherwise the work shall continue without amendment.

Web Service Provision

On condition that the Customer fulfils its obligations under this agreement (including the payment of Fees) then from the date of Acceptance Company shall make the Web Services available to the Customer in accordance with the service levels provided in this clause 4.

Company shall endeavour to ensure that the Web Services are available 24 hours per day without any unscheduled interruptions. The Web Services are provided over the internet and Company can accept no responsibility for degradation or disruption of the Web Services consequential upon the performance of the internet, from acts or omissions by the Customer, including the introduction of a virus or uploading inappropriate content.

It is technically impracticable to provide fault free Web Services and Company does not agree to do so and the Customer understands that the Web Services may be suspended at short or no notice for essential maintenance or for reasons of Force Majeure.

Occasionally Company may:

change the technical specification of the Web Services, provided that any change to the technical specification does not materially adversely affect the performance of the Web Services; or

22

suspend the Web Services for operational reasons such as repair, maintenance or improvement of the Web Services. Company will restore the Web Services as soon as it reasonably can after any suspension; or

give the Customer instructions which it believes are necessary for the proper operation of the Web Service.

Before doing any of the acts described in clause 4.4, Company will endeavour to give the Customer notice and whenever practicable will agree with the Customer when the Web Services will be suspended.

Customer obligations

The Customer agrees that:

this Agreement does not include the provision of equipment, telecommunications or other services necessary to access the Web Services and the Customer is responsible for providing and maintaining suitable equipment, telecommunications and support services to facilitate access to the Web Services;

to keep all Passwords secret at all times and to inform Company and change the password if the Customer believes that an unauthorised person has become aware of any of the Passwords;

to only use the Web Services for lawful purposes; and

to keep backups of all data contained on the Site or which form part of the Web Services.

The Customer agrees that it will not:

knowingly or recklessly post, link to or transmit any material that is unlawful, threatening, abusive, harmful, malicious, libellous, defamatory, obscene, pornographic, profane or otherwise objectionable in any way; or any material containing a virus or other hostile computer program; or

post, link to or transmit any material that shall constitute or encourage a criminal offence, give rise to civil liability or that violates or infringes any trade mark, copyright, other Intellectual Property Rights or similar rights of any person, firm or Customer under the laws of any jurisdiction.

Payment

Company shall invoice the Customer and the Customer shall pay the Fees and any other charges due to Company within thirty (30) days of the invoice date. All Fees and other charges are subject to VAT at the prevailing rate and are payable in Pounds Sterling. All Fees described herein are exclusive of any taxes, including any excise, sales, use, value added (VAT), withholding and similar taxes. Customer shall be liable and shall pay all applicable taxes associated with Fees. Customer shall gross up any payments to compensate for any withholding tax payable and Company shall credit Customer with any tax credit received within six (6) months by Company in respect of such withholding.

If any sum due to Company remains outstanding after thirty (30) days from the invoice date then, without prejudice to any other rights and remedies of Company, such sums shall attract interest at the then current rate of [Bank] plus two percent, before and after judgement, from the invoice date until payment is made in full, compounded at monthly intervals.

In the event that Company has to resort to collection enforcement as a result of the non-payment of its charges, Company will charge any reasonable expenses it has incurred associated with such collection including, but not limited to reasonable legal costs, lawyers' fees, court costs and collection agency fees.

Warranties

Each party warrants to the other that it has the full right, power and authority to enter into and perform this Agreement and has not entered into any arrangement which in any way conflicts with this Agreement or inhibits, restricts or impairs its ability to perform its obligations under this Agreement.

The Customer warrants that it has sufficient rights (including Intellectual Property Rights) in the Content to grant to Company the rights set out and contemplated in this agreement and has obtained and will maintain and renew, as appropriate, all necessary licences, authorisations and consents which are necessary for Company to provide the Web Services.

The Customer warrants to Company that the Content complies with all applicable law including all relevant consumer protection legislation and advertising codes and does not contain material that is obscene, blasphemous, defamatory, infringing of any rights of any third party or otherwise legally actionable under any civil or criminal laws in force in any legal jurisdiction from which the Web Services may be accessible or which might bring Company into disrepute.

Except as expressly provided in this agreement, each party expressly disclaims any further representations, warranties, conditions or other terms, express or implied, by statute, collaterally or otherwise, including but not limited to implied warranties, conditions or other terms of satisfactory quality, fitness for a particular purpose or reasonable care and skill.

24

Intellectual Property Rights

Nothing in this Agreement gives the Customer any right (including Intellectual Property Right), title or interest in the Web Services or Company Brand Features and their online implementation and any part thereof.

The Customer warrants that the Intellectual Property Rights in the Content and the Customer Brand Features do not infringe the Intellectual Property Rights of any third party.

Nothing in this Agreement gives Company any right (including Intellectual Property Right), title or interest in Content or the Customer Brand Features and any part thereof.

Company warrants that the Intellectual Property Rights in the Company Brand Features when used as part of the Web Services do not infringe the Intellectual Property Rights of any third party.

The Customer hereby grants Company a non-exclusive, royalty free, non-transferable world-wide licence to store, reproduce, transmit and display Content and Customer Brand Features for the purpose of this Agreement and to permit third parties to download, print, store and use Content and the Customer Brand Features.

Term

The Agreement shall commence on the Commencement Date and shall continue for a period of one year unless and until terminated in accordance with clause 14 ("Term"). On each anniversary of the Commencement Date this Agreement shall renew for a further period of one year unless either party gives the other not less that three months' prior written notice to expire on or before such anniversary.

Indemnities

Each party shall indemnify and keep the other party fully and effectively indemnified on demand against any liability, damage, expense, claim or cost (including reasonable legal costs and expenses) suffered by the other party as a result of any breach by the first party of the warranties set out in clause 7 of this Agreement, provided that where products are concerned the latest version of the products have been used in normal circumstances without modification.

To take benefit of an indemnity, that party shall: (i) notify the other party promptly in writing and in any event within ten (10) business days of first learning of any such claim, lawsuit, action or proceeding; (ii) consent to the other party having the sole authority to control the defence and/or settlement of any such claim, lawsuit, action or proceeding; and (iii) provide reasonable co-

25

operation and assistance to the other party, at that party's expense, in defending any such claim, lawsuit, action or proceeding.

Limitation of Liability

Save as provided in clause 11.3, neither party shall be liable in contract, tort (including negligence), statutory duty, pre-contract or other representations (other than fraudulent or negligent misrepresentations) or otherwise arising out of or in connection with this Agreement for: (a) consequential, indirect or special loss or damage; or (b) any loss of goodwill or reputation; or (c) any economic losses (including loss of revenues, profits, contracts, business or anticipated savings). In each case whether advised of the possibility of such loss or damage and howsoever incurred.

Save as provided in clause 10.1 and 11.3, both parties agree that the maximum liability of either party in contract, tort (including negligence), statutory duty, pre-contract or other representations (other than fraudulent or negligent misrepresentations) or otherwise arising out of or in connection with this Agreement, and each part thereof, including its execution and performance; shall, in respect of any one or more events or series of events (whether connected or unconnected) taking place within any twelve month period, be limited to the Licence Fees paid by Licensee in such period or [£10,000], whichever is the greater.

Nothing in this Agreement shall exclude or limit liability for death or personal injury resulting from the negligence of either party or their servants, agents or employees acting in the course of their duties.

Force Majeure

Either party will not be liable for any failure or delay in performing its obligations under this Agreement to the extent that this failure or delay is the result of any cause or circumstance beyond the reasonable control of that party including acts of god, war, civil commotion or industrial dispute and that failure could not have been prevented or overcome by that party acting reasonably and prudently. If either party is prevented from performing its obligations for a period exceeding six (6) months due to Force Majeure then the other party may terminate this Agreement on one month written notice.

Confidentiality and Data

During the term of this Agreement and for two (2) years thereafter, each party will treat as confidential all information that they obtain concerning, but not limited to, the business, finances, technology and affairs of the other,

("Confidential Information"). Each of the parties will use at least the same degree of care (and not less than a reasonable degree of care) it uses to prevent the disclosure of its own confidential information of like importance, to prevent the disclosure of Confidential Information of the other party. Each party will promptly notify the other party of any actual or suspected misuse or unauthorised disclosure of the other party's Confidential Information.

The provisions of this clause 13 shall cease to apply to: (i) information that has come into the public domain other than by breach of this clause or any other duty of confidence; (ii) information that is obtained from a third party without breach of this clause or any other duty of confidence; and (iii) information that is required to be disclosed by a regulatory or government body or court of competent jurisdiction with power to compel the disclosure.

In the event of termination or expiration of this Agreement, each party shall return or on request of the other party, destroy the Confidential Information of that party.

Each party will comply with its obligations pursuant to the Data Protection Act 1998 and any subordinate legislation and official guidelines.

Termination

Each party shall have the right to terminate this Agreement on written notice in the event that the other:

commits any material breach of the terms of this Agreement which, in the case of a breach capable of remedy, is not remedied within thirty (30) days of service of a notice specifying the breach and stating the intention to terminate the Agreement if not remedied; or

holds any meeting with or proposes to enter into or has proposed to it any arrangement or composition with its creditors (including any voluntary arrangement as described in the Insolvency Act 1986); has a receiver, administrator, or other encumbrancer take possession of or appointed over or has any distress, execution or other process levied or enforced (and not discharged within 7 days) upon the whole or substantially all of its assets; ceases or threatens to cease to carry on business or becomes unable to pay its debts within the meaning of Section 123 of the Insolvency Act 1986.

Forthwith upon the termination of this Agreement each party shall return all licensed and/or confidential materials, and all copies in whole or part, of the other or if requested by the other party, shall destroy them and certify in writing to the Licensor that they have been destroyed.

Termination or expiry of this Agreement shall be without prejudice to any rights, liabilities or remedies of a party accrued before termination nor shall it

27

affect any provision of this Agreement which is expressly intended to come into or continue in force after termination or expiry.

Severance
To the extent that any provision of this Agreement is found by any court or competent authority to be invalid, unlawful or unenforceable in any jurisdiction, that provision shall be deemed not to be a part of this Agreement, it shall not affect the validity, lawfulness or enforceability of the remainder of this Agreement nor shall it affect the validity, lawfulness or enforceability of that provision in any other jurisdiction.

Waiver
No failure or delay by any party in exercising any right, power or remedy under this Agreement will operate as a waiver of that or any other right, power or remedy nor will any single or partial exercise by either party of any right, power or remedy preclude any further exercise of any other right, power or remedy.

Time of the Essence
Any times, dates or periods specified in the agreement may be extended or altered by agreement in writing between the parties. However, time shall not be of the essence except where it is expressly stated to apply.

Insurance
Each party must have in force and maintain with a reputable insurance company professional indemnity insurance exceeding [£1,000,000].

Further Assurance
Each party shall at the cost and expense of the other party use all reasonable endeavours to do all such further acts and things and execute or procure the execution of all such other documents as that party may from time to time reasonably require for the purpose of giving that party the full benefit of the assets, rights and benefits to be transferred to the other party under this agreement.

Relationship
Nothing in this Agreement shall or shall be deemed to create a partnership or joint venture or contract of employment of any kind between the parties nor shall it be deemed to grant any authority to the other not expressly set out in the Agreement or create any agency between the parties.

28

Assignment and Sub-contracting

Either party shall not be entitled to assign, transfer, charge or license the whole or any part of its rights and/or obligations under this Agreement to any party without consent of the other party [which shall not be unreasonably withheld or delayed].

[Neither/either] party may engage any person, firm or company as its sub-contractor to perform any of its obligations, but shall not be released from any liability therefor.

Rights of Third Parties

Nothing in this Agreement shall create or confer any rights or other benefits whether pursuant to the Contracts (Rights of Third Parties) Act 1999 or otherwise in favour of any person other than the parties to this Agreement.

Notices

Any notice given under this Agreement will be in writing and shall be deemed served if hand delivered to the other party or sent by pre-paid post, facsimile transmission or confirmed email copy to the address or transmission number of that party specified on page 1 of this Agreement or such other address or number as may be notified under this Agreement by that party from time to time for this purpose. Notices will be deemed to be effective on personal delivery, within 48 hours of posting (if the address is in the UK or within 96 hours otherwise), or upon confirmation of receipt of facsimile or email.

Entire Agreement

Each party confirms that this Agreement sets out the entire agreement and understanding between the parties and that it supersedes all previous agreements, arrangements and understandings between them relating to the subject matter of the Agreement. Each party confirms that it has not relied upon any statement, representation or understanding that is not an express term of this Agreement and shall not have any remedy in respect of any statement, representation or understanding which is not an express term unless made fraudulently.

Governing Law and Jurisdiction

This Agreement shall be governed by and construed in accordance with the law of England and each party hereby irrevocably submits to the non-exclusive jurisdiction of the courts of England.

Dispute Resolution

Each party shall ensure that a Representative is appointed for the duration of this Agreement.

If any dispute arises between the parties out of this Agreement, the parties shall follow the dispute resolution procedure set out in Schedule 1.

If the parties have not settled the dispute pursuant to Schedule 1 within [60] days from the initiation of the procedure, the parties shall attempt to settle it by mediation in accordance with the Centre for Dispute Resolution (CEDR) Model Mediation Procedure.

If the parties have not settled the dispute by mediation within [42] days from the initiation of the mediation the dispute shall be referred to arbitration under the Rules of the London Court of International Arbitration in force at the date of this Agreement. The parties hereby agree that:

The tribunal shall consist of [one/three] arbitrator[s] who [specify qualifications/nationalities etc.];

If the parties do not agree on the appointment of the arbitrator[s], the London Court of International Arbitration shall determine the arbitrator[s];

The place of arbitration shall be London; and

The language of the arbitration shall be English.

General

The rights and remedies of the parties under this Agreement are cumulative and in addition to any rights and remedies provided by law. Any variation to this Agreement must be in writing and agreed by the parties. This agreement may be executed in counterpart.

This Agreement has been signed on the date appearing at the head of page 1.

Signed by	)	
for and on behalf of	)	Director
Company	)	
	)	Director/Secretary
Signed by	)	
for and on behalf of	)	Director
Customer	)	
	)	Director/Secretary

30

Schedule 1 – Dispute Resolution Procedure

In respect of any failure or dispute relating to this Agreement, the parties may carry out the following steps. References to "days" shall be to calendar days.

1.1 The matter shall be notified by the Representative of one party to the Representative of the other. The Representatives shall agree on a procedure and timescale for rectifying the failure or resolving the dispute.

1.2 If either:

    (a) the parties fail to agree the procedure and timescale referred to above within thirty (30) days of notification; or

    (b) the fault is not rectified or dispute resolved in accordance with the procedure and timescale

    (c) then the non-defaulting party shall be entitled to serve a notice on the other requiring the other to rectify such matter within a further period of thirty (30) days of receipt of such notice.

1.3 During the second thirty (30) day period (or the period agreed) as referred to in clause 1.2 above, if the matter is not resolved within the first 10 days of such period (the "Escalation Period"), then each party shall immediately require its CEO (or equivalent) to meet with the equivalent person from the other party to attempt to rectify the matter.

31

Schedule 2 to contain details of:
- Brand Features
- Commencement Date
- Content
- Fees
- Specification
- Project Plan

32

A2.4   Hosting Agreement

This Agreement is made the [   ] day of [   ]

Between:

(1) [Company Name] a company incorporated in England under registration number [   ], the registered office of which is at [   ] ("**Company**"); and

(2) [Customer Name] a company incorporated in England under registration number [   ], the registered office of which is at [   ] ("**Customer**").

Definitions and Interpretation

In this Agreement the following words and expressions shall have the meaning set out below:

"**Agreement**" means this Agreement and any Schedule;

"**Brand Features**" means Marks, logos, insignias, devices and other distinctive brand features (whether registered or unregistered) including those set out in the Schedule;

"**Commencement Date**" means the commencement date for the Services as set out in the Schedule;

"**Confidential Information**" has the meaning set out in clause 11.1;

"**Content**" the information, data and software provided to Company by the Customer for incorporation into the Services as specified in the Schedule;

"**Commencement Date**" means [/the date of this Agreement];

"**Force Majeure**" has the meaning set out in the clause 10.1;

"**Fees**" has the meaning set out in the Schedule;

"**Intellectual Property Rights**" means any and all registered and unregistered copyright patents, design rights, database and compilation rights, Marks (and related goodwill), trade secrets and other intellectual property rights, howsoever arising and in whatever media, and any applications for their protection or registration and all renewals and extensions anywhere in the world;

"**Improper Use**" has the meaning set out in clause 3.2;

"**Marks**" means any and all names, brands, logos, trade marks, service marks, trade names and domain names; and

"**Password**" means the codes which facilitate access to the Services and their configuration;

33

"**Services**" means the services provided by the Company on the terms and conditions of this Agreement as described in the Schedule;

"**SLA**" means the Service Level Agreement for the Services set out in the Schedule;

"**Users**" means any third party who makes use of the Services; and

"**Term**" has the meaning set out in clause 7.1.

Except where the context otherwise requires, words denoting the singular include the plural and vice versa, words denoting any gender include any other genders, and words denoting persons include firms and corporations and vice versa.

Unless otherwise stated, a reference to:

a Clause or Schedule is a reference to a clause of or schedule to this Agreement. Clause headings are for ease of reference only and do not affect the construction of this Agreement;

"include" and "including" shall be construed without limitation; and

any Act of Parliament shall be deemed to include any amendment, replacement or re-enactment thereof then in force and to include any bye-laws, statutory instruments, rules, regulations, orders, notices, directions, consents, licences, conditions or permissions made thereunder.

Company Obligations

On condition that the Customer fulfils its obligations under this agreement (including the payment of Fees) then from the Commencement Date, Company agrees to provide the Services using reasonable endeavours and in accordance with the SLA.

The Services are provided via the internet and Company can accept no responsibility for apparent or actual degradation or disruption of the Services consequential upon the performance of the internet or from Improper Use.

It is technically impracticable to provide fault free Services and Company does not agree to do so and the Customer understands that the Services may be suspended at short or no notice for essential maintenance or for reasons of Force Majeure.

At any time the Company may:

change the technical specification of the Services, provided that any change to the technical specification does not materially adversely affect the performance of the Services;

suspend the Services for operational reasons such as repair, maintenance or improvement of the Services. Company will restore the Services as soon as it reasonably can after any suspension;

34

disable any software or script provided by the Customer to form part of the Service if it materially adversely affects the performance of the Service or Company's network or computer systems; and

suspend or modify the Services until further notice if there is Improper Use, if the Customer is in breach of a material obligation of this Agreement or if required to do so by any governmental, regulatory or other competent authority. Before doing any of the acts described in clause 2.4, Company will endeavour, but shall not be obliged, to give the Customer notice and whenever practicable will agree with the Customer when the Services will be suspended and/or modified and to what extent.

The Company shall notify the Customer when access to the Service exceeds or is likely to exceed the specified bandwidth or allocated storage as set out in the Schedule.

Customer Obligations

The Customer agrees and shall ensure that the Users understand:

that the Service does not include the provision of equipment, telecommunications or other services necessary to access the Services and the Customer and/or the Users are responsible for providing and maintaining suitable equipment, telecommunications and services to facilitate access to the Services;

to keep all Passwords secret at all times and to inform Company and change the password if the Customer or Users believe that an unauthorised person has become aware of any of the Passwords;

to only use the Services for lawful purposes; and

to keep up to date and accurate backups of all Customer data and User data which forms part of the Services.

The Customer agrees that it will not itself and it will require that the Users shall not:

upload, post, link to or transmit any material that is unlawful, threatening, abusive, harmful, malicious, libellous, defamatory, obscene, pornographic, profane or otherwise objectionable in any way; or any material containing a virus or other hostile computer program;

upload, post, link to or transmit any material that shall constitute or encourage a criminal offence, give rise to civil liability or that violates or infringes any trade mark, copyright, other Intellectual Property rights or similar rights of any person under the laws of any jurisdiction; and

interfere with or disrupt the Service or any computer systems or networks which either form part of the Service or are accessible via the Service.

35

The Customer shall at all times:

comply with all reasonable directions from time to time issued by Company in relation to the Services;

provide Content in an agreed format and on a timely basis;

comply with all applicable law and guidelines and codes of practice issued by regulatory authorities regarding on-line sales, marketing, conduct and content; and

ensure that a valid contact name, telephone number and email address for the Customer is available to users of the Service.

The Customer undertakes that:

all goods and services made available via the Services are consistent with the description of them, of satisfactory quality and reasonably fit for purpose;

the Customer has title to or is duly authorised to supply such goods or services; and

it shall take full responsibility for checking the accuracy of each transaction entered into by Users using the Service including any dealings relating to credit and/or debit cards.

Notwithstanding anything else in this Agreement, the Customer shall indemnify and keep the Company fully and effectively indemnified on demand against any liability, damage, expense, claim or cost (including reasonable legal costs and expenses) suffered by the other party as a result of any breach by the Customer of clauses 3.2 and 3.4.

Payment

Company shall invoice the Customer and the Customer shall pay the Fees and any other charges due to Company within thirty (30) days of the invoice date. All Fees and other charges are subject to VAT at the prevailing rate and are payable in Pounds Sterling. All Fees described herein are exclusive of any taxes, including any excise, sales, use, value added (VAT), withholding and similar taxes. Customer shall be liable and shall pay all applicable taxes associated with Fees. Customer shall gross up any payments to compensate for any withholding tax payable and Company shall credit Customer with any tax credit received within six (6) months by Company in respect of such withholding.

If any sum due to Company remains outstanding after thirty (30) days from the invoice date then, without prejudice to any other rights and remedies of Company, such sums shall attract interest at the then current rate of [Bank] plus two percent, before and after judgement, from the invoice date until payment is made in full, compounded at monthly intervals.

36

In the event that Company has to resort to collection enforcement as a result of the non-payment of its charges, Company will charge any reasonable expenses it has incurred associated with such collection including, but not limited to reasonable legal costs, lawyers' fees, court costs and collection agency fees.

Warranties

Each party warrants to the other that it has the full right, power and authority to enter into and perform this Agreement and has not entered into any arrangement which in any way conflicts with this Agreement or inhibits, restricts or impairs its ability to perform its obligations under this Agreement.

The Customer warrants that it has sufficient rights (including Intellectual Property Rights) in the Content to grant to Company the rights set out and contemplated in this agreement and has obtained and will maintain and renew, as appropriate, all necessary licences, authorisations and consents which are necessary for Company to provide the Services.

The Customer warrants to Company that the Content complies with all applicable law including all relevant consumer protection legislation and advertising codes and does not contain material that is obscene, blasphemous, defamatory, infringing of any rights of any third party or otherwise legally actionable under any civil or criminal laws in force in any legal jurisdiction from which the Services might be accessible or which might bring Company into disrepute.

Customer agrees that it will notify Company immediately if Customer becomes aware of any actual or potential claims, suits, actions, allegations or charges that could affect either party's ability to fully perform its duties or to exercise its rights under the Agreement.

Except as expressly provided in this agreement, each party expressly disclaims any further representations, warranties, conditions or other terms, express or implied, by statute, collaterally or otherwise, including but not limited to implied warranties, conditions or other terms of satisfactory quality, fitness for a particular purpose or reasonable care and skill.

Intellectual Property Rights

Nothing in this Agreement gives the Customer any right (including Intellectual Property Right), title or interest in the Services or Company Brand Features and their online implementation and any part thereof.

The Customer warrants that the Intellectual Property Rights in the Content and the Customer Brand Features do not infringe the Intellectual Property Rights of any third party.

37

Nothing in this Agreement gives Company any right (including Intellectual Property Right), title or interest in Content or the Customer Brand Features and any part thereof.

Company warrants that the Intellectual Property Rights in the Company Brand Features when used as part of the Services do not infringe the Intellectual Property Rights of any third party.

The Customer hereby grants Company a non-exclusive, royalty free, non-transferable world-wide licence to store, reproduce, transmit and display Content and Customer Brand Features for the purpose of this Agreement and to permit third parties to download, print, store and use Content and the Customer Brand Features.

Term

The Agreement shall commence on the Commencement Date and shall continue for a period of one year unless and until terminated in accordance with clause 10 ("Term"). On each anniversary of the Commencement Date this Agreement shall renew for a further period of one year unless either party gives the other not less that three months' prior written notice to expire on or before such anniversary.

Indemnities

Each party shall indemnify and keep the other party fully and effectively indemnified on demand against any liability, damage, expense, claim or cost (including reasonable legal costs and expenses) suffered by the other party as a result of any breach by the first party of the warranties set out in clause 5 of this Agreement, provided that where products are concerned the latest version of the products have been used in normal circumstances without modification.

To take benefit of an indemnity, that party shall: (i) notify the other party promptly in writing and in any event within ten (10) business days of first learning of any such claim, lawsuit, action or proceeding; (ii) consent to the other party having the sole authority to control the defence and/or settlement of any such claim, lawsuit, action or proceeding; and (iii) provide reasonable co-operation and assistance to the other party, at that party's expense, in defending any such claim, lawsuit, action or proceeding.

Limitation of Liability

Save as provided in clause 9.3, neither party shall be liable in contract, tort (including negligence), statutory duty, pre-contract or other representations (other than fraudulent or negligent misrepresentations) or otherwise arising out

38

of or in connection with this Agreement for: (a) consequential, indirect or special loss or damage; or (b) any loss of goodwill or reputation; or (c) any economic losses (including loss of revenues, profits, contracts, business or anticipated savings). In each case whether advised of the possibility of such loss or damage and howsoever incurred.

Save as provided in clause 8.1 and 9.3, both parties agree that the maximum liability of either party in contract, tort (including negligence), statutory duty, pre-contract or other representations (other than fraudulent or negligent misrepresentations) or otherwise arising out of or in connection with this Agreement, and each part thereof, including its execution and performance; shall, in respect of any one or more events or series of events (whether connected or unconnected) taking place within any twelve month period, be limited to the Licence Fees paid by Licensee in such period or [£10,000], whichever is the greater.

Nothing in this Agreement shall exclude or limit liability for death or personal injury resulting from the negligence of either party or their servants, agents or employees acting in the course of their duties.

Force Majeure

Either party will not be liable for any failure or delay in performing its obligations under this Agreement to the extent that this failure or delay is the result of any cause or circumstance beyond the reasonable control of that party including acts of god, war, civil commotion or industrial dispute and that failure could not have been prevented or overcome by that party acting reasonably and prudently. If either party is prevented from performing its obligations for a period exceeding six (6) months due to Force Majeure then the other party may terminate this Agreement on one month written notice.

Confidentiality and Data

During the term of this Agreement and for two (2) years thereafter, each party will treat as confidential all information that they obtain concerning, but not limited to, the business, finances, technology and affairs of the other, ("Confidential Information"). Each of the parties will use at least the same degree of care (and not less than a reasonable degree of care) it uses to prevent the disclosure of its own confidential information of like importance, to prevent the disclosure of Confidential Information of the other party. Each party will promptly notify the other party of any actual or suspected misuse or unauthorised disclosure of the other party's Confidential Information.

39

The provisions of this clause 11 shall cease to apply to: (i) information that has come into the public domain other than by breach of this clause or any other duty of confidence; (ii) information that is obtained from a third party without breach of this clause or any other duty of confidence; and (iii) information that is required to be disclosed by a regulatory or government body or court of competent jurisdiction with power to compel the disclosure.

In the event of termination or expiration of this Agreement, each party shall return or on request of the other party, destroy the Confidential Information of that party.

Each party will comply with its obligations pursuant to the Data Protection Act 1998 and any subordinate legislation and official guidelines.

Termination

Each party shall have the right to terminate this Agreement on written notice in the event that the other:

commits any material breach of the terms of this Agreement which, in the case of a breach capable of remedy, is not remedied within 30 days of service of a notice specifying the breach and stating the intention to terminate the Agreement if not remedied; or

holds any meeting with or proposes to enter into or has proposed to it any arrangement or composition with its creditors (including any voluntary arrangement as described in the Insolvency Act 1986); has a receiver, administrator, or other encumbrancer take possession of or appointed over or has any distress, execution or other process levied or enforced (and not discharged within 7 days) upon the whole or substantially all of its assets; ceases or threatens to cease to carry on business or becomes unable to pay its debts within the meaning of Section 123 of the Insolvency Act 1986.

Forthwith upon the termination of this Agreement each party shall return all licensed and/or confidential materials, and all copies in whole or part, of the other or if requested by the other party, shall destroy them and certify in writing to the Licensor that they have been destroyed.

Termination or expiry of this Agreement shall be without prejudice to any rights, liabilities or remedies of a party accrued before termination nor shall it affect any provision of this Agreement which is expressly intended to come into or continue in force after termination or expiry.

Severance

To the extent that any provision of this Agreement is found by any court or competent authority to be invalid, unlawful or unenforceable in any

40

jurisdiction, that provision shall be deemed not to be a part of this Agreement, it shall not affect the validity, lawfulness or enforceability of the remainder of this Agreement nor shall it affect the validity, lawfulness or enforceability of that provision in any other jurisdiction.

Waiver
No failure or delay by any party in exercising any right, power or remedy under this Agreement will operate as a waiver of that or any other right, power or remedy nor will any single or partial exercise by either party of any right, power or remedy preclude any further exercise of any other right, power or remedy.

Time of the Essence
Any times, dates or periods specified in the agreement may be extended or altered by agreement in writing between the parties. However, time shall not be of the essence except where it is expressly stated to apply.

Insurance
Each party must have in force and maintain with a reputable insurance company professional indemnity insurance exceeding [£1,000,000].

Further Assurance
Each party shall at the cost and expense of the other party use all reasonable endeavours to do all such further acts and things and execute or procure the execution of all such other documents as that party may from time to time reasonably require for the purpose of giving that party the full benefit of the assets, rights and benefits to be transferred to the other party under this agreement.

Relationship
Nothing in this Agreement shall or shall be deemed to create a partnership or joint venture or contract of employment of any kind between the parties nor shall it be deemed to grant any authority to the other not expressly set out in the Agreement or create any agency between the parties.

Assignment and Sub-contracting
Either party shall not be entitled to assign, transfer, charge or license the whole or any part of its rights and/or obligations under this Agreement to any party without consent of the other party [which shall not be unreasonably withheld or delayed].

41

[Neither/either] party may engage any person, firm or company as its subcontractor to perform any of its obligations, but shall not be released from any liability therefor.

Rights of Third Parties
Nothing in this Agreement shall create or confer any rights or other benefits whether pursuant to the Contracts (Rights of Third Parties) Act 1999 or otherwise in favour of any person other than the parties to this Agreement.

Notices
Any notice given under this Agreement will be in writing and shall be deemed served if hand delivered to the other party or sent by pre-paid post, facsimile transmission or confirmed email copy to the address or transmission number of that party specified on page 1 of this Agreement or such other address or number as may be notified under this Agreement by that party from time to time for this purpose. Notices will be deemed to be effective on personal delivery, within 48 hours of posting (if the address is in the UK or within 96 hours otherwise), or upon confirmation of receipt of facsimile or email.

Entire Agreement
Each party confirms that this Agreement sets out the entire agreement and understanding between the parties and that it supersedes all previous agreements, arrangements and understandings between them relating to the subject matter of the Agreement. Each party confirms that it has not relied upon any statement, representation or understanding that is not an express term of this Agreement and shall not have any remedy in respect of any statement, representation or understanding which is not an express term unless made fraudulently.

Governing Law and Jurisdiction
This Agreement shall be governed by and construed in accordance with the law of England and each party hereby irrevocably submits to the non-exclusive jurisdiction of the courts of England.

Dispute Resolution
If any dispute arises between the parties out of this Agreement, the parties shall attempt to settle it by mediation in accordance with the Centre for Dispute Resolution (CEDR) Model Mediation Procedure.

42

If the parties have not settled the dispute by mediation within [42] days from the initiation of the mediation, the dispute shall be referred to arbitration under the Rules of the London Court of International Arbitration in force at the date of this Agreement. The parties hereby agree that:

The tribunal shall consist of [one/three] arbitrator[s] who [specify qualifications/nationalities etc.];

If the parties do not agree on the appointment of the arbitrator[s], the London Court of International Arbitration shall determine the arbitrator[s];

The place of arbitration shall be London; and

The language of the arbitration shall be English.

General

The rights and remedies of the parties under this Agreement are cumulative and in addition to any rights and remedies provided by law. Any variation to this Agreement must be in writing and agreed by the parties. This agreement may be executed in counterpart.

This Agreement has been signed on the date appearing at the head of page 1.

Signed by	)	
for and on behalf of	)	Director
Company	)	
	)	Director/Secretary
Signed by	)	
for and on behalf of	)	Director
Customer	)	
	)	Director/Secretary

43

Schedule to contain details of:
- Bandwidth/Storage
- Brand Features
- Commencement Date
- Content
- Fees
- Services
- SLA

44

A2.5 Content Provision and Linking

This Agreement is made the [   ] day of [   ]

Between:

(1) [Company Name] a company incorporated in England under registration number [   ], the registered office of which is at [   ] ("**Company**"); and

(2) [Customer Name] a company incorporated in England under registration number [   ], the registered office of which is at [   ] ("**Customer**").

Definitions and Interpretation

In this Agreement the following words and expressions shall have the meaning set out below:

"**Affiliate**" means in respect of a party its "holding company", its "subsidiary company" or a subsidiary company of its holding company, as those terms are defined in section 736 of the Companies Act 1985;

"**Agreement**" means this Agreement and any Schedule;

"**Commencement Date**" means [/the date of this Agreement];

"**Company Brand Features**" means all Marks and other distinctive brand features of the Company or its Affiliates that form part of the Company Property or are set out in the Schedule;

"**Company Property**" means any or all of Company's or its Affiliates' worldwide web sites, software, products, services accessible via the internet or otherwise;

"**Confidential Information**" has the meaning set out in clause 12.1;

"**Content**" means all the information, data and software made available to Company or its Affiliates by the Content Provider including that Content specified in the Schedule;

"**Content Provider**" has the same meaning as Customer and vice versa;

"**Content Provider Brand Features**" means all Marks and other distinctive brand features of Content Provider that form part of the Content or are set out in the Schedule;

"**Fees**" has the meaning set out in the Schedule;

"**Force Majeure**" has the meaning set out in the clause 11.1;

"**Intellectual Property Rights**" means any and all registered and unregistered copyright patents, design rights, database and compilation rights, Marks (and related goodwill), trade secrets and other intellectual property rights,

45

howsoever arising and in whatever media, and any applications for their protection or registration and all renewals and extensions anywhere in the world;

"**Marks**" means any and all names, brands, logos, trade marks, service marks, trade names and domain names;

"**Term**" has the meaning set out in clause 8.1; and

"**Web Site**" the Company Property at www.Company.com or such other address notified to Content Provider by Company.

Except where the context otherwise requires, words denoting the singular include the plural and vice versa, words denoting any gender include any other genders, and words denoting persons include firms and corporations and vice versa.

Unless otherwise stated, a reference to:

a Clause or Schedule is a reference to a clause of or schedule to this Agreement. Clause headings are for ease of reference only and do not affect the construction of this Agreement;

"include" and "including" shall be construed without limitation; and

any Act of Parliament shall be deemed to include any amendment, replacement or re-enactment thereof then in force and to include any bye-laws, statutory instruments, rules, regulations, orders, notices, directions, consents, licences, conditions or permissions made thereunder.

Content Provider's Responsibilities

Content Provider shall deliver to the Company on a date to be agreed between the parties (which shall be a date as soon as reasonably practicable after the date of this Agreement) an electronic copy of the Content in a format specified by the Company.

The Content Provider shall up-date the Content at least once a week by uploading by FTP to the site specified by the Company.

Content Provider shall use its best endeavours to ensure that the Content is timely, accurate, comprehensive and updated regularly as set forth in this Agreement. Content Provider will ensure that in no event will the Content be less up to date and accurate than that which is available on any site owned, managed or controlled by Content Provider.

During the Term, Content Provider must maintain a graphic hypertext link to the Company Property. Such link must contain the Company Brand Features and be placed as agreed between the Company and the Content Provider.

46

Company's Responsibilities

The Company will be solely responsible for the design, layout, look-and-feel and maintenance of any and all aspects of the Company Properties, including the Content.

Company has the sole right to sell or license any and all advertising and promotional rights which relate to the Company Properties or any part, and Company shall be entitled to retain any and all revenue generated from any sales or licences of such advertising or promotional rights.

Company agrees to provide with the Content any links, attributions and notices of the Content Provider in an agreed format, however, the Content Provider's logo shall be no greater than [200 pixels by 50 pixels] and which the Content Provider shall provide in GIF format.

Licence Grants

Content Provider grants to Company and its Affiliates for the duration of the Term:

a non-exclusive, worldwide, royalty free licence to use, copy, translate, adapt, distribute, transmit, publish, publicly display and perform the Content in whole or in part via any means, in connection with any Company Property save that Company's and its Affiliates' right to modify the Content is limited to modifying the format but not substantially the editorial content;

a non-exclusive, worldwide, royalty free licence to use, copy, translate, adapt, distribute, transmit, publish, publicly display and perform the Content Provider Brand Features: (i) in connection with the presentation of the Content on the Company Properties; and (ii) in connection with the marketing and promotion of the Content and/or the Company Properties; and

the right to sub-license the licences set out in clauses 4.1(a) and 4.1(b) to any third parties who host, in whole or in part, the Company Property or any derivative work, including under a co-branded arrangement or otherwise.

Company grants to Content Provider during the Term a non-exclusive, worldwide licence to use, copy, distribute, transmit, publish and publicly display the Company Brand Features as part of the hypertext link specified in clause 2.4.

Payment

Content Provider shall invoice the Company and the Company shall pay the Fees and any other charges due to Content Provider within thirty (30) days of the invoice date. All Fees and other charges are subject to VAT at the prevailing rate and are payable in Pounds Sterling. All Fees described herein are exclusive

47

of any taxes, including any excise, sales, use, value added (VAT), withholding and similar taxes. Company shall be liable and shall pay all applicable taxes associated with Fees. Company shall gross up any payments to compensate for any withholding tax payable and Content Provider shall credit Company with any tax credit received within six (6) months by Content Provider in respect of such withholding.

If any sum due to Content Provider remains outstanding after thirty (30) days from the invoice date then, without prejudice to any other rights and remedies of Content Provider, such sums shall attract interest at the then current rate of [Bank] plus two percent, before and after judgement, from the invoice date until payment is made in full, compounded at monthly intervals.

In the event that Content Provider has to resort to collection enforcement as a result of the non-payment of its charges, Content Provider will charge any reasonable expenses it has incurred associated with such collection including, but not limited to reasonable legal costs, lawyers' fees, court costs and collection agency fees.

Warranties

Each party warrants to the other that it has the full right, power and authority to enter into and perform this Agreement and has not entered into any arrangement which in any way conflicts with this Agreement or inhibits, restricts or impairs its ability to perform its obligations under this Agreement.

The Content Provider warrants that it has sufficient rights (including Intellectual Property Rights) in the Content to grant to Company the rights set out and contemplated in this agreement and has obtained and will at its own cost maintain and renew, as appropriate, all necessary licences, authorisations and consents which are necessary for Company to provide and publish the Content in accordance with this Agreement.

The Content Provider warrants to Company that the Content complies with all applicable law including all relevant consumer protection legislation and advertising codes and does not contain material that is obscene, blasphemous, defamatory, infringing of any rights of any third party or otherwise legally actionable under any civil or criminal laws in force in any legal jurisdiction from which the Company Properties might be accessible or which might bring Company into disrepute.

Content Provider agrees that it will notify Company immediately if Content Provider becomes aware of any actual or potential claims, suits, actions, allegations or charges that could affect either party's ability to fully perform its duties or to exercise its rights under the Agreement.

48

Except as expressly provided in this agreement, each party expressly disclaims any further representations, warranties, conditions or other terms, express or implied, by statute, collaterally or otherwise, including but not limited to implied warranties, conditions or other terms of satisfactory quality, fitness for a particular purpose or reasonable care and skill.

Intellectual Property Rights

Nothing in this Agreement gives the Content Provider any right (including Intellectual Property Right), title or interest in the Company Properties, Web Site or Company Brand Features and their online implementation and any part thereof.

Nothing in this Agreement gives Company any right (including Intellectual Property Right), title or interest in Content or the Content Provider Brand Features and any part thereof. Company will own the Intellectual Property in any derivative works created by it that are based upon or incorporate Content, but excluding the Content itself.

Term

The Agreement shall commence on the Commencement Date and shall continue for a period of one year unless and until terminated in accordance with clause 13 ("Term"). On each anniversary of the Commencement Date this Agreement shall renew for a further period of one year unless either party gives the other not less that three months' prior written notice to expire on or before such anniversary.

Indemnities

Each party shall indemnify and keep the other party fully and effectively indemnified on demand against any liability, damage, expense, claim or cost (including reasonable legal costs and expenses) suffered by the other party as a result of any breach by the first party of the warranties set out in clause 6 of this Agreement, provided that where products are concerned the latest version of the products have been used in normal circumstances without modification.

To take benefit of an indemnity, that party shall: (i) notify the other party promptly in writing and in any event within ten (10) business days of first learning of any such claim, lawsuit, action or proceeding; (ii) consent to the other party having the sole authority to control the defence and/or settlement of any such claim, lawsuit, action or proceeding; and (iii) provide reasonable co-operation and assistance to the other party, at that party's expense, in defending any such claim, lawsuit, action or proceeding.

49

Limitation of Liability

Save as provided in clause 10.3, neither party shall be liable in contract, tort (including negligence), statutory duty, pre-contract or other representations (other than fraudulent or negligent misrepresentations) or otherwise arising out of or in connection with this Agreement for: (a) consequential, indirect or special loss or damage; or (b) any loss of goodwill or reputation; or (c) any economic losses (including loss of revenues, profits, contracts, business or anticipated savings). In each case whether advised of the possibility of such loss or damage and howsoever incurred.

Save as provided in clause 9.1 and 10.3, both parties agree that the maximum liability of either party in contract, tort (including negligence), statutory duty, pre-contract or other representations (other than fraudulent or negligent misrepresentations) or otherwise arising out of or in connection with this Agreement, and each part thereof, including its execution and performance; shall, in respect of any one or more events or series of events (whether connected or unconnected) taking place within any twelve month period, be limited to the Licence Fees paid by Licensee in such period or [£10,000], whichever is the greater.

Nothing in this Agreement shall exclude or limit liability for death or personal injury resulting from the negligence of either party or their servants, agents or employees acting in the course of their duties.

Force Majeure

Either party will not be liable for any failure or delay in performing its obligations under this Agreement to the extent that this failure or delay is the result of any cause or circumstance beyond the reasonable control of that party including acts of god, war, civil commotion or industrial dispute and that failure could not have been prevented or overcome by that party acting reasonably and prudently. If either party is prevented from performing its obligations for a period exceeding six (6) months due to Force Majeure then the other party may terminate this Agreement on one month written notice.

Confidentiality and Data

During the term of this Agreement and for two (2) years thereafter, each party will treat as confidential all information that they obtain concerning, but not limited to, the business, finances, technology and affairs of the other, ("Confidential Information"). Each of the parties will use at least the same degree of care (and not less than a reasonable degree of care) it uses to prevent the disclosure of its own confidential information of like importance, to prevent

50

the disclosure of Confidential Information of the other party. Each party will promptly notify the other party of any actual or suspected misuse or unauthorised disclosure of the other party's Confidential Information.

The provisions of this clause 12 shall cease to apply to: (i) information that has come into the public domain other than by breach of this clause or any other duty of confidence; (ii) information that is obtained from a third party without breach of this clause or any other duty of confidence; and (iii) information that is required to be disclosed by a regulatory or government body or court of competent jurisdiction with power to compel the disclosure.

In the event of termination or expiration of this Agreement, each party shall return or on request of the other party, destroy the Confidential Information of that party.

Each party will comply with its obligations pursuant to the Data Protection Act 1998 and any subordinate legislation and official guidelines.

Termination

Each party shall have the right to terminate this Agreement on written notice in the event that the other:

commits any material breach of the terms of this Agreement which, in the case of a breach capable of remedy, is not remedied within 30 days of service of a notice specifying the breach and stating the intention to terminate the Agreement if not remedied; or

holds any meeting with or proposes to enter into or has proposed to it any arrangement or composition with its creditors (including any voluntary arrangement as described in the Insolvency Act 1986); has a receiver, administrator, or other encumbrancer take possession of or appointed over or has any distress, execution or other process levied or enforced (and not discharged within 7 days) upon the whole or substantially all of its assets; ceases or threatens to cease to carry on business or becomes unable to pay its debts within the meaning of Section 123 of the Insolvency Act 1986.

Forthwith upon the termination of this Agreement each party shall return all licensed and/or confidential materials, and all copies in whole or part, of the other or if requested by the other party, shall destroy them and certify in writing to the Licensor that they have been destroyed.

Termination or expiry of this Agreement shall be without prejudice to any rights, liabilities or remedies of a party accrued before termination nor shall it affect any provision of this Agreement which is expressly intended to come into or continue in force after termination or expiry.

51

Severance

To the extent that any provision of this Agreement is found by any court or competent authority to be invalid, unlawful or unenforceable in any jurisdiction, that provision shall be deemed not to be a part of this Agreement, it shall not affect the validity, lawfulness or enforceability of the remainder of this Agreement nor shall it affect the validity, lawfulness or enforceability of that provision in any other jurisdiction.

Waiver

No failure or delay by any party in exercising any right, power or remedy under this Agreement will operate as a waiver of that or any other right, power or remedy nor will any single or partial exercise by either party of any right, power or remedy preclude any further exercise of any other right, power or remedy.

Time of the Essence

Any times, dates or periods specified in the agreement may be extended or altered by agreement in writing between the parties. However, time shall not be of the essence except where it is expressly stated to apply.

Insurance

Each party must have in force and maintain with a reputable insurance company professional indemnity insurance exceeding [£1,000,000].

Further Assurance

Each party shall at the cost and expense of the other party use all reasonable endeavours to do all such further acts and things and execute or procure the execution of all such other documents as that party may from time to time reasonably require for the purpose of giving that party the full benefit of the assets, rights and benefits to be transferred to the other party under this agreement.

Relationship

Nothing in this Agreement shall or shall be deemed to create a partnership or joint venture or contract of employment of any kind between the parties nor shall it be deemed to grant any authority to the other not expressly set out in the Agreement or create any agency between the parties.

Assignment and Sub-contracting

Either party shall not be entitled to assign, transfer, charge or license the whole or any part of its rights and/or obligations under this Agreement to any party without consent of the other party [which shall not be unreasonably withheld or delayed].

[Neither/either] party may engage any person, firm or company as its sub-contractor to perform any of its obligations, but shall not be released from any liability therefor.

Rights of Third Parties

Nothing in this Agreement shall create or confer any rights or other benefits whether pursuant to the Contracts (Rights of Third Parties) Act 1999 or otherwise in favour of any person other than the parties to this Agreement.

Notices

Any notice given under this Agreement will be in writing and shall be deemed served if hand delivered to the other party or sent by pre-paid post, facsimile transmission or confirmed email copy to the address or transmission number of that party specified on page 1 of this Agreement or such other address or number as may be notified under this Agreement by that party from time to time for this purpose. Notices will be deemed to be effective on personal delivery, within 48 hours of posting (if the address is in the UK or within 96 hours otherwise), or upon confirmation of receipt of facsimile or email.

Entire Agreement

Each party confirms that this Agreement sets out the entire agreement and understanding between the parties and that it supersedes all previous agreements, arrangements and understandings between them relating to the subject matter of the Agreement. Each party confirms that it has not relied upon any statement, representation or understanding that is not an express term of this Agreement and shall not have any remedy in respect of any statement, representation or understanding which is not an express term unless made fraudulently.

Governing Law and Jurisdiction

This Agreement shall be governed by and construed in accordance with the law of England and each party hereby irrevocably submits to the non-exclusive jurisdiction of the courts of England.

Dispute Resolution

If any dispute arises between the parties out of this Agreement, the parties shall attempt to settle it by mediation in accordance with the Centre for Dispute Resolution (CEDR) Model Mediation Procedure.

53

If the parties have not settled the dispute by mediation within [42] days from the initiation of the mediation, the dispute shall be referred to arbitration under the Rules of the London Court of International Arbitration in force at the date of this Agreement. The parties hereby agree that:

The tribunal shall consist of [one/three] arbitrator[s] who [specify qualifications/nationalities etc.];

If the parties do not agree on the appointment of the arbitrator[s], the London Court of International Arbitration shall determine the arbitrator[s];

The place of arbitration shall be London; and

The language of the arbitration shall be English.

General

The rights and remedies of the parties under this Agreement are cumulative and in addition to any rights and remedies provided by law. Any variation to this Agreement must be in writing and agreed by the parties. This agreement may be executed in counterpart.

This Agreement has been signed on the date appearing at the head of page 1.

Signed by	)	
for and on behalf of	)	Director
Company	)	
	)	Director/Secretary
Signed by	)	
for and on behalf of	)	Director
Customer	)	
	)	Director/Secretary

54

Schedule to contain details of:
- Content Provider Brand Features
- Company Brand Features
- Description of Content
- Fees

55

APPENDIX 3

Summary of cases cited

The information below has kindly been provided by Pillsbury Winthrop.

Demon case   14, 15, 17, 24, 74

Godfrey v. *Demon Internet Ltd* [1999] NL JR 609

Line One case   96

Naomi Campbell case   205

Napster cases   101, 288

Significant Napster cases are indicated below with an asterisk:

*A&M Records, Inc. v. *Napster, Inc.*, 114F. Supp. 2d 896, 908 (N.D. Cal. 2000)

Complaint of 6 December 1999 by A&M Records and 17 other record companies for contributory and vicarious copyright infringement against Napster, and requesting injunction preventing Napster from 'engaging in or facilitating others in copying, downloading, uploading, transmitting, or distributing plaintiffs' copyrighted works'.

A & M Records, Inc. v. *Napster, Inc.*, 2000 WL 1055915, *1 (9th Cir. July 28, 2000)
Rejection by Court of Appeal of injunction granted following injunction.

**A&M Records, Inc.* v. *Napster, Inc.*, 239 F.3d 1004 (9th Cir. 2001)
February 2001 affirmation by the Ninth Circuit of findings of fact and grant of injunctive relief.

A&M Records, Inc. v. *Napster, Inc.*, 2001 WL 227083 (N.D. Cal. March 5, 2001)
Modified preliminary injunction entered on 5 March 2001.

A&M Records, Inc. and others v. *Napster, Inc.*, Order No. C 99-5183 MHP (N.D. Cal. March 5, 2001)

Jerry Lieber and others v. *Napster, Inc.*, Order No. C 00-0074 MHP (N.D. Cal. March 5, 2001)

Casanova Records and others v. *Napster, Inc.*, Order No. C 00-2638 MHP (N.D. Cal. March 5, 2001)

Metallica and others v. *Napster, Inc.*, Order No. C 00-4068 MHP
(N.D. Cal. March 5, 2001)
Injunction orders of 5 March 2001.

**In re Napster, Inc. Copyright Litig.* 191 F. Supp. 2d 1087 (N.D. Cal.
February 22, 2002)
Partial grant of stay of summary judgment against Napster in order
to allow for further discovery.

Norwich Union case   28

Western Provident Association v. *Norwich Union Health Care and
Norwich Union Life Insurance* [unreported, 1997]
This case settled out of court for £450,000 and was not reported at
the time.

NTL case   18

R (NTL Group Ltd) v. *Crown Court at Ipswich* QBD [2002] 3 WLR
1173

Road Tech case   74

Roadtech Computer Systems Ltd v. *Mandata (Management and Data
Services) Ltd* (2000) ChD (Bowman) Lawtel 22/6/00

Shetland Times case   81, 82, 276

Shetland Times Ltd v. *Wills and another* [1997] FSR 604
This is the 'Shetland Times *v.* Shetland News' case. Wills was the
publisher of the *Shetland News*.

APPENDIX 4

Internet glossary

Browser
Web browsing software such as Microsoft Internet Explorer (often referred to as 'IE') or Netscape Navigator and so on.

Cookie
A cookie is a small file that may be placed on the hard disk of a Web surfer's computer for record-keeping purposes. Consequently, when he/she returns to that website, the cookie will enable the website to tailor information according to his/her consumer preferences. A web surfer may set his browser to notify him when he receives a cookie, thus giving him the chance to decide whether or not to accept it.

Framing
The practice of linking into a third party's website or content sites but presenting the site or information within the originating site's framing text and graphics and possibly with that site's own URL or domain name displayed at the top of the screen. Users will not necessarily know they have left the original site.

HTML	HyperText Markup Language. A system of additions to plain text which act as instructions to web browsers or other HTML compliant programs. The browser acting on the instructions will convert the marked up text into formatted pages including hypertext links.
HTTP	HyperText Transmission Protocol. The Internet protocol which enables the transmission of a HTML document across the Internet.
Hyperlink	(Also referred to as 'hypertext link', 'hot link', 'page link', 'link', etc.) Underlined or otherwise high-lighted text in web pages which, when clicked on, takes you to other web pages (most often outside the website containing the hyperlink).
Hypertext	A hypertext document includes highlighted text which, when clicked upon, causes the user to jump to another place in the same document, to another document on the same computer, or (if HTML is used on a network with HTTP-compliant computers), to a document on another computer altogether. On the Internet hypertext links can exist between documents on computers anywhere in the world.
ISDN	Integrated Services Digital Network. A telephony standard designed to deliver medium bandwidth digital voice and data. After a slow start, ISDN is becoming popular for Internet connections where more than the capacity of a dial-up modem connection is required but the expense of a leased line connection cannot be justified.

Internet	(Also referred to as 'Net'.) A network of computers linked via telecommunications systems.
Java	A programming language originating from Sun Microsystems designed to be usable across many different types of computer and operating system. Many websites now employ small programs ('applets') written in Java, which are downloaded to the user's computer when he accesses the site. These applets may perform functions such as animating parts of the website, or providing more sophisticated user interfaces than can be readily built using HTML. Another technology capable of performing similar functions on Window-based systems is ActiveX from Microsoft.
Java Script	A language in which a web page can be written and which a web browser will interpret to display the page. It is a sophisticated alternative to HTML, but which unlike Java does not require the user's computer to download a separate program from the website.
Server	(Also referred to as 'Domain Name Server' or 'DNS'.) Strictly, a server is a piece of software which delivers data from the computer on which it resides across the network in response to requests from elsewhere. Thus a web server delivers web pages, a Domain Name Server delivers IP addresses in response to domain name requests, and so on. The term server is often used to denote the computer itself as well as the software.

DNS – A computer which maintains a list of domain names and corresponding IP addresses. On receipt of a request from another computer it will deliver the IP addresses corresponding to the requested domain name if it has an authoritative list for that domain name. Otherwise, it will refer the request elsewhere in the DNS system until a computer is found which can give an authoritative response.

Spam

Unsolicited commercial communications sent by e-mail designed to promote directly or indirectly the goods, services or image of a company, organisation or a person.

An inappropriate attempt to use a mailing list, or USENET or other networked communications facility as if it was a broadcast medium by sending the same message to a large number of people who did not ask for it.

TCP/IP/SLIP/PPP

Transmission Control Protocol, Internet Protocol, Serial Line Internet Protocol, Point to Point Protocol. The set of standards which govern how computers communicate with each other over the Internet.

URL

Uniform Resource Locator. The address of a website, e.g. http://www.mwe.com or http://www.mweglobal.com.

Web

(Also referred to as 'World Wide Web' or 'www'.) The Web is a global collection of hypertext-linked HTML pages which a user equipped with a web browser can view and browse.

Website   (Also referred to as 'site'.) A cohesive collection of
                               web pages, usually maintained by or on behalf of
                               one entity (e.g. an individual or a company).

In addition to the above, the following two sites provide user-friendly
glossaries to a wide range of Internet terms:

http://www.webopedia.com/

http://www.onelook.com/index.html

APPENDIX 5

Contact details

A5.1   The author

Amanda C. Brock can be contacted via the Publishers.

A5.2   Lawyers and law firms specialising in e-commerce

A5.2.1   *England*

Duane Morris

Contact:

Susan Laws, Partner
Duane Morris Solicitors
4 Chiswell Street, London EC1 4UP

Kemp Little LLP

Kemp Little is a City-based law firm specialising in business and technology. Contact:

> Richard Kemp / Jonathon Little / Kenneth Mullen
> Kemp Little LLP, Solicitors
> Saddlers House, Gutter Lane, London EC2V 6BR
> Tel: +44 (0)207 710 1606
> Fax: +44 (0)207 600 7878
> Mobile: 07932 695 616
> Website: www.comlegal.com

McDermott, Will & Emery

Rafi Azim-Khan, Partner heading the e-Business Group at McDermott, Will & Emery, London, has advised clients ranging from major ISPs and technology companies to multinational manufacturers and media companies on a wide range of marketing, commercial, data protection and intellectual property issues and on all aspects of conducting business on the Internet. Rafi has co-authored numerous texts on such topics and is listed in Legal Experts, Legal 500 and, as one of the world's leading e-commerce lawyers, in Chambers Global Directory 2002–2003. Contact:

> Rafi Azim-Khan,
> McDermott, Will & Emery
> 7 Bishopsgate, London EC2A 3AR
> Tel: 020 7577 6900
> Fax: 020 7577 6950
> E-mail: razimkhan@europe.mwe.com

Olswang

Olswang is a full-service law firm with a particular focus and unrivalled experience in the areas of e-commerce and emerging technologies. Contact:

Clive Gringas, Partner
Olswang
90 High Holborn, London WC1V 6XX

Pillsbury Winthrop

Ashley Winton, Partner in Pillsbury Winthrop, provided the precedents in Appendix 2. Contact:

Ashley Winton
Pillsbury Winthrop
54 Lombard Street, London EC4V 9DH
Tel: 0207 648 9212
Fax: 0207 283 1656
E-mail: awinton@pillsburywinthrop.com
Website: www.pillsburywinthrop.com

Singletons, Solicitors

Singletons provides IT/commerce, data protection and commercial legal advice. Contact:

Susan Singleton
Tel: 0208 866 1934
E-mail: susan@singlelaw.com
Website: www.singlelaw.com

Tite & Lewis

Contact:

Mark Lewis, Partner
Tite & Lewis
10 Noble Street, London EC2V 7TL
E-mail: mark.lewis@titeandlewis.com

A5.2.2   Scotland

Wright, Johnston & Mackenzie

302 St Vincent Street, Glasgow G2 5RZ
Tel: 0141 248 3434
Fax: 0141 221 1226
Website: www.wjm.co.uk

A5.3   Further information, publications and updates

Electronic Business Law is is published 12 times a year, price £290 per annum, by Lexis Nexis Butterworths Tolley. For further enquiries or sample copies please call the editor, Elsa Booth, on 020 7400 2566.

A5.4   Lawyers and law firms specialising in employment

Berwin Leighton Paisner

Contact:

Paul Mander, Partner, Employment Department
Adelaide House, London Bridge, London EC4R 9HA
DX: 92 London Chancery Lane, London WC2
Tel: 020 7760 1000
Fax: 020 7760 1111
Email: paul.mander@blplaw.com
Website: www.blplaw.com

A5.5 Government and regulatory

Direct Marketing Association

DMA House, 70 Margaret Street, London W1W 8SS
Tel: 020 7291 3300
Fax: 020 7323 4165
E-mail: dma@dma.org.uk
Website: www.dma.org.uk

Information Commissioner

Wycliffe House, Water Lane, Wilmslow, Cheshire SK9 5AF
Fax: 01625 524 510
DX: 20819 Wilmslow
Enquiry/Information Line: 01625 545745
Notification Line: 01625 545740
Switchboard: 01625 545700

Internet Services Providers' Association, UK

23 Palace Street, London SW1E 5HW
Tel: 020 7233 7234
Fax: 020 7233 7294
E-mail: admin@ispa.org.uk

Internet Watch Foundation

5 Coles Lane, Oakington, Cambridgeshire CB4 5BA
Tel: 01223 237700
Fax: 01223 235870/235921
Website: www.iwf.org.uk/hotline/report.htm

Office of Fair Trading

Public Liaison Unit
Tel: 08457 22 44 99
E-mail: enquiries@oft.gsi.gov.uk

Trading Standards

Website: www.tradingstandards.gov.uk

TrustUK

2nd Floor, DMA House
70 Margaret Street, London W1W 8SS
Tel: 020 7291 3345
Fax: 020 7323 4165
Website: www.trustuk.org.uk

Which? Web Trader

Castlemead, Gascoyne Way, Hertford SG14 1YB
Tel: 01992 822888
Fax: 020 7770 7485
E-mail: webtrader@which.net

Index

cookies, 129, 214–15

cooling off periods, 156–7

copyright, 26, 45–6, 57
protection of, 81, 83, 100, 128

country of origin, 97–8

credit agreements/payments, 161,
166

credit cards, 166
authentication/verification,
193–4
children, 114
chip protected, 192–3
fraud, 161–2, 188–92, 196
and Secure Sockets Layer (SSL),
194–5

customer relationships, 117–20
business-to-business (B2B),
170–1
legal relationships, 120–1

customers
complaints by, 109–10
and content provision, websites,
96
contracts, 102–4, 105, 121–6
information provision, durable
form, 150–4, 155
information requirements, pre-
sale, 144–9
'ownership' of, and linking
contracts, 281–2
registration, 130–2
and security, 188–96
terms and conditions, binding,
121–6
terms of use, 126–30
see also terms of sale

CVZ numbers, 193

cybercrimes, 196–7, 200

cybersquatting, 64, 67–9

data
cleansing, 221
personal, definition, 210
secure storage, 182, 196
third party requests, 222
usage, opt-in/opt-out, 212–13
see also data protection; Data
Protection Act 1998

data collection, 171, 201–2, 204–5
from children (US), 115
click boxes, 211
databases, functionality, 216–17
and download contracts, 293–4
interactive television (iTV) service
providers, 304
and linking contracts, 282
notices, 130–1, 210–11, 315
opt-in/opt-out, 212–13
privacy policies, 222, 316–17
by third parties, 219–20
unsubscribing, 220–1
viral marketing, 218–19

data protection, 17–18, 47, 202
checklist, 226
cross-border transfers, 223–4
e-mail, 224–5
and linking contracts, 282
padlock system (Information
Commissioner), 224
see also security

Data Protection Act 1998, 42–3,
186, 202–3
collection principles, 204–5
compensation, 208
data access, 207
data controller, 204
data processing, conditions to be
met, 205
notification, 203, 209
offences, 209

prevention of processing, 208
rectification, 207, 208
rights, data subjects, 207–9
sensitive data/uses, 206, 209
third party data requests, 222

databases
and data collection, 216–17
rights, 55–7

deep links, 81, 279

defamation, 14–15, 17, 28–9

Demon, 14–15, 24

design and build contracts *see* web
design and build contracts

digital rights management (DRM),
101

digital signatures/encryption, 31,
178–84, 194

Direct Marketing Association,
preference service/opt out
registers, 217

disclaimers
e-mail, 32, 40, 45, 184, 334–6
websites, 99–100

disclosure, requirement for, 17

Distance Selling Regulations, 142
applicability of, 162
compliance with, 307
contract of sale, requirements
checklist, 164
cooling off periods/cancellation
rights, 156–8, 159, 160–1
duty to supply goods/services,
155
exempt transactions, 142
failure to comply with, 162, 165
fraudulent transactions,
cancellation of, 161–2

gift sales, 154–5
guide to/full text of, where to
obtain, 172
information provision, durable
form, 150–4, 155
information requirements, pre-
sale, 144–9
product withdrawal, 105
refunds, 160–1
return of goods, 158–60
software sales, 294, 297
stock availability, 106–7
substitute goods, 156
summary, 163
see also E-Commerce (EC
Directive) Regulations
2002

Dixons, terms of sale/terms of use,
337–9

Domain Name Service (DNS)
attacks, 177–8

domain names
country codes, 59, 60, 62
cybersquatting, 64, 67–9
definition, 58
disputes, 67–9
hijacking, 78
legal cases, 64
length of ownership/renewal,
65–6
ownership identification, 68, 70
primary/top-level, 58–9, 60, 61,
63–4
registration, 59, 60–7, 70, 252,
254
secondary, 58–9
sub-category names, sale of,
59–60
typosquatting, 64, 67

and intellectual property, 45
Internet, use of, 25–7
liability for, 26, 27, 28–9
monitoring of, 39–44, 185–7
and security, 185–8

encryption/digital signatures, 31,
178–84, 194

filing systems, and data access rights,
207

film, downloading, 101

financial services, 108

'force majeure', contracts, 231

framing, 82–3, 304–5

fraud, 78, 80, 173–4, 197
credit/payment cards, 161–2,
188–96
'gagging orders', 187
and secure data storage, 182, 196
see also security

Freeserve, sample policies, 311–29

gift sales, 154–5

Godfrey v. *Demon*, 14–15, 24

goods *see* products

hacking, 178, 190

hijacking, domain names, 78

hosting *see* web hosting

Human Rights Act 1998, 39, 41–2,
186

identity theft, 190

Independent Television Commission
(ITC), 91, 307
Codes, 91–2, 273, 305–6

Information Commissioner, 38–9,
42–3, 47, 202, 203, 224

information society services
codes of conduct, 111–12
and E-Commerce (EC Directive)
Regulations 2002, 143–4

intellectual property, 45–6
advertising, 271–2, 273
contract clauses, 233–5, 238,
248–9, 261–2, 278
database rights, 55–7
protection of, 100–1, 128
see also copyright; trade marks

interactive television (iTV),
regulation, 91–2, 305–7

interactive television (iTV) contracts,
299–300
checklist, 309
content, modification of existing,
301–2
customer issues, 303–4
framing, 304–5
legal compliance, 305–7
licences, 302–3
linking, 305
menu placement, 305
payment, 308
private networks (ëwalled
gardensí, 300
specification, 301
term/termination, 308
testing/acceptance, 308
warranties/indemnities, 307

interest, late payments, 248

Internet
access, 11–12, 22–3
employees, use by, 25–7
glossary of terms, 405–9
policies (employers), 30, 35–9,
43, 44, 175–6, 185, 330–4
regulation, 306

Office of Communications
(OFCOM), 92–3, 306–7

parody websites, 80

passwords, 131–2

payment, 166–7
authentication/verification,
193–4
by children, 114
fraudulent transactions, 161–2
and security, 183, 188–96

PIN numbers, 193–4

Playboy, 75

pricing, 104–6, 107–8
errors, 135–7

privacy, 186
policies, 222, 316–17

products
age-restricted, 88, 114
information, 105–6
product-specific provisions, 104
quality, 103–4
return of, 158–60
substitutes, 156
withdrawal, 104–5

pubs247.co.uk, user terms, 340–3

refunds, 160–1
downloaded software, 294
for fraud, 191–2

registration, customers, 130–2

regulation
advertising, 89–91, 260, 272–3,
306, 307
broadcasting, 91–2, 273, 305–7
content, 87–93, 103
interactive television (iTV), 91–2,
305–7

Internet, 306
Internet Service Providers (ISPs),
13–14, 16, 19–22
trading, 87–9, 96–8, 102–8
websites, 96–8
see also Distance Selling
Regulations; E-Commerce
(EC Directive) Regulations
2002

Regulation of Investigatory Powers
Act (RIPA) 2000, 39, 40–1,
185, 186

return of goods, 158–60

Road Tech Computer Systems Limited
v. *Mandata*, 74–5

search engines, 71–2
and meta tags, 72–6

Secure Sockets Layer (SSL), 194–5

security, 173–4, 198
British Standard, 196
checklist, 199
confidentiality, 31–3, 179, 184,
187–8
customers, 188–96
data storage, 182, 196
Domain Name Service (DNS)
attacks, 177–8
e-mail, 31–3, 184
employees, 185–8
encryption/digital signatures, 31,
178–84, 194
passwords, 131–2
payment systems, 183, 188–96
Secure Sockets Layer (SSL),
194–5
secure systems/VPN (Virtual
Private Networks), 182–3
terrorism/cybercrimes, 196–7,
200

codes of conduct, 110–13
dispute resolution, 98
law/regulation, 87–9, 96–8, 102–8
pricing, 104–6, 107–8, 135–7
stock availability, 106–7
terms of agreement, 102–4
see also terms of sale

trading standards, 88–9, 306

Trust UK, 112, 116

typosquatting, 64, 67

unbundling (local loop), 22–3

Unfair Contract Terms Act (UCTA) 1977, 99–100, 102

Unfair Terms in Consumer Contracts Regulations 1999, 102

unsubscribing, 220–1

URL (Uniform Resource Locator), definition, 58

US
children, data collection from, 115
data protection/transfer, 223
taxation, 168–9

VAT, 167–9

viral marketing, 217–19

viruses, 29–30, 33, 175–7

VPN (Virtual Private Networks), 182–3

waivers, contracts, 230

'walled gardens', 300

warranties/indemnities (contracts), 234–5, 251, 263, 268, 280–1, 296, 307

web content, 254–5
European Commission website, 116
liability for, 14–17, 19–22, 94–6, 99–100
protection of, 100–1
regulation, 87–93, 103
third-party, 93–6, 280

web content contracts, 254–5
advertising/sponsorship, 262–3
checklist, 264
cost/payment terms, 263, 265
delivery of content, 257–8
exclusivity of content, 256–7
intellectual property rights, 261–2
legality of content, 259–61, 262
sample, 389–99
service levels, 258
specification of product/service to be provided, 255–6
use of content, 258–9
warranties/indemnities, 263

web design and build contracts, 93, 241–2
additional services, 252, 254
changes, provision for, 246–7
checklist, 253
functionality, 242–3
intellectual property/code, 248–9
key personnel, 247
look and feel, 245
maintenance/training, 250–1
modifications/upgrades, 249–50
payment terms, 247–8
site specification, 244
testing/acceptance, 252
timing/milestones, 245–6
two phase, 242–3
warranties/indemnities, 251